PASCAL
His Life and Works

PASCAL, mathematician and mystic, is the most fascinating, the most enigmatic, the most controversial figure among Frenchmen.

Here is a life which is as interesting to the ordinary reader as to the scholar It contains delightful descriptions of the background into which the infant prodigy was born, gives an account of the amazingly modern way in which he was educated, studies his relationship with his father and his sisters. It follows his intellectual achievements, his friendships, his enmities, his spiritual development.

There is much original thought and criticism in this book by a well-known French scholar, a great deal to interest, excite and disturb students of Pascal, but if one had never heard of Pascal, the book would stand comparison with any story about an exceptionally sensitive and gifted human being whose life bore witness to all the reactions which characterize genius: succ cution, devoted friends, l times of doubt and rea enduring integrity. Al against the vivid backgro of Paris in the seventeen

Monsignor Ronald Knox's foreword will stimulate readers to an appreciation of the many problems aroused by any study of Pascal.

PASCAL
HIS LIFE AND WORKS

PASCAL

From the original Picture by Philippe de Champagne

PASCAL

his Life and Works

By JEAN MESNARD

Preface by
MONSIGNOR RONALD KNOX

Translated by
G. S. FRASER

LONDON
HARVILL PRESS

Published, 1952,
by Harvill Press
23 Lower Belgrave Street, London, S.W.1

Translated from *Pascal, l'homme et l'œuvre*,
by Jean Mesnard
Collection : " Connaissance des lettres "

PRINTED IN GREAT BRITAIN BY THE ALCUIN PRESS, WELWYN GARDEN CITY HERTS.

CONTENTS

FOREWORD

THERE will always be room for more books about Pascal. And they will always be written; the French have a genius for reinterpretation, they prefer to reinterpret their fellow-countrymen, and among those—even among those—Pascal takes indisputably high rank. In some ways, he has a rarity which one is tempted to write down as uniqueness. If there is such a thing—how *he* would have hated the phrase!—as "a religious genius", Pascal, evidently, must be so described. And what other "religious genius" in all history is there, whose name would have been written among the Immortals even if he had never written a word, never entertained a thought, on the subject of religion? Here is a mathematician, a scientist, of world consequence, to whom, in his innermost thoughts, science and mathematics were dross.

Again, what other recipient of a mystical experience has served it up for posterity (if the expression may be allowed) hot from the oven? Père Poulain tells us of a philosopher who thought to read the riddle of existence by putting himself under the influence of a certain drug, leaving paper and pencil handy so that he could write down the great secret just before the fumes overpowered him. When he came to, and staggered back to the table in search of the revelation, he found that he had written down the words "A strong smell of turpentine prevails throughout". That is the crux of the matter—How to be sure that our impressions of the irrecoverable moment have not been falsified by reflection? The revelations made to Saint Gertrude, John Wesley's memories of his conversion—they were written down afterwards; they are emotion remembered in tranquillity. But the *Memorial*, that scrap of paper which Pascal wore round his neck in memory of 23rd November,

1654, bears all the marks of being fresh from the mint. He wrote when the experience was over, since he can tell us how long it lasted, from half-past ten till about half an hour after midnight. But the loosely connected texts, the fragmentary aspirations, are seen to spring from the unconscious mind, in which all inspiration, true or false, must needs be focused. The variations in the size of the handwriting (Brémond gives you the document in facsimile) tell the same story. Rigidly an experimentalist, Pascal could not even pass through the crisis of his soul without wanting to get it down, at the first possible moment, on paper.

But it is not only his rare qualities that make him a subject for perpetual reinterpretation; it is also the elusiveness of his personality. We are for ever trying to see the man behind the message, and it is a baffling exercise because we are not quite sure that we have fixed the attitude of his mind exactly right. Here there is a tempting parallel in the case of Newman. There is much in common between the two men; the admirably limpid style which makes it all too easy for the reader—and perhaps for the writer—to be carried away by the argument; the want of sympathy for scholastic methods; the destiny which allotted to either dangerous comrades-in-arms, with whom he was not altogether in sympathy. But especially there is this quality of elusiveness; what did Pascal, what did Newman feel *behind* it all? Critics have not been wanting who claimed that either man was, at the roots of him, an atheist.

And yet, what a vast difference in our apparatus for getting a personal impression of the two men! Newman so intimately self-revealed, so jealously scrutinized by friend and foe, who have left their impressions on record—and yet nobody, least of all himself, has really made it clear what happened to Newman's outlook between 1828 and 1830. How, then, are we to get any glimpse into the inner thoughts of Pascal, so anonymous in his influence, so much a figure behind the scenes, alternately whitewashed by Jansenist and by orthodox admirers? Port-Royal had a regular vice for hagiography; all its geese were swans, and Pascal must be written up as something next door to a Saint. If you would know anything about a man's *naturel*, you do not go to the annalists of Port-Royal for it; they disapproved, *ex hypothesi*, of the *naturel*. Only a stray allusion in a letter from his sister allows us to guess that Pascal had an atrabilious temperament, kept under control with difficulty; and yet how can your judgments on a man be valid if a fact like that is left out of sight?

The Pascal of the *Memorial*, and the Pascal of *The Provincial Letters*—how are we to bridge the gap between them? Fourteen months have elapsed, and a John Wesley suddenly reappears as a Jonathan Swift. If you take them in detail, the criticisms levelled at *The Provincial Letters* can be disposed of. You may say that the extracts chosen from the casuists, though not representative, were nevertheless characteristic. You may say that the *volte-face* by which the Thomist view of grace, at first ridiculed, is later on pressed into the service of Jansenism was due to a change in Nicole's attitude, not in Pascal's. You may say that Port-Royal was forced into a polemical frame of mind by the determined attacks made on it, and Pascal with the rest— even in his *Memorial* he will have it that God is not the God of the philosophers or the *savants*. You may defend his statement that he did not belong to Port-Royal on the ground that he did not belong to any Jansenist organization (but did Arnauld? Did Nicole?). You may think that Mère Angèlique and M. Singlin were only shocked by the *Letters* because they terribly lacked a sense of humour. But you cannot get over the impression that a false note has been struck. A man of first-class mind, newly converted to a religion of desperate seriousness, has brought theology down to the level of the man in the street; has taken up a weapon of raillery which will be fatally borrowed by Voltaire.

There is fresh ground for speculation about Pascal's

later years, not least about the conflict between his Catholic
and his Jansenist loyalties. Did he really help to draft the
Mandement; did he lend himself to that compromise by
which the religious of Port-Royal were to disown Jansen's
condemned propositions without committing themselves
to the assertion that these propositions were to be found
in Jansen's writings? That compromise broke the heart
of Jacqueline, his own sister, was his conscience so much
less tender than hers? Later, it was notoriously Pascal who
held out for a more intransigent policy, when Nicole and
Arnauld were for conciliation. To be sure, there was no
logical inconsistency in that; but it looks as if there had been
a psychological development at which we can only guess.
Thenceforward, Pascal and the Port-Royalists drew apart;
was it, as some hold, because he thought they had been too
complaisant? Or did he, as others think, draw back from
his Jansenist position? Or did he draw back from his Jansenist position on the ground that the cause was not worth
fighting for at all unless you were prepared to fight for it *à
l'outrance*? These questions were not solved on his deathbed,
because the priest who attended him, Père Beurrier, first
gave an edifying account of his Catholic dispositions, then
retracted, then retracted his retractation. The biographers
are left to wrangle.

Meanwhile, Pascal had bequeathed to the world a whole
collection of disjointed fragments, some of which—but how
many of them? Nobody is quite sure—were to be incorporated in his projected apology for the Christian religion.
That it would have been a masterpiece of literature, there
can be no doubt; if Pascal had never written anything
else, he would still be remembered by his fragments. But
would it have been a convincing apology? Quite certainly,
it would not have followed the traditional lines of theodicy.
Pascal distrusted *a priori* arguments; had he not shown
that the vacuum existed, when Père Noël had proved that
it could not? And he would solve a more momentous
question, whether that Plenum exists without which all our

human life would be a vacuum, on other lines than the scholastic thinkers who had gone before him. He would appeal to facts; to the facts of human nature, in its heights and in its depths, to the facts of Jewish history, to the facts of the Incarnation. What appeal would such an Apology have for our own day? Would it have satisfied the modern mind by its revolt from metaphysics? Or would it have antagonized the modern mind by its reliance on a fundamentalist view of Scripture? All this can be argued and re-argued, as we fit together, now this way now that, the dazzling fragments of that tessellated pavement which Pascal never lived to finish.

And behind it all lies the doubt whether he was attempting the impossible, or whether he was solving at a blow the age-long difficulty of apologetics, when he set out to convince man's mind and man's heart at a single stroke, instead of appealing first to the one and then to the other. Would the finished work have been a rival to the *Summa contra Gentes*, or a rival to the *Exercises*? Or would it, miraculously, have been a rival to both? Posthumously, as in life and in death, Pascal remains an enigma; there can be no certainty how the work would have grown in such hands as his. All he has left us is the ruins of a temple which was never built.

M. Mesnard's book is a marvel of compression and of lucidity. It is not to be expected that everybody will agree with all his conclusions. But two things emerge, fascinatingly, from the reading of it; the veiled figure of a man, and the clear-cut outlines of a problem.

RONALD KNOX.

INTRODUCTION

FOR some time past, there has been a great deal of new
and deep research into the problems raised by the life and
work of Blaise Pascal. Brunschvicg's great edition of Pascal, a
remarkable achievement when it first appeared, can no
longer be regarded as the last word in scholarship. Unpublished documents have been found and the manuscript of
the "Pensées" has revealed unsuspected secrets. We have a
better knowledge, to-day, also of the mental climate that
Pascal moved in; the *salons*, the circles of the learned and of
the free-thinkers, the religious life of the time, the Jansenist
movement, all stand out in bolder relief. This little book
aims merely at serving as an introduction to the serious study
of Pascal. It does, however, attempt to indicate, with the aid
of recent researches, what are the main problems connected
with his life and work. For each of these problems, we shall
outline the solution that seems most plausible in the light
of a critical examination of all Pascal's own work and all the
other relevant documents. Such a cautious approach as this
will naturally lead us to question certain accepted ideas
based on a superficial knowledge of the sources.

Here, let us deal with one large preliminary problem: to
what extent can we trust Pascal's earliest biographers?

The most important of these is Pascal's own sister,
Gilberte, the wife of Florin Périer. We owe to her a biography which would be remarkable even if only for the
literary talent displayed in it. Always sober and natural,
Gilberte evokes the atmosphere of Pascal's last years in
particular with notable skill. She wrote her biography
shortly after her brother's death; manuscript copies were in
circulation long before the life was published in 1684. Very
much admired—Bayle enthusiastically praised it—it became
inseparable from the various editions of the *Pensées*. In

our own time, its documentary value has been vigorously questioned. It has been thought of as a piece of hagiography, with all the defects of its kind, silent about weaknesses, exaggerating virtues. The Pascal family wanted to leave a portrait of their great man that would conform with the Jansenist ideal of the saintly life. This is the modern explanation of certain palpably mistaken statements in Gilberte's work, such as her claim that Pascal abandoned science after his first conversion.

Another source of information is Gilberte's daughter, Marguerite Périer. Marguerite Périer had been cured in her childhood of a serious eye complaint by the Miracle of the Holy Thorn, and in later life she earned the esteem of her friends by her life of charity and retirement from the world. She did not, however, possess her mother's superior intelligence. Making use of her childhood memories and of family traditions, she composed, towards the end of the seventeenth century, various memoirs concerning her uncle Blaise, his family, and his friends. Where Gilberte leads us to the heights of the spiritual life, Marguerite is content to report odd anecdotes, of a rather facile picturesque quality, and to accumulate realistic details about her uncle's illness. Does not, however, her very simple-mindedness guarantee the truth of what she is telling us? Some critics might be tempted to agree that it does.

Should we prefer Gilberte's testimony or Marguerite's? That problem might be insoluble, if there did not exist a third class of documents, those offering testimony that is involuntary and therefore all the more trustworthy. In this class, apart from Pascal's own writings, we may mention the letters of his family and friends, known to us either through the originals or through reliable copies. We can also give great weight to public records and legal documents, much more numerous and more suggestive in relation to the Pascal family than they are generally believed to be, and more unquestionably authentic than any of our other documents. Such documents give us a more concrete and exact idea of the real Pascal; we shall lean on them more than on the biographies properly so called.

Thanks to the points of comparison with which such documents furnish us, we can also use them to verify the assertions of Gilberte and Marguerite about particular events and thus try to arrive at an idea of the reliability of both. Here, without an attempt to justify them by detailed arguments, are the conclusions to which such an objective investigation leads. Marguerite Périer's anecdotes ought to be considered with the greatest distrust. Thus her story that Pascal was converted by a sermon of Singlin's is contradicted by essential facts; as we shall see later, Pascal had already announced his conversion at the date when Marguerite says the sermon was delivered, and moreover at that date Singlin was too ill to preach. Marguerite is lavish both with dates and with exact details, but when these can be checked they are often found to be inaccurate. Here is an example: "In 1630, Etienne Pascal sold his post as Second President of the Court of Aids to his brother Blaise Pascal, and also sold the greater part of his property, which he invested in bonds on the Hôtel de Ville in Paris, whither he retired to superintend the education of his children, and especially that of Blaise." This fairly short sentence, often taken over word for word by biographers, contains at least five errors of fact.

The corresponding passage by Gilberte, while more vague, remains, after checking, perfectly accurate: "In the year 1631"—"1632" according to one manuscript, and in fact the Pascals were not strictly speaking installed in their new house in Paris till 1st January, 1632—"my father retired to Paris, took us all with him, and established his home there. My brother, who was then only eight, derived great advantage from this retirement, through the plan my father had for bringing him up." Outside documents, which add to and enrich Gilberte's text, leave almost nothing of Marguerite's standing: that one can state as an almost general rule. The details of Gilberte's story very rarely contradict the facts established by objective research. Let us therefore reconstitute Gilberte's life of Pascal in its entirety. The seventeenth-century editors cut it considerably, and it has received only very imperfect publication since and was truncated even by Brunschvicg. Let us supplement it by the memoir which Gilberte wrote of her sister Jacqueline, which in places is much more detailed and exact. Let us be careful also not to attribute to Gilberte the errors of scholars: Gilberte, for instance, does not really tell us that her brother rediscovered the first thirty-two theorems of Euclid. If there is a Pascal legend, she is not wholly responsible for it. It remains true that her narrative, taken as a whole, gives an incomplete and inexact portrait of her brother. Undoubtedly she writes with edification in mind. She does not observe due proportion between the various periods of Pascal's life or between the various branches of his activity. It was only Pascal the Christian who seemed to her worthy of interest. Pascal the scientist remains in the shadow; yet if he felt some scruples about pursuing his researches, did he ever abandon them entirely? Again, in Gilberte's narrative, Pascal, the man of the world, appears, however brilliantly, only briefly; yet Pascal never lived far from the world. The real Pascal was a more complex and a more human creature than the Pascal Gilberte describes for us. Let us try to see him in his living reality.

CHAPTER ONE

CHILDHOOD AND YOUTH

THE childhood and youth of Blaise Pascal are one of the periods of his life about which there is least argument. There is the detailed narrative of his sister, Gilberte, and we owe other particulars to the researches of learned local historians. One figure dominates the earlier life of Pascal, that of his father. Etienne Pascal had certainly a profound influence on his son, though it is hard to be sure of its exact nature.

I. *Clermont*

On 19th June, in 1623, Blaise Pascal was born at Clermont, the capital of Auvergne, at that time a small town with about 9,000 inhabitants. Some years later when Pascal's sister Jacqueline was about to take up residence in Clermont, intending to live a life of contemplative retirement in her room, she was alarmed by the thought that she was known to "everybody" in the town. As an administrative centre, Clermont was not so important as its neighbour and rival, Riom, the headquarters of the Generality, or general administration of the province. The Court of Aids, which was sovereign in matters of taxation, was at Montferrand, still an independent city. Strangers, especially those from Paris, who passed through Clermont at this period have left, like Fléchier a few years later, unflattering descriptions: they found the town gloomy, its streets narrow and smelly: the rue des Gras, where Etienne Pascal's house stood, was certainly such a street. Nor, of course, did the masterpieces of medieval art of which the town can boast attract these seventeenth-century visitors; the church of Notre Dame du Port struck them as chilly and dark.

B   I

It was, nevertheless, in Clermont, when they could, that the high officials or "officers" of the Office of Finances at Riom and the Court of Aids at Montferrand preferred to reside. The town possessed an intellectual *élite* belonging to the upper classes of the *bourgeoisie* and the legal nobility. This group had already produced such a figure as Jean Savaron, who was deputy of the Third Estate in the States General of 1614. It was to produce an eminent legal scholar, Domat, born two years after Pascal. Moreover, these legal and financial officials did not disdain, in imitation of their colleagues in Paris, to gather together in order to discuss literature or mathematics. In Clermont, at the time of Pascal's birth, a few *salons* and a few academies were undoubtedly already in existence.

The Pascals belonged to this intellectual *élite*. There were, however, two separate families of this name. One of these, whose chief was the Seigneur de Mons, had been ennobled by Louis XI in 1480. The other, originally from Cournon in Limagne, had included several rich merchants in its ancestry and had reached the highest ranks of the burgess class. The two families formed an alliance around 1580, when Marguerite Pascal of Mons married Martin Pascal, of the humbler clan. The latter, after having been receiver of taxes on the commonalty at Clermont, became secretary to Queen Louise, the wife of Henry III, and was finally, in 1586, granted the important post of Counsellor of the King, Treasurer of France, and General of the King's Finances in the Generality of Riom. Did these various promotions suffice to make him a member of the nobility? It is difficult to be sure, but, with the following generation, the situation clarifies. Two of his sons, Etienne, the father of Blaise, and another Blaise successively exercised the functions of the Presidency of the Court of Aids, a sovereign court, and by assuming this post became members of the hereditary nobility; Etienne Pascal sometimes describes himself as the Chevalier Pascal; Blaise, like his cousins, Robert and Martin Pascal, was always to bear the title

2

of Squire. Thus the Pascals became members of that *petite noblesse* which was as distinct from the ancient nobility as from the common people and which formed at that time, along with certain of the higher *bourgeois* elements, a new and original social setting, characterized especially by its interest in the things of the mind.

Of his marriage, "General" Martin Pascal had at least seven children, of whom three were sons. Etienne, the eldest, was born, possibly, in 1588. His father sent him to pursue his legal studies in Paris and, according to Marguerite Périer, recommended him to his compatriot, the advocate Antoine Arnauld, whose sons and daughters were to play such an important part in the history of Port-Royal. But this story is rather too *ben trovato*, and appears to me to be of doubtful authenticity: what we do know is that though Etienne Pascal, while living in Paris, was a neighbour of the Arnaulds, he visited them rather infrequently. When he came back to Clermont in 1610 he bought himself a post as one of the elected representatives in the Clermont election: these "elected representatives" formed the lowest court of judgment in disputes concerning taxation. In 1624 both his capacity and his wealth led to his being chosen as Deputy President of the Court of Aids at Montferrand; he became one of the most prominent figures in the general life of his province.

In 1616 or 1617, he had married Antoinette Begon, born in 1596, the daughter of Victor Begon, a burgess and merchant of Clermont, and of Antoinette de Fontfreyde, his wife. Of four children born of Etienne Pascal's marriage, three survived; Gilberte, born in 1620, Blaise, born in 1623, and Jacqueline, born in 1625. In 1626, Antoinette Begon died. Her husband was grief-stricken and from that moment, perhaps, began to dream of retiring and settling in Paris.

About the childhood of Blaise Pascal in Clermont, we know very little. His mother, who died when he was three, cannot have exercised any marked influence on him; so far as we can make out, she was a pious and charitable lady.

According to his sister Gilberte, Blaise, from his earliest years, "gave signs of an intelligence quite out of the ordinary, not only by the very apt little answers he gave to other people's questions, but even more by his own questions about the nature of things, which used to surprise everybody". Did Pascal's passion for science, then, make its appearance at such an early age, combined with the irony from which *The Provincial Letters* were to spring? Marguerite Périer has information with a more factual flavour, but how far can we believe it? According to her, when he was only one year old, Pascal fell into a kind of apathy and this state was accompanied by two curious circumstances; he could not bear the sight of water and he started to cry when he saw his father and mother draw near to each other. How far is either of these reactions of a one-year-old child really out of the ordinary? But we must add that, according to Marguerite, this apathy, which lasted for a year, was attributed to an evil spell cast by a witch. Etienne Pascal, at first incredulous, finally accepted this explanation and gave the poor sorceress a bad time. Blaise's cure was finally also effected through sorcery, which involved the sacrifice of two cats. This whole story, perhaps is proof less of the credulity of Etienne Pascal than of that of Marguerite Périer. What we can accept in it is that the first symptoms of Pascal's life-long malady appeared very early. The nature of that malady remains even to-day unexplained, and this is a subject to which we shall have to return.

At the end of 1631, Etienne Pascal, accompanied by his three children, left Clermont and settled in Paris. The reasons underlying this change of scene remain mysterious. Perhaps to his grief for the loss of his wife we ought to add disappointed ambition and the desire for a more intense intellectual life. In addition, a kind of migratory instinct had already drawn many of his closest relations from Auvergne to the capital. However, this breaking of the links with his native place was in easy stages and in fact never became final. Till 1636 at least, Etienne Pascal used to return each year in the autumn to spend two or three months at Clermont. He did not sell his house in the rue des Gras till 1633 or his post as President in the Court of Aids till 1634, both to his brother Blaise. Then he invested a great part of his wealth in bonds on the Hôtel de Ville, which, he believed, would assure himself and his family future ease and tranquillity.

II. *Paris*

Across the Paris of 1631 a fresh wind was blowing. The strengthening of the central power was to be noted in the very physical structure of the city. New districts were rising, their streets laid out in harsh rectangles. Open squares, built with a view to a fine general architectural effect, were being used as promenades for the gentry, *les honnêtes gens*. Richelieu was building the Palais-Cardinal. The aristocracy and the great financiers of the *bourgeois* class were adorning the neighbourhood of the Louvre and the Marais with their new mansions. A whole flowering of convents and monasteries bore witness to a religious reawakening; among them Port-Royal, already profoundly transformed under the direction of Mère Angélique, but still very little known to the outside world, had been transferred from its first unhealthy low-lying site to the Faubourg Saint-Jacques. If, among all this new magnificence, there were poverty and wretchedness everywhere, few people took any notice: though St. Vincent de Paul had already begun his work of evangelization and charity.

In this setting of relative calm and peace, the life of the intellect was opening out like a flower: still, however, as a fashionable life, glittering in the *salons* and above all in the Hôtel de Rambouillet. The ideal of the *honnête homme*, the honourable and cultivated gentleman, was being worked out but, still hampered by Italian models, had not yet found its perfect form. A society of the elect had nevertheless come into being, the society that, in applauding the comedies of Corneille, applauded itself. This society already felt itself capable of imposing its own taste in literary matters and of assuring the success of the works that met with its favour. The life of learning, on the other hand, was a little more shut off from the fashionable world. It gathered together into groups or "academies" all those who had any kind of scientific curiosity: curiosity about genealogy or grammar, natural history or mathematics. These groups discussed with equal eagerness the discovery of an ancient manuscript, the news of a distant exploration, the carrying out of an interesting experiment in physics. Such, for instance, was the famous "Cabinet" of the Brothers Dupuy. It was in these circles that what was called "free-thinking" was developed; with all its shades from mere breadth of mind to frank unbelief, and with a range of attitudes in which boldness and submissiveness to authority were mingled in the most ambiguous fashion.

It was in this atmosphere which left so much to intellectual choice that the young Pascal, now eight years old and already exceptionally gifted, was to begin his education.

It is difficult to be exact about the chronology of Blaise's first stay in Paris. Our easiest course is still to follow Etienne Pascal in his successive changes of residence.

Shortly after their arrival, the family settled in the rue de la Tissanderie, in an old district, at the edge of the busy streets that lay around the Port de la Grève, and at the edge, also of the fine new mansions of the Marais district. To look after his young children and act as a housekeeper, Etienne Pascal—who, in contrast to the general custom of his time, had not remarried—engaged a governess. Louise Default was of a lower-middle-class family, originally of Coulommiers, and connected with the family of La Fontaine. She kept her post for twenty years and remained strongly attached to the children she had brought up; just before her death in 1658, she asked Blaise to draw up her will. Etienne Pascal, however, did not abandon his authority in the family to the new governess; on the contrary—and this is a fresh mark of originality in his character—he had a

6

passionate interest in his children and managed to create between himself and them an atmosphere of mutual confidence which is strangely in agreement with the demands of the most modern theories of education. He delighted, while they were still very young, to take them out visiting with him, to keep them abreast of his work, and even to make them responsible for household and educational tasks; Gilberte, for instance, had the task of teaching her younger sister to read, she was her father's companion on a journey, she was in charge of the household during his absence. This atmosphere of mutual confidence did not, however, exclude paternal authority; on the contrary, the father's authority was sometimes felt severely. It is easy to understand how, growing up with so exceptional a background, the three children should each have developed a strong personality. But Etienne Pascal's greatest originality lay in his scheme for educating his children himself, without employing any tutor. It would be very hard to find precedents for this attitude; in the eyes of Pascal's social superiors it might even have implied, in a man of his rank, a certain arrogance. It bears witness to his family sense and his passion for the cultivation of the intellect.

Blaise Pascal's education began in 1632 and followed out a plan laid down in advance. We know about this plan and the details of its application through the narrative of Gilberte, who was her father's first pupil and who owed to him that superiority of mind which was later to strike Madame de Sablé so strongly. We may regret the absence of other testimony but what Gilberte has to say has never, in its general drift, been questioned, and it is confirmed in some points of detail by independent documents.

"The chief maxim in this plan of education," writes Gilberte, "was that of keeping the child in a state of superiority to his tasks," that is to say of waiting, before instructing him in some new kind of knowledge, till he had passed the age when he would be sufficiently advanced to assimilate it. This was the maxim of a profound educational theorist, and it explains the order of Pascal's early studies. Etienne Pascal, in whom one feels the living spirit of the Renaissance, wished first and foremost to make his son a humanist but, in conformity to his own maxim, he forbade himself to teach Blaise Latin or Greek till he was twelve; the study of these languages began very much earlier at the Jesuit colleges, in one of which the mind of Descartes has been formed. A new stage was to be reached when Blaise was fifteen or sixteen; he would then learn mathematics, which were to be the crown of his education. In working out his plan, therefore, Etienne Pascal was seeking to avoid all painful effort on the pupil's part and to develop the suppleness of the mind.

But how was the time of the teacher and the pupil to be employed between the ages of eight and twelve, that is to say, during the period with which we are now dealing? The child received lessons on the most varied topics, but always lessons within his capacity and of a sort likely to strike his young imagination; he learned, for instance, the effects of gunpowder as used in cannons. Current events often formed the starting points of his lessons and, in addition, the child, in whom the desire for knowledge had been awakened very early, often gave his lessons their starting point by his own questions: the noise made by a porcelain plate struck, by accident, with a knife provided material for a lesson on the theory of sound. Young Blaise's education proceeded even at meal-times, as in Rabelais, whose accounts of the education of Gargantua and Pantagruel Etienne Pascal often seemed to remember, even though his primary inspiration was Montaigne.

At the same time, preparations were made for the study of languages, that was to commence later. In general terms, the father explained to his son "what languages were; he showed him how they had been reduced to grammars, containing certain rules; how these rules, however, admitted exceptions, which had also been carefully noted down; and how a method had been found in this way to make all languages communicable from country to country." Is this the first sketch of the idea of a *general grammar*, valid for all languages, which Port-Royal attempted to bring into being, and which was very dear to the philosophers of the Enlightenment? In any case, Etienne Pascal's attitude to language illustrates the rationalistic character of his whole scheme of instruction.

The Pascals remained at the rue de la Tissanderie till 1634. To evoke the atmosphere of this period, we would have to sketch President Pascal's earliest circle of acquaintances in Paris. It seems, then, that he chiefly visited his fellow-provincials. The documentation that we possess for these years shows him always in the company of Auvergnats either settled in Paris or passing through the capital: the Champflours, the Ribeyres, or members of his own family. It was at this period also, certainly, that he made the acquaintance of the famous actor, Montdory, the son of a cutler of Thiers, who was in a position to introduce him into intellectual circles. Finally, with his passion for mathematics and physics, he began to frequent the gatherings of the learned.

During the years 1634 to 1635, however, the situation changed; Etienne Pascal's links with Auvergne grew looser and his circle of purely Parisian acquaintances grew wider. The Pascals established themselves in the aristocratic Faubourg Saint-Germain, facing the Hôtel de Conde, and almost next door to the Luxembourg. Was President Pascal received by his great neighbours? It seems rather improbable. He was perhaps introduced to Madame de Combalet, the future Duchesse d'Aiguillon, Richelieu's niece, who lived at the Petit-Luxembourg. But above all he frequented the near-by *salon* of Madame Sainctot. The latter, a woman of remarkable beauty, had become famous through her affairs with the Comte d'Avaux and, more especially, with Voiture; through her contact with that poet she had refined an originally rather uncultivated intelligence and some of her letters do not lack charm. In 1634, however, she had been long since abandoned by Voiture and all her attempts to recapture the fickle poet had been unsuccessful. Her husband, the Treasurer of France at Tours, had died young, leaving her one son, Nicolas, and two daughters, Anne and Catherine, whose education she very much neglected; they were the playmates of the Pascal children.

Among the company at Madame Sainctot's, Etienne Pascal rediscovered a friend of his earlier years, no doubt an old fellow-student, called Jacques le Pailleur. The son of a Lieutenant in the Election of Meulan, the Intendant of a superannuated flirt, the Maréchale de Thémines, and scrupulously honest in the exercise of that function, a considerable mathematician though he had not gathered his studies together into any work of continuous application, le Pailleur was also a good fellow, fond of music, poetry, and dancing. He was attached to a group of poets that numbered among them Saint-Amant, Benserade, and d'Alibray. The last named lived with Madame Sainctot, who was his sister, and was a particularly close acquaintance of the Pascals. In this group of poets, underlying the passion for wine and good cheer which they so often celebrated, there could be perceived an open-mindedness, a taste for study, and a certain boldness of thought. There survives to-day an epistle addressed by le Pailleur to d'Alibray on "Galileo's opinion concerning the movement of the earth": it is an ironic eulogy of ignorance which alone preserves us from the risk of heresy, an irreverent mixture of Gospel texts and invitations to the pleasures of the table. But the essential note of this group was a hatred of pedantry and a horror of dogmatism; they had been formed by Montaigne.

The dignity and gravity of the magistral office made of Etienne Pascal a very different man. But he enjoyed the company of these poets and showed sufficient indulgence towards their boldness to allow him to introduce his still very young children into this atmosphere of free speech.

While Etienne Pascal was making these lighter social contacts, his more serious scientific reputation was, at the same time, growing. At the beginning of 1634, Richelieu named him one of five commissioners charged with an investigation into the discoveries of the Sieur Morin, the inventor of a method for determining longitudes. In 1635, Father Mersenne, a Friar Minor, founded an important "academy" which, in contrast with that of the Dupuy brothers, sought to gather together genuine scientists rather than merely learned men. Etienne Pascal was one of the first members along with, among others, Mydorges, Desargues and Roberval. We can estimate the high regard in which this assembly was held by the dedication to it of one of the books of Mersenne's *Universal Harmony*; he speaks of the group's "very deep learning in all the branches of mathematics". Mersenne kept up an assiduous correspondence with foreign and provincial scientists, notably with Descartes in Holland, and with Fermat, then Counsellor in the Parliament of Toulouse. His Academy thus became the first centre of purely scientific life in Europe.

It was, perhaps, to be near Father Mersenne, who lived at the Monastery of the Friars Minor in the Place Royale that, in the very year of the foundation of Mersenne's Academy, Etienne Pascal left the rue de la Condé for the rue Brisemiche, near the church of Saint-Merri. He retained this new residence till 1648, taking care to renew his lease even while living at Rouen.

How, meanwhile, was the education of the young Blaise developing? The time had come for him to begin his study of languages. But the plan of education, as laid out in advance, underwent a profound transformation as a sequel to a famous event about which there has been a great deal of scholarly argument.

This is Gilberte's story. Strictly following out his own method, Etienne Pascal refused to teach his son mathematics till, at the age of fifteen or sixteen, his mind should be ripe for this subject. Blaise Pascal, mildly thwarted by this refusal, and seeing his father always in the company of mathematicians, succeeded one day in extorting from Etienne a definition of the science. This was as follows:

mathematics was "the method of making correct figures and of discovering the proportions which they bear to each other". Thereupon, Blaise set himself to reflect and to draw figures on the tiles of his playroom. "But as his father had taken so much care to conceal these things from him that he did not even know their names, he was forced to make up names for himself. He called a circle a 'round', a line a 'bar'; and so with other figures. Having invented these names, he went on to make axioms for himself and finally perfect demonstrations; and as in these things one is led from one stage to the next, he passed on and pushed his researches so far that he reached the thirty-second theorem of the first book of Euclid." Etienne then surprised him at work; "His father having asked him what he was doing, he said that he was seeking for something, which was in fact the thirty-second theorem of the first book of Euclid." Carried away with admiration, President Pascal rushed out to describe his joy and astonishment to his intimate friend, le Pailleur.

The above quotations from Gilberte's account bring out the blunder made by the majority of commentators. We are *not* told that the child had discovered all the theorems of Euclid up to the thirty-second: that would be genuinely miraculous and incredible. No, he was surprised by his father at the very moment *when he was seeking to demonstrate the thirty-second theorem,* namely: "The sum of the angles of a triangle is equal to two right angles." A very small number of axioms and preliminary demonstrations are all that is necessary for the postulation of this theorem. If one were seeking to minimize the importance of the anecdote—but there are plenty of similar cases of precocity in the lives of other mathematicians—one might acknowledge that the young Pascal seems to have been following out a chain of intuitions rather than of reasonings properly so called: we are authorized to say so by the phrase, "he was *seeking* for something": the result to be obtained appeared more clearly to him than the method of obtaining it. In every mathematical discovery, for that matter, intuition has the primary role.

Tallemant des Réaux, the author of the *Historiettes*, reports the actual facts rather differently. According to him the son of President Pascal had been reading secretly, at night, the earlier books of Euclid: and that in itself would be a striking achievement at the age of twelve, and with no assistance. But all the reality of childish life, every detail taken "from the life", has disappeared from this new version of the story. And one can understand very well how, passing from *salon* to *salon*, the story would be distorted, some speakers embellishing it out of family pride, others, by a natural reaction, trying to reduce it to plausibility. What is certain, in any case, is that the young Pascal gave very early signs of a lively passion for science, a passion supported by exceptional natural endowments.

His father understood this, put Euclid's *Elements* into his hands, and undertook his scientific education. But what direction did he give to this education?

Etienne Pascal had a mind that attached itself to the material reality of things; he had reacted against the principles of Aristotelian physics and so was able to spare Blaise that scholastic training which was still the rule in the colleges. He set a high value, above all, on the work of Roberval. In 1636, the two friends were to address a letter to Fermat on the problem of gravity, which reveals their mental attitudes very clearly. According to them gravity was not a quality residing within bodies, but a phenomenon analogous to the attraction of iron by a magnet. Above all, in this letter, they managed to define some aspects of an excellent scientific method. They declared that no hypothesis should be accepted unless it is demonstrable and no principles of reasoning "except those which experience, assisted by good judgment, has certified for us".

One can understand why the importance of the *Discourse on Method*, published a year later, should have escaped the attention of scientists already so modern in their outlook.

They were rather severe on the mathematical and physical treatises which accompanied the *Discourse*, especially on the *Dioptrics*, reproaching Descartes for reasoning on the basis of confused ideas and not making a sufficient appeal to experience. This criticism was formulated by Roberval, but it equally expressed the opinion of Etienne Pascal. The two friends entered into a sharp conflict with Descartes, arising out of his controversy with Fermat, in which they energetically took the side of the latter. An esteem for Fermat, a prejudice against Descartes, the feelings of Etienne and the scientific principles that supported them, were all later to be found in Blaise.

The latter was now making rapid progress in mathematics; the bent of his genius, avid for clarity and eager to know the reason for everything, could have found no more satisfying subject to study. Very soon, Etienne was introducing Blaise into the scientific circles which he frequented. The child took his share in the examination of new works and even sometimes put together little works himself. People took notice above all of a *Treatise on Conics*, which he wrote at sixteen. We do not possess this treatise in its original state, since Pascal later perfected it, but there remain two copies of an *Essay on Conics*, a little placard in poster form, printed in Paris in 1640. This essay, which defines the properties of conics or conic sections, the circle, the ellipse, the parabola, the hyperbola, bear witness to a great power of intuition and synthesis. All the properties of conics and conic sections are deduced from a single theorem, later called that of "the mystic hexagram": if a six-sided figure is inscribed within a conic section, the meeting points of opposite sides are in a straight line with each other. Blaise Pascal had taken his inspiration, on his own admission, from the work of a geometrist of Lyons, Desargues. This was in itself an originality, for the true value of Desargues' work was not recognized till much later; and Desargues nevertheless acknowledged that Pascal himself was the sole inventor of the mystic hexagram. It is interesting to note that, amid the chorus of praise which greeted the young man, the voice of Descartes alone was disdainful and reserved.

We can see now how deep was the intellectual impression which Etienne Pascal made on his son. Etienne's scientific ideas furnished Blaise with a foundation on which his genius could easily build itself up. If Pascal reached intellectual maturity with unusual rapidity, the reason is that, unlike Descartes, he did not have to effect a revolution within himself; he had only to follow a path already traced out.

Meanwhile, however, neither the study of languages nor that of philosophy was neglected. Finally, an important place was assigned to religious instruction.

In matters of religion, once more, Etienne Pascal's attitudes can be explained by setting him against the background of his time; in his character there was a mingling of that gravity proper to the legal nobility and of the free thinking characteristic of learned society.

No doubt he was very exact in carrying out the religious practices which his social position demanded. He was able to teach his children a great respect for religion, perhaps more an outward respect than a deep inner piety; his daughter Jacqueline, for instance, was not confirmed until she was twenty-one. The few facts that are available about the spirit of his religious teaching still bear witness to the humanistic spirit of the Renaissance. The scholastic and abstract side of theology was neglected in favour of reading of, and direct meditation upon, passages from the Bible, and a small number of texts from the Fathers and essential decisions of the Councils. The non-metaphysical, the positivistic nature of such teaching was in agreement, before Jansenism existed, with certain aspects of Jansenism. The latter movement was similarly hostile to scholasticism.

To Gilberte, we owe another very valuable detail. Etienne Pascal "held it as a maxim that anything which is the concern of faith cannot be the concern of reason". This was a convenient maxim to avoid possible conflicts between reason and faith and it was very popular in certain free-thinking circles, where, of course, it would be completed by the converse maxim: that anything that was the concern of reason could not be the concern of faith. Thus, this protestation of respect for faith could also become one of independence in matters of reason. However, this principle seems to have freed Blaise Pascal, in his youth, of every tendency towards doubt, and, after his conversion, he was to include it in his own system, having found an analogous distinction in Jansenius.

There is a very revealing page, also, in which Gilberte describes the reflections of Jacqueline, while still a child, on conventual and monastic life: for this life of withdrawal and contemplation, Jacqueline felt "a great estrangement and even contempt, as she believed that in that life people carried out practices that were not capable of satisfying a reasonable mind". In these words of Jacqueline's we surely see an indirect and unintentional result of the attitude of her father. This hostility towards the monastic life recalls the Renaissance cult of the life according to nature, a cult kept alive both by learned men and by that Gallicanism, that wish to restrict so far as possible the direct influence of Rome on the Catholic Church in France, which was common among the great magistrates. This Gallican and anti-monastic sentiment should not be confused with mere hostility to religion. Within the bosom of the Church itself, a very definite movement was taking shape against the life of the monastic rule. Led partly by Jean-Pierre Camus, the friend of Saint François de Sales, whom the Pascals were to know at Rouen, it had received the support of a fiery theologian who hid his identity under the pseudonym "Pétrus Aurelius": the Abbé de Saint-Cyran.

To sum all this up, we can say that, without neglecting the religious education of his children, Etienne Pascal did not do much to incline them towards piety, but that his own bent of mind prepared them to sympathize with some of the tendencies of the Jansenist movement.

As they grew up, Blaise and his sisters more and more

often accompanied their father on his visits to his friends in the fashionable world. Though Etienne was now living well away from the Faubourg Saint-Germain, he had kept up his contacts there. In 1636, when leaving Paris for Auvergne with Gilberte, he did not hesitate to confide Jacqueline, then aged eleven, to Madame Sainctot. The two daughters of the latter shared with Jacqueline her passion for poetry. Together they composed a play in five acts, observing all the unities. "They acted it themselves twice with other actors they got to help them, and there was a crowd of spectators." A few poems written by Jacqueline as a child still survive; very much admired by Benserade and Scudéry, they were sometimes included in printed verse miscellanies. The desire to shine was Jacqueline's from birth, as it was Blaise's.

In the neighbourhood of Saint-Merri, the Pascals made new acquaintances. They were often to be found at the Barillons', a great parliamentary family, members of whom had held the highest administrative posts. The atmosphere here was both more austere and more aristocratic than at Madame Sainctot's. Antoine Barillon, Seigneur de Morangis, Master of Requests and Counsellor of State, was at first one of the administrative counsellors of the Church of Saint-Merri and later a warm defender of Duhamel, the Jansenist priest of the parish. For the time being, Monsieur and Madame de Morangis were above all taken with the sweetness of Jacqueline. In 1638, the child had written some verses on the pregnancy of the Queen—a "noble" subject, if ever there was one!—and Madame de Morangis took her to Saint-Germain to present her to Anne of Austria. While in expectation of this visit, Jacqueline managed to improvise an epigram to present to Mademoiselle, the King's sister, and another to present to Madame de Hautefort. Later, she was to pay several return visits to the Court. It is interesting to see how much freedom, at that time, such very young children might enjoy.

It was at this period also that the Pascals made their first acquaintance with the great family of Roannez. The future

Duc de Roannez and his sister Charlotte were known by the Pascals when they were still children. This explains the familiar intercourse which later became habitual between two families so unequal in rank.

Thus, from about 1638, Blaise Pascal had a very complete experience of "the great world". He had been to Court. He knew the atmosphere both of high society with its deliberate preciosity, its affectation, and of the smaller *salons* of the rich middle-class. He enjoyed the amusements and the brilliant life of such a society. Has not "the libertine", the man of free life and free thought, in the *Pensées*, his models, among others, in such men as d'Alibray or le Pailleur, the friends of Pascal's father: types rediscovered, and known more thoroughly, in the young man's own social investigations? Perhaps such men as these led Blaise towards Montaigne, if his father, who perhaps preferred the more masculine lessons of Epictetus, had not already done so. We can be sure at least, that while he was studying the sciences Blaise was also studying man.

Towards the end of 1638, a series of rather romantic events transformed the life of Etienne Pascal and his children. The state of the royal treasury, depleted by wars, no longer permitted the regular payment of interest on bonds on the Hôtel de Ville. Etienne Pascal and other people who lived on the interest of their investments and to whom this measure struck harshly home protested violently to the Chancellor Séguier. When informed of this, Richelieu ordered the ring-leaders in the protest to be sent to the Bastille. Fearing for his own safety, Etienne Pascal at first went into hiding and then fled to Auvergne.

However, in February, 1639, the Cardinal wanted to have a comedy acted by children, for the amusement of his guests. His niece, the Duchesse d'Aiguillon, had the task of gathering a company together. She asked for the assistance of one of Madame Sainctot's daughter and of Jacqueline Pascal. The friends of the Pascal family saw in this an opportunity to put an end to the disfavour into which Jacqueline's father had fallen. The Duchesse d'Aiguillon promised to help. The performance took place and Jacqueline was heartily applauded. But, as they forgot to present her to the Cardinal after the play, she went to see him alone. Richelieu took her on his knees, kissed her, and, seeing that she was crying, asked her what was the cause of her grief. She explained, and Etienne Pascal was swiftly restored to favour. On his return to Paris he paid a grateful visit, with his children round him, to the Cardinal at Rueil. In the autumn of the same year, he was appointed an assistant to the Intendant of Normandy with the title of "His Majesty's Deputy Commissioner for the imposition and levying of taxes on the commonalty".

III. *Rouen*

The mission thus confided to President Pascal was a delicate one; Richelieu was counting on his financial experience but even more on his devotion to the central power. For several years, Normandy had been in a state of latent rebellion. The excesses of the "soldiery", the increase in taxes, levied by pitiless methods, and finally a serious outbreak of the plague, had reduced the population to such wretchedness that the gentry themselves were taking to banditry, and insecurity reigned throughout the province. The war against the House of Austria made new taxes endlessly necessary; but both the Parliament and the Court of Aids at Rouen were refusing to accept these. Towards the end of August, 1639, Rouen was the scene of a riot caused by an edict controlling the manufacture of dyes. Killing and looting which the authorities were unable to control forced the Intendant, Claude de Paris, to withdraw to Gisors. It was there that Etienne Pascal joined him. While together they sought to spread out a levy of 150,000 livres over the town and neighbourhood of Rouen, the Government had decided to make an example of the city. The Chancellor Séguier came in person to Gaillon to make contact with the Intendant and his new colleague. In spite of the supplication of the Archbishop, François de Harlay, Marshal Gassion's troops entered Rouen on 2nd January, 1640. Séguier, no doubt accompanied by Claude de Paris and Etienne Pascal, followed close on their heels and gave the signal for the putting into effect of repressive measures. These repressive measures were bloodthirsty; Corneille, who witnessed them, perhaps wished, when a little later he composed his *Cinna*, to appeal for clemency towards the people of Rouen. Did the young Blaise witness these dramatic episodes? We may doubt it. But the echo of them reached him; Gassion's repressive measures had not wholly damped down the fires and trouble broke out again several times after Blaise and his sisters had joined their father in Rouen. These memories, and his memories of the Fronde, explain the horror of popular uprisings which Blaise Pascal was to express later, and that fidelity to the central monarchical power which was the last word of his political philosophy.

Etienne Pascal seems to have aroused little sympathy among the people of Normandy; which, given the circumstances of his arrival, is what one would expect. Intendants, Commissioners, and other agents of the central power were loathed throughout the province and were to suffer from the reaction which followed on Richelieu's death in 1643. The very tasks with which Etienne was entrusted were of a sort to make him enemies; they are rather hard to define, but they consisted chiefly in parcelling out taxation between the different parishes of the Generality. This was an onerous duty at first, but it became progressively lighter as the old organizations, the Office of Finances and the Court of Aids, gradually recovered their authority. Etienne Pascal carried out his duties with scrupulous care, working late into the night, travelling about to estimate the taxable resources of different parishes, and having, at the end of his administration, foreborne to enrich himself. The Court recognized his merits by conferring on him on 27th December, 1645, letters of appointment as Counsellor of State.

For the Pascals life in Rouen was in its broad patterns very like life in Paris. Their house lay behind the walls of Saint-Ouen, in the parish of Sainte-Croix, the district of the "functionaries" and magistrates, among whom they made their closest acquaintances. The atmosphere was still that of high and good society, though no doubt more austere and less varied than in Paris. The characteristic simplicity of the Pascals marked Gilberte's marriage ceremony. She was married, on 13th June, 1641, to her cousin, Florin Périer, for whom Etienne Pascal had obtained a post in Normandy.

Jacqueline meanwhile continued to work at her poetry, encouraged by the great Corneille, who had become a family friend. In 1640, on 8th December, she carried off the prize at the competition for Palinodes. During the ensuing years, her gift acquired more strength; the tone of her poems became more robust and personal. Possibly the influence of Corneille revealed to her the lofty and forceful nature of her temperament; her *Stanzas Against Love* exalt the victory of reason and virtue over that tyrannic passion.

Blaise was closely associated with his father's work and interests. Etienne, tied to Rouen by his official duties, would sometimes send his son to Paris or even Clermont to look after urgent business matters; thus Blaise from time to time would revisit the rue Brisemiche and rediscover his old Paris friends. At Rouen, he took his share in the endless task of dividing out taxes between different parishes. It was the sight of the tedious calculations this entailed which suggested to him the invention of his famous arithmetical machine. He thought of it in 1642 but it required two years of toil to bring it into practical existence. We still possess at least six machines built under Pascal's instructions. Most of them are still in working order and can add, subtract, multiply, and divide. How far was this an original invention? The *idea* of an automatic calculating machine had occurred to several scientists, but none of their projects had wholly eliminated the need for mental labour on the part of the operator. There were two main obstacles in the way, one mechanical, one technical. The mechanical difficulty was that of making the machine itself record its results; for this purpose, Pascal invented a new piece of machinery called a "jumper", which was the most notable novelty in his instrument. The technical difficulty did not demand genius so much as a great deal of patience. Many preliminary gropings and a very close collaboration with the Rouen craftsman who had the job of building the model were necessary before Pascal could get a machine that worked perfectly.

There was another originality in the invention: its practical, utilitarian character. Most of the machines built under Pascal's orders are intended not for abstract arithmetical operations but for calculations in livres, sols, and deniers. The inventor sought, also, to exploit his machine commercially. In 1645, Blaise Pascal printed an "Epistle Dedicatory" to Chancellor Séguier, followed by an explanation of the working of his instrument. This was rather like a company prospectus, showing a quite modern sense of the value of publicity, and emphasizing the merits of Pascal's own machine and the shortcomings of all imitations and counterfeits. The machine was put on show by Roberval who, where there was any demand, accepted orders for it. But its high price—100 livres—meant that there could be no extensive commercial demand for it. It remained among the class of expensive intellectual toys or museum exhibits.

But if this invention did not bring Blaise Pascal fortune, it certainly brought him fame. The young man's reputation passed beyond the circles of the learned and reached the great world. In February, 1644, Bourdelot, a doctor of medicine, begged Pascal, then on his way through Paris, to demonstrate the machine to the Prince de Condé. Mersenne and Huygens praised the invention in prose, d'Alibray and the gazeteer Loret, the latter in a sonnet, in verse. A hundred years later, Diderot still felt it necessary to include a detailed sketch of the machine among the plates of his encyclopedia.

Blaise Pascal took a passionate delight in his own growing fame. His consciousness of his own superiority, the pleasure he took in being admired, are expressed magnificently, and

not without a certain boyish naïvety, in his "Epistle Dedicatory". With what a genuine glow of triumph does this young
scientist praise "the first attempt of a man of twenty!" With
what confidence in his own genius he must have awaited the
future!

Meanwhile, throughout Normandy, there were signs of the
growth of a movement of intense religious feeling. The
growing poverty and wretchedness of life in the province
excited a wonderful spirit of devotion in those who sought to
relieve it. In some parts of Normandy, this rebirth of
Catholicism had taken a deeply mystical form. Such mysticism, in fact, is not really unknown among very hard-
headed people, such as the Normans are reputed to be. It
was not a mere matter of chance that *Polyeucte*, that
tragedy of Christian martyrdom, was conceived by a Nor-
man dramatist; the character of his hero may have been
suggested to Corneille by the attitudes of some of his country-
men. This movement of religious revival was centred, in the
first instance, upon the famous Company of the Blessed
Sacrament. But there were also in Normandy some friends
of the Abbé de Saint-Cyran, among others Father Maignart,
a preacher of the Oratory and priest of the church of Sainte-
Croix in Saint-Ouen, the Pascals' own parish. In 1643,
having felt the call of a life of retreat, he gave up his parish
and this decision aroused great interest in Rouen. About the
same time, Jean Guillebert, who was pursuing his studies at
the Sorbonne in the company of the great Arnauld, received
from Saint-Cyran, director of his conscience, an order to
go to his parish of Rouville, near Rouen; like many parish
priests of the time, he had been habitually non-resident. The
presence of Guillebert wrought magic changes throughout
the whole region; through him, the spirit of Saint-Cyran was
widely diffused and many great families were "converted"—
the term constantly used by the great director of Port-Royal
to describe the transition from a life of dutiful religious practice without fervour to one of austerity and penitence.
Among those who took Guillebert as their director were

Thomas du Fossé, the Master of Accounts, a neighbour and almost a colleague of Etienne Pascal's, and two members of the nobility, the Deschamps brothers, one Seigneur des Lands, the other Seigneur de la Boutellerie. The latter two, formerly men "mad on the point of honour, always ready to draw their swords", turned the natural ardour and fieriness of their temperaments towards works of charity. Each of them had founded a little hospital, and they had become skilful surgeons.

Though the Pascals were close witnesses of this religious revival, they were not at first in the least affected by it. Then in January, 1946, Etienne Pascal who had slipped on the ice and put his thighbone out of joint, asked for the assistance of the Deschamps brothers. These two remained for three months as guests in the Pascal household. Full of admiration for the personalities they encountered there, they determined to win them over to a deeper life. They interested themselves especially in Blaise, whose passion for science and appetite for worldly fame was bound to strike them. They lent him devotional works whose reading, little by little, worked a profound change in him. He, in his turn, tried to win over his sister Jacqueline, then these two together "converted" their father. At the end of the year, Gilberte and her husband came to stay in Rouen, and altered their way of life in a similar fashion. The whole family placed itself under Guillebert's direction.

What then was this doctrine which the whole Pascal family embraced? It would be extremely inaccurate to describe it as Jansenism: unless in a sense in which that term is taken to designate a much wider movement of which Jansenius himself represents only a single tendency. The *Augustinus* of the famous Doctor of Louvain, which had appeared six years previously, had already, indeed, excited many controversies, but it was a book which was discussed much more than it was actually read. The activating doctrine, transmitted by Guillebert, was rather that of Saint-Cyran. The latter, especially since his imprisonment at

Vincennes in 1638, had turned away from theology and polemics to devote himself, till his death in 1643, to the direction of souls. He was a master of the interior life, inspired above all by the work of Bérulle, and his attitude had been already crystallized in his letters and in little devotional pamphlets with such titles as *The New Heart*. Such a title is symptomatic, for it was towards a "conversion", towards a renewing of his whole nature, that Saint-Cyran primarily directed the Christian penitent. For the love of "objects of sense" to which our "natural heart" is inclined there had to be substituted "charity and the love of God", the essence of the "new heart" sanctified by grace. The Christian must detach himself, at least at the spiritual level, from all the good things of this world. The convert must then attempt to carry out his "vocation", that call from God towards some significant field of activity, some high ideal of life, which the soul waits for in silence and prayer. No authentically good act, not even receiving the sacraments, could be carried out unless provoked by this supernatural attraction, by this movement of grace which can allow us to escape from routine and from merely human motives. What followed from these premises was abandonment of oneself to God but also submission to the Church, as represented by one's spiritual director; it is the director who has the task of discovering, for every soul submitted to him, those practices of penitence which are indispensable for the achievement of a true conversion and which will reveal to each soul its vocation. These are the fundamental aspects of a doctrine which is complex, makes great demands, aims at perfection and appeals to an *élite*, but is capable, in practice, of adapting itself to very various circumstances.

A similar spirit to that of Saint-Cyran inspired Jansenius's little work, translated in 1644 by Arnauld d'Andilly, the *Disquisition on the Reformation of the Inner Man*, whose title makes its scope clear; and above all it inspired the *Frequent Communion* of Antoine Arnauld, which was published in 1643, and met with enormous success.

What changes did the reading of such works bring about in the soul of Blaise Pascal? Gilberte's narrative is defaced, at this point, by serious inaccuracies: "God so cleared his understanding by such reading that he perfectly understood that the Christian religion obliges us to live only for God, and to have no concern but God. And this truth appeared to him so obvious and needful and useful that he brought all his scientific investigations to an end. So that, from this time onwards, he renounced all other sorts of knowledge to apply himself to the one thing called needful." This passage is all the more disquieting because Gilberte, before relating Pascal's conversion, has described investigations which he undertook *after* his conversion; we are bordering here on hagiography. What were the facts?

Two facts are equally certain; Pascal's scientific researches were not interrupted and yet certain attitudes and certain writings of his at this period betray a profound religious disquiet. But do these two facts really contradict each other, and do we not sometimes unreasonably exaggerate the austerity of Jansenism? No doubt Jansenius did insist on the war which the Christian must wage against "the lust of the eyes", or the desire for knowledge, but in such passages he is condemning rather a vain curiosity, an intellectual arrogance leading to forgetfulness of God, than the search for scientific or historical truth: or else, since he was himself an historical scholar, he would stand self-condemned. We have, of course, found traces of this blameworthy intellectual arrogance in Pascal's "Epistle Dedicatory"; we shall find further traces even before arriving at the heart of Pascal's fashionable or "worldly" period. But in so far as scientific curiosity as such, as distinguished from intellectual arrogance, is concerned, at Port-Royal itself, Arnauld did not despise mathematics; a Monsieur de Rebours, with whom we shall shortly be dealing as an example of excessive austerity, had close relations with Mersenne and had a good many scientific books in his library. Gilberte, in the passage we have quoted, seems to display an exceptional narrowness of mind; or else she is picturing Blaise's "first conversion" to herself on the model of his second, which in fact did for a period of time effectively interrupt his scientific work.

But we have to go deeper. In a letter written on the 25th September, 1647, Jacqueline speaks of "a person who is no longer a mathematician", thus apparently alluding to her brother. How are we to explain away this unexpected piece of evidence in Gilberte's favour? An explanation on the following lines may, perhaps, help us to get our bearings. To use the language of Saint-Cyran, Pascal had already felt the abandonment of his researches as a *vocation*. But, whether the feeling of his own immaturity had made him decide to postpone till some years later a complete detachment from science, or whether he considered the sciences as an innocent amusement of the kind which his doctors recommended for his health, he had not really at this time responded to this vocation, except during intermittent periods of religious fervour. So this first conversion remained an incomplete one and allowed Pascal to slip gradually and without being aware of it into his period "in the world".

The religious development of other members of the Pascal family, moreover, throws light on Blaise's. No doubt they all renounced a certain taste for the more superficial social pleasures, and practised a more inward piety; but without achieving or perhaps even aiming at that frigid perfection which, in any case, the reader who studies such topics from the outside is likely to picture to himself in too simple-minded a way. Jacqueline herself whom, since she decided to become a nun, we must consider as the most deeply affected member of the family, took two years to arrive at that decision, after much inner struggle. The Périers did not renounce their attempts to improve their social position. Soon they became Seigneurs de Bien-Assis, after having purchased this important property at the gates of Clermont. Finally, Etienne Pascal was violently opposed to the idea of his daughter's becoming a nun. In a word, we are dealing here with slow conversions, with lives which remained imperfect, but with souls which had certainly been profoundly transformed.

Pascal returned to his scientific investigations in August 1646, in the following circumstances. Pierre Petit, Intendant-General of the Ports and Fortifications of France, a learned mathematician and a friend of the neo-Epicurean atomist philosopher, Gassendi, passed through Rouen on his way to Dieppe, where he was going to inspect a machine which was a sort of early diving-bell. He met the Pascals and talked with them about the experiments of the Italian scientist, Torricelli. The proper interpretation of Torricelli's results was at that time a topic of lively controversy. A glass tube, full of mercury, and open at the top, is plunged perpendicularly, the closed end upwards, into a bowl already full of mercury. Some, but not all, of the mercury goes into the bowl. A column of mercury remains suspended at a certain height in the tube. What remains at the closed end of the tube? Is it a vacuum? Is it air? Or is it some other substance? The disciples of Aristotle postulated it as an axiom that nature abhors a vacuum; students of physical science with a more modern point of view tend to accept the idea that a vacuum can exist in nature. On his way back from Dieppe, Petit attempted to reproduce Torricelli's experiment, with the assistance of Etienne and Blaise Pascal. The attempt was successful, and a written account of the experiment was addressed to Pierre Chanut, a fellow-countryman and friend of the Pascals, then the Agent-General of France in Sweden. Only one remark of Blaise Pascal's on the experiment is reported, but it is very significant. He was prejudiced, like his father and Petit, in favour of the vacuum, but he nevertheless risked an objection: "It might be said that the space in the tube which seemed to be empty was really air which, in order to avoid a vacuum, had penetrated the glass and entered through its pores." Blaise, in this influenced by the attitude of his father, wished to allow a fair field to traditional ideas in science and to propose new explanations only after the old ones had been proved either self-contradictory or contradictory to experience. Pascal did not stop here. In a most ingenious fashion, he devised other experiments, involving tubes of various shapes and sizes, and various liquids, such as wine, water, and oil. These experiments, which were laborious, expensive, and spectacular—one of them involved the use of two tubes forty feet high, attached to the mast of a ship—aroused a great deal of interest.

About the same time, Blaise gave a most striking demonstration of his zeal in matters of religion. At the beginning of 1647, there had arrived in Rouen, with the hope of finding a benefice, a former Capuchin friar, Jacques Forton, the Sieur de Saint-Ange. Between 1637 and 1643, not without finding some difficulty in obtaining the approval of the Doctors of the Sorbonne, Forton had published three volumes entitled, *The Conduct of Natural Judgment*, in which he had pushed to an extreme point the principle of "the fundamental agreement of faith and reason": in his attempt to resolve the conflict between reason and faith, Forton showed a tendency to do away with the mysterious element in Christianity, and in consequence to make both Revelation and Grace seem unneedful. There was a real profundity in some of Forton's views, but he was above all a man of adventurous and sometimes extravagant temperament. In Paris, before coming to Rouen, he had already caused some unpleasantness, by his outspokenness, in the *salon* of the Vicomtesse d'Auchy.

When Forton sought to expound his ideas in Rouen he found savage opponents in the persons of Blaise Pascal and two of his young friends, the mathematician Adrien Auzoult, and the son of a magistrate, Raoul Hallé de Monflaines, who intended to enter the Church. The three men left a written record of their discussions with Forton. The latter flattered himself that he could demonstrate the existence and nature of the Trinity so as to satisfy natural reason. He asserted that the purpose of Faith was to supply the absence of Reason in men of feeble intelligence. He held that the body of Christ was not formed from the blood of the Virgin. And he had other odd ideas. When pressed to give his opinion on Jansenius, he was evasive. Pascal and his friends asked the Sieur de Saint-Ange to make a private retraction of his views. He refused, and they submitted the case to the coadjutor of the Archbishop, Jean-Pierre Camus, the former Bishop of Belley. The latter, who wanted to keep the matter quiet, contented himself with vague reassurances and exculpated Forton. The three friends, thoroughly dissatisfied, now addressed themselves to the Archbishop, who was living in retirement at Gaillon. After a number of interviews, they managed to obtain from Forton a retraction of his rasher theses, which, however, left his fundamental philosophy intact; and the Sieur de Saint-Ange managed to obtain his benefice.

What does this business teach us about Pascal? His role in the drawing up of the written record of objections was secondary; but in the approaches to ecclesiastical authority it was, because of his father's high position, primary. The fierceness of his opposition to the Sieur de Saint-Ange has been rather harshly judged on the pretext that, if Pascal and his friends were successful, Saint-Ange risked being burned alive. This however, is an unrealistic picture of the actual state of affairs; rash though Saint-Ange was, he had the parish priests of Rouen, the Parliament, and the Archbishop's coadjutor on his side. The silent and effective devices by which this coalition sought to avoid a public retraction fully justified the obstinacy with which Pascal and his friends demanded one. The only practical intention of Pascal and his friends was, not to have Saint-Ange burned, but to see that a man of fantastic opinions was not allowed to carry off an important benefice. If we admit that Saint-Ange did genuinely hold the opinions attributed to him—and there can be no question of denying it—and if we remember his troubled past, there is nothing surprising in the attitude taken up by Blaise Pascal and his friends. We need not invoke Jansenism and its distrust of reason. This distrust, for that matter, as we shall see later, was never fully shared by Pascal himself. It may be said, however, that it is not for the laity to intrude into spiritual matters. But, if Pascal judged that there was a scandal, he owed it to himself to intervene. And in fact the initiative probably came from Hallé de Monflaines, who was going to become a priest, and the three friends had the support of a Doctor of the Sorbonne, le Cornier. In this affair, also, Pascal showed himself as thoroughly under the influence of Saint-Cyran who, following Bérulle, had insisted strongly on the high dignity of the priest as such and on his responsibility towards the faithful. To most of Pascal's contemporaries, the granting of a benefice appeared merely an administrative matter; Pascal emphasized the spiritual side of the problem. That is probably the simplest explanation of an episode many of whose details still remain shrouded in obscurity.

During the year 1647, Pascal's health, which had deteriorated as a result of his long labours on his arithmetical machine, took a striking turn for the worse. Headaches, pains in the stomach, and paralysis of the legs are the essential symptoms noted by the biographers. Forceful remedies, including repeated purgings, led to a partial cure. Was it at this moment that the doctors, hoping to achieve a more complete recovery, advised the sick man to avoid all excessive mental or nervous strain and to seek out opportunities for amusement and relaxation? In any case, towards the middle of the year, Pascal left Rouen to continue his treatment in Paris. He was accompanied by Jacqueline.

CHAPTER TWO

THE WORLDLY PERIOD

THERE is a great deal of confusion about what is commonly called "the worldly period" in the life of Blaise Pascal. First of all, when did it begin? The narratives of Gilberte and Marguerite Périer agree. Following on Pascal's serious illness of 1647, but at a date which it is not possible to fix exactly, the young man's doctors forbade him "any prolonged intellectual tasks" and advised him to seek distractions. We are therefore obliged provisionally and as a hypothesis to be tested by further research, to make the beginning of the worldly period coincide with the return of Blaise and Jacqueline to Paris. But what was the nature of this worldly period, and what meaning are we to give to the term "world"? The term, obviously borrowed from the vocabulary of religion, indicates, in a vague fashion, everything that is opposed to Christian perfection. It may imply vices and impiety; it may on the other hand merely imply an eagerness about business, ambition, a taste for amusement, and, of course, the frequentation of *salons*. Gilberte and Marguerite make it clear that in Pascal's case the idea of worldliness has not its more serious implications. He remained always "without vices or disorders". This statement, however, has sometimes been contested, and will have to be checked with the ascertainable facts. But even if we accept the milder interpretation of the idea of worldliness, how many difficulties and uncertainties there are when we wish to analyse the state of mind of Pascal as a man of the world! The only safe way is to follow Pascal step by step with the aid of what documents we have. In regard to the nature of these documents, two periods can be distinguished. Till Etienne Pascal's death, we have a good number of firmly dated texts, and of pious letters regularly alternating with scientific writing. After the death of Etienne Pascal, conjecture has a much larger part to play. Finally, a detailed study of the circumstances of Blaise's "second conversion" will show us the scope and significance of his period in the world.

I. *Before Etienne Pascal's Death*

An important small work, a fragment of a preface for a *Traité du Vide* which Pascal must have been meditating since the autumn of 1647, plunges us into the atmosphere of this first period. Pascal in this fragment raises the problem of the relationships between reason and authority, between respect for the ancient and the rights of the moderns. In historical matters, which depend purely on memory, the ancients are the only witnesses worthy of belief, we are not permitted to add anything to what their books teach us; in theology notably, a region inaccessible to reason, truth remains inseparable from authority: only the Holy Scriptures reveal theological truth to us, immutable and eternal. But "as for the subjects that fall under the senses or the reasoning power . . . it is the task of reason alone, to acquire knowledge of them". In physics, the reasoning power itself must submit to the facts and confine its ambitions to co-ordinating results ascertained by experiment. Thus in the scientific field the ancients are of no use to us, since, to whatever experimental knowledge they possessed, each succeeding generation has added its own discoveries. Humanity as a whole might be compared to a single man whose knowledge increases from century to century: thus "those whom we call the ancients were really new to everything, and formed the very infancy of mankind. . . . It is in ourselves that we ought to revere that antiquity which we revere in others".

These reflections, which explored more deeply the teaching of Etienne Pascal, link up on the one hand with the views of such a man as Bacon and on the other hand are perfectly in agreement with the teachings of Jansenius.

Jansenius, repudiating every kind of scholastic argument of abstract construction, acknowledged only "positive" theology, that is the historical study of the doctrine of the Scriptures, the Fathers, and the Councils. Has Pascal thus resolved the conflict of the religious and the scientific attitudes within himself? On the contrary, he notes that these two attitudes are opposed. And so his own life will be divided; he will profess the Christian faith with the most perfect submission but will remain deeply attached to the sciences. And for Gilberte and Marguerite this attachment no doubt constitutes a first indication of his "worldliness".

An examination of the scientific researches carried out by Pascal between 1647 and 1651 will enable us to discover not only his real scientific genius but also certain revealing attitudes of mind surprising in a fresh convert and really describable as "worldly".

Pascal continued to work at all the scientific tasks which he had been engaged in before his conversion. He went ahead with his researches on conic sections and at least partly completed them; of these labours, which excited the admiration of Mersenne, and which Leibniz succeeded with great difficulty in having communicated to him in 1675, there only remains to-day the final portion, which has been preserved thanks to a copy made by Leibniz, and which bears the title, *Generatio Conisectionum*. At the same time, the arithmetical machine was perfected and on 22nd March, 1649, the manufacture of it was reserved by royal privilege to Pascal; the inventor was still thinking of commercially exploiting his machine. But Pascal's more important researches were connected with the problem of the vacuum. Between 1647 and 1651, four episodes stand out in this connection: the publication of Pascal's *Nouvelles Expériences touchant le Vide*, his polemical exchanges with Father Noël, the experiment of the Puy-de-Dôme, and the letters to Monsieur de Ribeyre.

On arriving in Paris, Pascal found that the problems raised by Torricelli's experiment were the leading topic in scientific circles, such as Mersenne's academy and the more recent academy of the Abbé Bourdelot, which had its meetings at the Hôtel de Condé. His experiments at Rouen had been followed in Paris with lively interest, the more so as they could not have been carried out in the capital itself for lack of technical instruments and skilful experimentalists. Roberval had made Pascal's experiments known in Poland, where a Capuchin, Valeriano Magni, was carrying out similar investigations. Fearing that the originality of his own experiments would be questioned, Pascal, who was pondering a general treatise on the vacuum, published his preliminary conclusions in a pamphlet, *Nouvelles Expériences touchant le Vide*, which appeared in October, 1647.

Shortly before this he had had occasion to discuss the problem with Descartes who, passing through Paris, had made a point of seeing him. It is difficult to get an exact idea of the two interviews which they had on 23rd and 24th September. During the first interview, the presence of Roberval, who hated Descartes and was famous for his black moods, spoiled the conversation. During the second, Descartes, who was proud of his knowledge of medicine, gave Pascal some advice about the restoration of his still precarious health. On matters relating to physics, however, the two geniuses could hardly understand each other: Descartes claimed that the top of Torricelli's tube was full of "subtle matter", and to Pascal this hypothesis seemed merely chimerical.

What strikes us in the *Nouvelles Expériences touchant le Vide* is the realism and prudence of Pascal as an experimentalist. The very plan of the book shows the strictness of his method. Pascal begins by accepting Nature's horror of a vacuum as a received principle. His experiments then oblige him to rectify this point of view and, at first, to postulate that bodies can be separated by an *apparent* vacuum. Then he points out that this apparent vacuum is, in fact, empty of all the kinds of matter that are accessible to the senses, therefore it is not only apparent, it is a mere and actual vacuum. Are we to conclude from this that Nature has no horror of a vacuum? No, merely that Nature has only a *limited* horror of a vacuum. That is all that can be asserted so far.

Yet do we not also find, in these few luminous pages, that Pascal too insistently claims his rights of priority? In this rather excessive concern for his own fame does he not show a development surprising in a fresh convert? Attitudes that are open to criticism also appear in his polemical exchanges with Father Noël. The latter—the first Jesuit whom Pascal was to engage in battle—was rector of the College of Clermont, the most important of the Jesuit establishments in Paris. He had taught Descartes at La Flèche; he defended the physics of Aristotle, but not unskilfully and not without keeping in touch with the latest research. Father Noël read Pascal's pamphlet and immediately sat down to write a refutation; according to him, the top of the tube is full of "purified air", which enters through the "pores" of the glass, a substance which recalls Descartes' "subtle matter". Like a good scholastic, Father Noël dwelt at length on the distinct qualities and the various combinations of the "four elements" and the "four humours". He drew down upon himself a wonderful reply, a masterpiece of clarity and method and, under a mask of perfect courtesy, a masterpiece of irony that sometimes borders on insolence. The venerable Father is not only refuted, point by point, but treated as a student, who must learn first principles, learn to distrust "presuppositions", to avoid confusing a mere "thought" with a "demonstration", and to avoid substituting words for thoughts, as in defining light as "a *luminary* motion of *luminous* bodies". Pascal concludes with this condescending judgment: "I find your letter a sign no less of the weakness of the opinion you are defending than of the strength of your own mind."

Father Noël felt the crushing superiority of his antagonist; in a measured reply, he conceded various points. But his attitude was somewhat equivocal: while begging Pascal not to make his own reply public, he allowed a pamphlet to be printed, ironically entitled *Le Plein du Vide*, in which he went back to his earlier theories; then he added an erratum to this which again took up some of Pascal's ideas. Though annoyed, Pascal did not reply directly, no doubt feeling himself incapable of preserving a tone of courtesy; but he re-affirmed his own position in a *Lettre à Le Pailleur* and asked his father, whose age and whose distinguished position exempted him from treating Father Noël with too much tenderness, to attack the Jesuit directly. The latter, however, fundamentally a modest and discreet man, did not wish to prolong the quarrel.

The existence of a vacuum is not the only problem raised by Torricelli's experiment. How, also, are we to explain the suspension of the column of mercury in the tube? In an important letter, written in 1644, Torricelli put forward the hypothesis that the weight of the air balanced the weight of the mercury. This hypothesis had been vigorously ques-tioned, but Pascal seems to have completely accepted it.

To verify the hypothesis, he thought out the experiment of the Puy-de-Dôme, whose history is to be found in his *Récit de la Grand Expérience de l'Equilibre des Liqueurs*, published in October, 1648. On 15th November, 1647, Pascal addressed to his brother-in-law, Florin Périer, Counsellor at the Court of Aids at Clermont-Ferrand, a letter in which, going beyond the provisional conclusions of the *Nouvelles Expériences*, he affirmed his conviction that the effects attributed to Nature's horror of a vacuum are due to the "weight and pressure of the air". To demonstrate this, it would be enough to repeat Torricelli's experiment on the same day at the foot and on the top of a mountain. If the height of the mercury is greater at the foot than on the top, the weight of the column of air will be the sole cause of the suspension of the mercury: "Nobody could say that Nature has more abhorrence of a vacuum at the foot of a mountain than at the top of it." Since Clermont was suitably situated at the foot of the Puy-de-Dôme, Pascal begged his brother-in-law to carry out the experiment.

Florin Périer, held back by a mission in Bourbonnais, did not reply till 22nd September, 1648. The experiment had been completely successful. The mercury, which rose to a height of $26\frac{7}{24}$ in. at Clermont, at the top of the mountain reached a height of only $23\frac{1}{6}$ in. Pascal repeated the experiment himself on the tower of the Church of Saint-Jacques de la Boucherie, again with success. He was able to conclude that "Nature has no repugnance towards a vacuum . . . all the effects that have been attributed to this horror proceed from the weight and pressure of the air. . . ."

Pascal did not stop at this point, as the title of his pamphlet proves. The results obtained were for him nothing but particular instances of the more general laws of the "equilibrium of liquids", which he proposed to define in a *Traité du Vide*. The latter was not put into its definitive shape till 1654.

We cannot help admiring the continuous progress, with no fresh starts and no failures, that had led Pascal from his first experiment at Rouen to these decisive conclusions, and also the clearness and brevity of the few pages in which the results of so many experiments are summed up. At this very period, scientists like Mersenne and Roberval were accustomed to sum up their results in long and confused Latin dissertations, thus often losing sight of the essential thread of their thoughts. Is this wonderful continuity merely a matter of appearances, due to the fact that Pascal concealed his own hesitations and dishonestly attributed to himself the merit of other men's discoveries? This thesis, which breaks down into a multiplicity of problems which it is impossible to tackle here, has been occasionally sustained. Though the question as a whole has not yet been thoroughly clarified, it does seem that there is nothing in these accusations. To mention only one particular point, Descartes claimed to have suggested to Pascal the idea of the experiment of Puy-de-Dôme, and Pascal proudly defended the priority of the conception with himself. In fact, the idea of such an experiment was in the air, but Descartes would certainly not have interpreted the experiment in the way that Pascal did, and only Pascal had enough faith in the experiment to take steps to see that it was carried out.

At the most, we can blame Pascal for his inventor's self-esteem. That nowhere asserts itself more violently than in his letters to Monsieur de Ribeyre.

A Jesuit of Montferrand, in a thesis sustained on 25th June, 1651, and dedicated to Monsieur de Ribeyre, First President in the Court of Aids and a friend of the Pascal family, had alluded to "certain persons" who described themselves as "the inventors of a certain experiment of which Torricelli is the author", clearly having Pascal in mind. It may seem a petty matter of controversy, but Pascal felt that his honour was at stake, and justified himself in a letter to Monsieur de Ribeyre; he fiercely denied that he had ever attributed to himself Torricelli's experiment and defined his own personal contribution to the researches into the question of the vacuum. There can be no doubt that Pascal was perfectly within his rights, but his insistence is excessive. Less than ever does he show in these letters a spirit of detachment from fame and worldly honours. The effect of the first letter was aggravated by its publication. Monsieur de Ribeyre, in a very wise reply, through which a little irritation shows itself, pointed out how very unimportant was the sentence which Pascal attacked: nobody had noticed it. Pascal, while still protesting that the matter was very important indeed, declared himself satisfied.

An attachment to science, an attachment to fame, a rather too imperious sense of his own genius, these are the first symptoms of "the worldly spirit" in Pascal.

But what path, meanwhile, was his religious life following? His letters to his sister Gilberte teach us. On their arrival in Paris, Blaise and Jacqueline had been conducted by Guillebert to the Abbey of Port-Royal and had got into the habit of going there regularly to hear the sermons of Singlin, the confessor of the nuns, a remarkable director of souls who had fully inherited the spirit of Saint-Cyran. Jacqueline decided to withdraw from the world into this convent and entered into close relationships with its two chiefs, Mother Angélique and Mother Agnès.

At the beginning of 1648, Pascal made the acquaintance of another confessor at Port-Royal, Antoine de Rebours. The latter, originally from Auvergne, was always to retain close ties with the Pascal family; in 1661, Florin Périer was the executor of his will. His first impression of Blaise, however, was one only of much qualified approval. Pascal had flung into the conversation a sentence of capital importance for the understanding of his whole line of thought: declaring himself a partisan of Port-Royal, he added "that one could, even following the mere principles of common sense, show that many things the adversaries of Port-Royal said were contrary to common sense, and that a well-conducted train of reasoning led one to believe the opposite principles, though one ought to believe them without the help of reasoning". Here is a point of view which foreshadows *The Provincial Letters*, the *Pensées*, and above all the *Ecrits sur la Grâce*. Monsieur de Rebours heard this statement with a great deal of distrust; the role that Pascal granted to reason seemed to him a mark of presumption and arrogance. Pascal protested his good faith and his submission to authority, but the misunderstanding persisted. Monsieur de Rebours' reservations about his brilliant new acquaintance foreshadow those of Singlin and Mother Angélique at the time of the publication of *The Provincial Letters*. Pascal had always a dominating and imperious air which took aback the "gentle souls", as they have been called, of Port-Royal. Later on, however, he was to be supported by leaders of Port-Royal like Arnauld and Nicole. But the misunderstanding with Monsieur de Rebours may at this time have somewhat disquieted him.

A very beautiful letter of 1st April, 1648, addressed to Gilberte, announces a theme which was to have important developments in Pascal's later work: "Corporeal things are only an image of spiritual, and God has represented the invisible in the visible." Deriving from Saint Augustine, this idea was dear to Saint-Cyran, and is at the basis of Pascal's own doctrine: the whole creation is an image of God, but only grace enables us to recognize the Creator behind the created. "We must consider ourselves as criminals in a prison full of images of their Liberator." From such a point of view as this, sin consists in "taking the representation for the reality". Every attachment to the created is a kind of idolatry. Thus in the *Pensées*, in accordance with this principle, Pascal will attempt to make the unbeliever pass from the earthly representation to the divine reality.

On the 5th of the following November, Pascal attempted to define the action of grace. He insisted on the difficulty of retaining the divine grace, on the efforts at perfection to which the soul must strain if to each grace already granted a new grace is to succeed; for not to acquire a new grace is equivalent to losing the old grace. This passage is interesting for the way in which it reconciles the action of divine grace and of the human will. But, above all, was not the scientist who had just acquired fresh fame by publishing the narrative of the experiment of Puy-de-Dôme aware of a certain "dryness of soul"? How otherwise explain the postscript: "If you know some good soul, ask her to pray to God for me"?

At this moment, Etienne Pascal rejoined his children in Paris; he had established his family in the rue de Touraine, in the Marais district. Though he was a fervent Christian, he formally opposed the entry of Jacqueline into Port-Royal; he could not bear to be separated from his daughter; he was at once an authoritarian and a man of feeling, as his son was to be. Blaise then took his sister's part and assisted her communications with Port-Royal, while she was living a life of withdrawal in her father's house.

Jacqueline continued to lead the same life at Clermont, where Etienne Pascal, fleeing from the troubles of the Fronde, had retired with his children from May, 1649, to November, 1650. During this period we have no letters recording Blaise's religious life. His zeal had not necessarily grown feebler, but he was living in the same house as his usual correspondent, Gilberte. Shortly after the return to Paris, Etienne Pascal died, on 24th September, 1651.

On the occasion of this death, Pascal wrote the most famous of his letters of piety. Dated 17th October, it is addressed to Gilberte and her husband, who were kept in Clermont by the birth of a son. The letter is a sermon on death, a consolation based on some of the grand principles of that Augustinian Christianity on which Pascal had nourished his soul. Let us enter into the purposes of God; every death seems to be in conformity with an order which He has willed. Following the example of Jesus Christ, let us consider human life as a sacrifice that is completed by death and that permits us to attain to that state of glory in which the will of man is absorbed in God; whoever dies commences truly to live. Death would be rightly held in horror if it separated a sanctified soul from a sanctified body; but as it delivers the soul from sin, we must hate this mortal life and aspire only to the divine life. Thus grief at the death of a father is permissible, but faith brings us consolation. It teaches us to fear, far more than the death of the body, that of the soul. It invites us to keep the memory of the dead alive by doing "what they ordered us to do when they were still in the world". And here is a disquieting avowal: "Had I lost him six years ago, *I* should have been lost." The tight logic of the reasoning and the oratorical amplitude of the style do not prevent real emotion from displaying itself.

Thus Pascal's pious letters from 1648 to 1651 reveal the existence in him of a profound religious life. Their tone is no doubt less personal and less moving than that of the famous letters to Mademoiselle de Roannez, but how much reading and meditation do they bear witness to: letters and pamphlets by Saint-Cyran, sermons by Singlin, and above all the Bible! They imply far more than an external knowledge of the spiritual life. Pascal in these letters becomes aware of some of his own fundamental ideas. How could the author of such letters remain, in the eyes of Gilberte and Marguerite Périer, possessed by a worldly spirit? The answer is that he had not yet been able to resolve that his religious life should be his whole life. He had returned to the sciences, and the sense of his value as a scientist had reawakened his pride; moreover, the repercussions of his labours opened the doors of the *salons* to him. Once again he was seeing le Pailleur and d'Alibray and perhaps forming a closer acquaintance with Mitton. Little by little his convert's fervour was cooling off, and some admissions of his show that he was aware of this. And this is all that the documents permit us to assert.

II. *After the Death of Etienne Pascal*

After the death of his father, Marguerite Périer tells us, Pascal "continued to go into the world, with even more ease, being now master of his own property". What documentary evidence is there to enable us to trace the growth of his "worldly spirit"?

Towards the end of October, 1651, Blaise and Jacqueline signed a series of contracts relating to inherited property of which no fully satisfactory explanation has yet been given; experts on Pascal have not been sufficiently versed in seventeenth-century custom and law. It was a matter of reciprocal donations; Jacqueline donates to her brother properties from her share of her father's estate; in exchange, Blaise promises her a yearly income of 1,600 livres. This bargain is a perfectly fair one; it even spares Jacqueline, who was anxious to live a life of religious retirement, the fatigue and anxiety inseparable from the division of inherited property. Moreover, the bargain gave Blaise no immediate advantage; it did not provide him with liquid assets but merely with credits on a number of his father's debtors. What, then, is the nice point? Simply this: Jacqueline's income from Blaise would legally come to an end once she became a nun, and Blaise would have full use, then, of what might have been her property; and Blaise knew that Jacqueline intended to enter Port-Royal as soon as she could. Therefore, Blaise did not intend to deprive his sister of part of her inheritance—especially since, at the same period, he had granted a yearly income of 400 livres to the old family servant, Louise Delfault, to be continued even if she became a nun.

But all this was perfectly in order. Surely Pascal's critics are aware that nuns make a vow of poverty? Moreover, their convents could not become heirs in their place; canon law and royal regulations—the latter aiming at curbing the ambition of religious communities and protecting family rights—both forbade it. In particular, neither a nun, nor her convent for her, could receive an income, unless, as in Louise Delfault's case, it was a mere subsistence allowance. Thus these contracts merely meant that Blaise became Jacqueline's heir-general at the expense of Gilberte, who had already been amply provided for under her marriage contract. Jacqueline did not even lose the power of disposing as she pleased of the properties that remained to her up to the day when she should become a nun. Quite other financial difficulties were soon to arise between the brother and sister but for the moment their relations were not troubled.

Or rather they were troubled, but for a quite different reason. When Jacqueline wanted to enter Port-Royal immediately, her brother implored her to remain with him for a few more years. Why this change of attitude after his support of Jacqueline in 1648? No doubt his religious ardour had cooled. But, above all, having already lost his father, he was afraid to be left utterly alone. But do not let us overwhelm him with reproaches. In relation to Jacqueline's profession, Etienne Pascal acted no differently, and yet on his death his parish priest pronounced a public eulogy on his piety. The Pascals had such strong family feelings, and Jacqueline was so fascinating both as a daughter and as a sister!

Jacqueline, however, decided to leave Blaise. Gilberte, who had come to Paris for the settlement of property under her father's will, has described the scenes which she witnessed, silent scenes, but moving and dramatic. Jacqueline had to leave on 4th February; she did not dare to warn her brother and asked Gilberte to break the news. Gilberte did so with all sorts of precautions and nevertheless Blaise "withdrew very sadly into his room". Jacqueline left very early in the morning, avoiding farewells. Blaise found great difficulty in accepting the accomplished fact. On 7th May, 1652, in a very beautiful letter, Jacqueline asked him to forget his resentment and agree that she should assume the nun's habit on Trinity Sunday. Blaise, at first indignant, asked for a delay, but finished by giving his consent.

At the same period, Blaise was pursuing his scientific activities, but in a much more fashionable setting. According to the chronicler Loret, at the beginning of April, 1652, Pascal gave a scientific lecture in the drawing-room of the Duchesse d'Aiguillon. He demonstrated his arithmetical machine, which he was still producing and publicizing; one of the machines still in existence is dated 12th May, 1652. He went on to talk about fountains and to touch on the problem of the vacuum. It is interesting to find him moving in the most exclusive circles; the Duchesse d'Aiguillon, however, was not a new acquaintance but an old family friend. More important than this lecture was Pascal's letter to Christina of Sweden, which should be dated somewhere in June, 1652. The young and learned Queen of Sweden had recently become the great patron of scholars and writers, who flocked to her court from all parts of Europe. She had chosen as her medical attendant the famous Abbé Bourdelot, who put her in touch with Pascal. Pascal sent her one of his arithmetical machines—it was a way of getting publicity—accompanied by a splendid letter, in which the old humanistic enthusiasm for science of the earlier *Epistle Dedicatory* reappeared: "The power of kings over subjects, as it seems to me, is a mere image of the power of superior over inferior minds. . . . And this second kind of dominion appears to me as much the loftier of the two as the order of minds is itself loftier than the order of bodies." This was a transposition into a profane key of Pascal's religious intuition of the material world as the image or symbol of the spiritual one; and also a first, truncated sketch of his famous theme of the "three orders", of body, of mind, and of charity. Intoxicated with success, Pascal was returning to the state of mind of the period preceding his first conversion—a period in which, as he himself admitted, he had almost become one of the lost.

In October of the same year, Pascal returned to Clermont, where he stayed till May, 1653. Several independent documents, consistent in essentials, bear witness to this journey. It enabled Pascal to take possession of what he had inherited from his father, who had lent out a good deal of money in Auvergne. Possibly it is to this journey that the allusions of Fléchier refer; he tells us that Pascal and another were "continually dancing attendance on a beautiful learned woman", the "Sappho of her province". To be sure about this, we should have to know more about Clermont *salons* of the period.

The end of this visit and Pascal's return to Paris were marked by serious financial disagreements between Pascal and Jacqueline. The latter now wished to make her vows and custom—in this going dead against canon law— demanded that she should receive a dowry. In principle, such a dowry would be donated by the nun's family, since nuns at that time generally made their profession before coming of age and could not dispose of their own property. But Jacqueline was of age and therefore, before making the profession which entailed her "civil death", could draw up her will. She wished to bequeath the greater part of the property that remained to her to Port-Royal. This was a generous decision and almost certainly she failed to see that it was against the rules; a prospective nun cannot make a donation to the convent which she herself is going to enter. Jacqueline's family complained that they were being disinherited, and this seems to be an exact statement of the case. On his side, Blaise, supported by Gilberte, showed a certain lack of understanding and of disinterestedness. On 8th July, 1652, he had donated to Port-Royal 4,000 livres on condition that he died childless—a purely formal and contingent donation—and he did not want to give anything more. Jacqueline underwent a violent nervous crisis; Mother Angélique offered to take her without a dowry, but her pride rejected such a humiliation. She was, however, about to decide to accept this offer, when Pascal, his own pride no doubt piqued by Mother Angélique's attitude, offered more than had been asked; but he felt very bitter about the whole business, and considered the convent had tricked him.

After the beginning of June, 1653, it is much harder to keep trace of Pascal. He was now at the heart of his "worldly period" and forming or developing his most important fashionable connections.

The most intimate of Pascal's fashionable friends was the Duc de Roannez. Artus Gouffier, born in 1627, in the highest ranks of the nobility, had inherited the Duchy-Peerage of Roannez, in Forez, in 1642. The greater part of his lands, however, were in Poitou and gradually his ancestors had got into the habit of establishing their provincial seat at the Château d'Oiron, near Thouars. At Paris, he lived in the cloister of Saint-Merri, with his mother, the Marquise de Boisy, who came of a parliamentary family. Widowed young, a narrow and strict devotee, and unfitted to manage a great estate, she had handed all his property over to him in 1647. Two of her children were then already nuns, and the third daughter, Charlotte, delicate and a martyr to physical suffering, remained with her.

Between 1640 and 1650, the Duke spent most of his time in the Army, took part in the fighting in Flanders, and was promoted to the rank of Maréchal de Camp, or Brigadier-General, in 1649. In 1651, he bought from the Duc de la Rochefoucauld the post of Governor of Poitou. In spite of the inherited debts of his family, a brilliant future was opening out before him. He shone at Court and dreamt of marrying the rich Mademoiselle de Mesmes. At the consecration of Louis XIV as King on 7th June, 1654, he bore the King's sword.

Pascal had known him when he was a child. But the rarity and brevity of the Duke's visits to Paris render any close acquaintanceship improbable before 1653. The Duke, who had a passion for mathematics, then attached himself strongly to Pascal who gained a powerful ascendancy over him. What, at this time, was the Duke's moral character? From a debauched grandfather, he had received a somewhat unedifying education, but we have no reason to doubt the judgment of Marguerite Périer who attributes to him, from his youth onwards, "religious feelings".

The Duke had made the acquaintance, perhaps in the Army, of a Poitou gentleman, long famous in the Paris *salons* for his wit and his fine manners, Antoine Gombaud, Chevalier de Méré. Méré is a mysterious person, and he was a person who cultivated mystery; it is difficult to picture him as he was at the period we are dealing with; his literary works were written long after the death of Pascal, and his letters cannot be precisely dated. Free both in his opinions and his morals, not without vanity and pretentiousness, he was nevertheless a man of delicate and subtle wit, who at a university might have held a "chair of polite behaviour". It is to him that we owe the perfection of the concept of the *honnête homme*. To the middle-class, moralistic conception of the *honnête homme*, defined by Nicolas Faret in 1630, he opposed a conception which was aristocratic and whose implied standards were wholly those of the "great world". For him "honesty" was to be identified with the art of pleasing, but pleasing in the deepest sense of the word, that is, making oneself loved. The *honnête homme* will always be of a gentle and playful humour, will avoid everything low and pedantic, and will refrain from appearing interested in, or even attached to, his business, his profession, or his opinions; finally, he will try to acquire a supple and easy distinction, an "indefinable noble and exquisite something", which we can feel rather than explain. Méré's

ideal was firmly opposed to the excesses of "preciosity"; it
was inspired at several points by Montaigne, and it did not
lack grandeur. Pascal was to attack the forgetfulness of God
and the unconscious egoism involved in this ideal of the
honnête homme, but not before recognizing it as the finest
of merely human ideals. But we must not exaggerate
the specific influence of Méré on Pascal; ideas like his were
more or less confusedly current in all the *salons*. The two
men were not to meet each other before 1653; Méré lived
most frequently in Poitiers either on his estate at Baussay,
near Melle, or at Poitiers; it was there, no doubt, in 1653
that Pascal saw him for the longest period.

Among Méré's correspondents there is a certain Damien
Mitton. Mitton, a fashionable figure, famous in his time, of
whom to-day little is known, seems to have particularly
struck Pascal who several times summons him, as it were,
to explain himself in the course of the *Pensées*. He was a
very rich *bourgeois*. Born around 1618, he possessed from
1646 onwards the very important office of Treasurer General
of Extraordinary War Funds for Flanders, Artois, and
Picardy. His youth had been one of debauchery but he
became a devotee at the end of his life. In the interval, he
was a tepid or indifferent Christian. He had married in
1653, kept open house for gamesters, and was supposed to
treat his guests very well. His reputation as a wit gained him
admission to the Court; in literary matters, his authority
was unquestioned. He has unfortunately left very few
literary memorials: three letters to Méré and a few small
pieces that were slipped into the *Oeuvres Mêlées* of Saint-
Evremond. The latter are disappointing both in thought
and style. The letters to Méré are more interesting and reveal
a profound scepticism, a disillusioned melancholy, which we
ought not perhaps to take too seriously. His mind
formed by Montaigne, and in some ways he recalls le
Pailleur and d'Alibray. We should expect to find him among
their circle. But there is no documentary evidence of
this; we know only that he knew Benserade and that he

bought his office as Treasurer from a brother of Madame Sainctot.

There is a famous passage in Méré's discourse *De l'Esprit*, about which we must ask whether it throws some light on Pascal's relationship with these three representatives of the worldly spirit. This is what Méré says. "I made a journey with the D— d— R—, who speaks such deep, sound sense, and whom I find rewarding company. Monsieur M., whom you know, and who pleases the whole Court, was of the company. ... Le D— d— R— has a mathematical turn of mind, and so as not to be bored on the way, he had brought along a man neither old nor young, then very little known, but who has since made a great name for himself. This man was a great mathematician, but at that time knew nothing about anything but mathematics. ... He admired, for instance, the wit and eloquence of Monsieur du Vair, and repeated to us some of the 'good things' of the Criminal-Lieutenant d'O.; we had not the least notion of disillusioning him, nevertheless we expressed our feelings sincerely. Two or three days passed by in this fashion, and our mathematician began to have a certain distrust of his former sentiments. ... By the time we arrived at P., his conversation consisted of almost nothing but genuine good things. ... After this journey, he thought no more of mathematics, which had always been his occupation, and the effect of the journey on him was as it were to make him abjure them." It cannot be denied that two of Méré's companions on this journey were the Duc de Roannez and Mitton. Their destination was no doubt Poitiers. But who is the fourth traveller, the mathematician? It is very tempting to identify him as Pascal and, for ourselves, we have no doubt that this is a true hypothesis. The superior air which the Chevalier affects in the presence of the mere scientist and the fashion in which he glories in having disillusioned him with mathematics can be found reproduced exactly in a letter of Méré's to Pascal himself. The hypothesis of Monsieur Strowski, who conjectures that the fourth traveller was Descartes, appears to us quite untenable. Marguerite Périer bears witness to the fact that Pascal did travel into Poitou. Unpublished documents prove that Pascal was a shareholder in a company for draining the Poitou marshes.

What remains to be determined is the date of the journey. Let us trace the movements of the Duc de Roannez, over the relevant period, between Paris and the province he governed. The Duke remained in Poitou from October to December, 1651, then again from March to November, 1652, and finally from September to December, 1653. The traditional opinion which favours Pascal's accompanying the Duke, Méré, and Mitton in July, 1652, runs up against insurmountable difficulties; for one thing, Mitton was then in Paris. Méré's narrative then refers to some date around mid-September, 1653. Pascal passed the whole autumn in Poitou, staying chiefly in Poitiers, but also at Oiron and Fontenay-le-Comte.

However, the portrait of Pascal which Méré sketches with his habitual self-sufficiency is a very inaccurate one. Pascal was not an out-of-date pedant, ignorant of the world. We accept far more readily the judgment of Gilberte, in an admirable unpublished fragment, recently discovered by Monsieur Lafuma: "There he was, then, in the world; he went several times to Court where some very able observers noted that he at once took on the air and the manners of the place as if he had been bred there all his life." But while it was the fame of Pascal as a scientist that attracted Madame d'Aiguillon and the Duc de Roannez, it is the scientist in Pascal that Méré affects to despise. Was Pascal, in fact, induced to revise his attitudes by the episode which Méré describes? He certainly did not interrupt his mathematical labours, on the contrary: but it is one thing to occupy oneself with mathematics—Méré, for that matter, flattered himself that he was an expert in this field—and another to see in mathematics the essential end and aim of all mental activity. It is remarkable that this renunciation of mathematics is attributed to Pascal in 1646 by Gilberte, and in 1653 by Méré, in both cases, it seems, quite gratuitously. Does not this prove that Pascal was constantly questioning himself about the human value of scientific research, and that the meeting with Méré deepened the problem for him by making him feel that, quite apart from his religious scruples, there might be a higher type of merely human knowledge? Without exaggerating Méré's influence, may we not admit that he helped Pascal to become aware of the development that was taking place in him and so to guide his thinking towards its full maturity?

When he came back from Poitou in January, 1654, Pascal kept in close touch with his old friends. He passed more and more time at the Hôtel de Roannez, where he sometimes stayed overnight. On the initiative of Méré, an eager gambler, he undertook the researches which were to give rise to the calculus of probabilities and which form the theme of an interesting correspondence with Fermat. At the beginning of 1654, moreover, Pascal was extending his scientific researches into a wide variety of fields. In an address to "The Parisian Academy of Sciences"—no doubt the old Academy of Mersenne, directed since 1648 by le Pailleur, who was to die this year, 1654—Pascal enumerates the works which he is composing, treatises on geometry, arithmetic, and physics. Some of these were to be completed in the next few months, notably the *Traité de L'Equilibre des Liqueurs* and the *Traité du Triangle Arithmétique*. The first was not published by Florin Périer till 1663 and the second appeared in 1665. Pascal has an important place in the history of the development of the infinitesimal calculus and of combinational analysis. These treatises, of a great scientific value, have less interest in relation to Pascal's state of mind; but they show the part which scientific investigation still played in his life during his "worldly period" and on the very eve of his second conversion.

Such are the hard facts that we possess about this period; but to make our picture complete, we must now touch on some controversial questions.

Did Pascal at any moment become an unbeliever? There is only one document which can give the slightest support to this supposition. Father Rapin, in his *Mémoirs*, associates Pascal with Méré, Mitton, and the mathematician Thevenot in relation to some experiments in witchcraft which he dates in 1649. At this date, however, it is very improbable either that Pascal knew Méré, or that Méré was in Paris. Rapin moreover imagines these friends of Pascal as being coarse scoffers, which they were not; Sainte-Beuve has shown us clearly what we ought to think of such calumnies. A few lines further on, indeed this Jesuit Father accuses Pascal of having plagiarized his *Apology* from a work which only appeared after he was dead!

Did Pascal yield to the temptations of sensuality? A curious document has been brought forward in support of this hypothesis: letters of legitimation in favour of Jean Pascal, natural son of Blaise Pascal, "Counsellor Notary and Secretary of the King, Royal House and Crown of France", and of Anne Charmat. Is the reference to the future Christian apologist? This thesis has rarely been taken seriously and cannot be sustained. Our Pascal was never "Secretary of the King"; this purely honorary duty was sought out only because it conferred ennoblement. But our Pascal was of noble rank already. Another Blaise Pascal, his cousin, was given the office in question by letters of 24th December, 1640, and thus became the ancestor of the future Seigneurs de Montel. He married three times and had at least twelve children, without counting the natural ones; Jean Pascal was one of the latter.

But was Pascal ever in love? The problem is raised by a famous document, the *Discours sur les Passions de l'Amour*. The manuscript, discovered by Victor Cousin as late as 1842, bears this simple inscription: "Attributed to Monsieur Pascal." This discourse is quite certainly the work of a man of the world who knows the spirit of high society; when he praises the ideal of a "tumultuous" life, passing from love to ambition, both "fiery passions", is he not thinking of some of the intrigues of the Fronde? The discourse is also the work of a philosopher, Cartesian in his general tendencies, who analyses in a penetrating way the relationships between thought and passion, between reason and love, who seeks to define the human ideal of beauty and occasionally slips in some pessimistic reflection on human nature. The discourse, finally, in spite of its state of incomplete finish, is the work of a writer of great talent, the most delicate impulses of love are described with subtlety and the thought often expresses itself in vigorous terse sentences. These are the arguments for attributing the discourse to Pascal, with the addition of one more point, of capital importance; between the text of the *Discours* and that of the *Pensées* we can establish numerous correspondences; thus the distinction between the geometric mind, and the tactful or sensitive mind, occurs in both. Victor Cousin therefore decided in favour of Pascal's authorship.

Subsequent criticism, on the whole, has sided with him. The final argument was even perfected as late as 1920 by Lanson. It was objected that the *Discours* might be later in date than the first printed version of the *Pensées* and the author might simply have imitated the *Pensées*. Lanson's train of reasoning is as follows. The seventeenth century knew the *Pensées* only in the Port-Royal edition, which departs notably from the autograph manuscript. If the passages of the *Discours* which recall the *Pensées* are nearer to the text of the manuscript than to this earliest printed text, then Pascal is undoubtedly the author of the *Discours*. That they are nearer to the manuscript is what Lanson seeks to establish by the examination of each particular case. All these arguments have been recently further elaborated by Monsieur Saulnier.

However, the opposite point of view is beginning to find more and more partisans. Earlier arguments against Pascal's authorship have been gathered together and largely transcended by the most recent researches of Monsieur Louis Lafuma. What, he asks himself, are the arguments in favour of the attribution of the *Discours* to Pascal really worth? If the manuscript discovered by Victor Cousin does suggest this attribution, it remains true that there is another manuscript which mentions no author's name. Why was criticism silent in the seventeenth and eighteenth centuries? Why did the enemies of Pascal from the Jesuits to Voltaire, make no mention of this work? Lanson's arguments are turned against himself: Lafuma asserts that, after all, the *Discours* does recall the Port-Royal edition rather than the manuscript of the *Pensées*; there is even one passage inspired by an editorial gloss. Indeed, we have to bring the date of the composition of the *Discours* a good deal forward; the author uses quite a number of works that appeared only after Pascal's death, including La Rochefoucauld's *Maximes*, the works of Méré, and Malebranche's *Recherche de la Vérité*. Finally, some parts of the *Discours* correspond exactly to the "questions on love" raised around 1666 by Bussy-Rabutin; the game of making up "maxims on love" through questions and answers was then all the rage in the *salons*. Having thus, as he feels, eliminated Pascal, Monsieur Lafuma proposes another claimant to the *Discours*, the Marquis d'Alluye.

Our own personal researches are not yet at a stage at which we can oppose Monsieur Lafuma's theory with one of our own. We shall confine ourselves to suggesting a few criticisms of his argument. The whole business, after all, of working out correspondences between texts is a very delicate one and such arguments often lack demonstrative force; we have seen that Lanson's argument based on textual correspondences can be turned against himself. To establish the fact that one text has been certainly derived from another, it is not enough to point out a marked resemblance, it is also necessary to eliminate every other possible influence; such resemblances may be explained by an imitation of a common model or by living in a common atmosphere. May, for instance, the influence on the *Discours* which Monsieur Lafuma attributes to Malebranche—the most striking of his suggestions—not be merely that of the Oratory, which, since Father Senault's time, took a great interest in the theory of the passions, or of some Cartesian of the second rank? As for the "questions on love" their origin goes back to the medieval literature of courtly love, a fashion which caught on again with the development of aristocratic politeness in the seventeenth century. Around 1650, such questions were frequently asked among the group gathered round Mademoiselle de Scudéry; and her novels contain a great number of such questions. One of them, which Bussy-Rabutin had not retained, is actually answered in the *Discours*; it has to do with the problem of love between persons of unequal social rank. It is therefore at least not impossible to put the composition of the *Discours* as far back as the neighbourhood of 1650. These are mere suggestions for further research, deriving from the labours of Monsieur Lafuma himself, who has put the problem on its proper basis by reducing it to a matter of a careful investigation of sources.

Whatever the results of such further research may be, we may agree that the *Discours* is at least a less original work than has been thought, and that it would be futile to turn to it for evidence about the "love-life" of Pascal. Since Faugère's time, all sorts of theories have been built up on the assumption that Pascal was in love with Mademoiselle de Roannez, the young sister of the Duke; the sole pretext for these theories is this single passage in the *Discours* which deals with the problem of love between persons of unequal social rank. The passage treats, in fact, a trite and obvious theme, a commonplace, closely tied up with the other trite and obvious theme of the relationships between love and ambition. There are those, however, who say that the feeling is described with too much subtlety to be the work of a writer who had not felt it personally; at that rate, we must suppose that Saint Thomas Aquinas, who has profound analyses of passion, must himself have been a lover! Let us await the discovery of fresh documents before pronouncing any judgment on this aspect of Pascal's life.

One last problem: did Pascal ever consider marrying anybody? Marguerite Périer says so; her uncle had resolved to
"obtain a post and to marry". For her, this is palpably the
culmination of Pascal's "commitment" to the world, and
later in his life Pascal was to take a similar point of view
himself about the projected marriage, of which he thoroughly disapproved, of his niece, Jacqueline Périer. He was then
to describe marriage as "the most dangerous and the lowest
of the conditions of life permitted to a Christian". Racine in
his *Abrégé de L'Histoire de Port Royal* is even more particular in his statements: Pascal "renounced a very advantageous
marriage which he was on the point of concluding" at the
time of his second conversion. It seems certain therefore that
Pascal considered marriage. Had he some definite project
in mind? We may regret that Racine was not more
explicit.

How, then, are we to define the worldliness of this second
period of Pascal's worldly life? As worldliness in the simplest
sense of the word, a growing habit of moving in that fashion-
world in which Pascal's reputation as a scientist made him
welcome. He had close ties with Madame d'Aiguillon and
even closer ones with the Duc de Roannez. He was presented
at Court. Did he also cultivate the society of the fashionable
freethinkers? Certainly he met some, but was theirs a coarse
impiety like that of Desbarreaux or Saint-Pavin? It is very
improbable. Those men of this type, like Méré and Mitton,
whom one can certainly number among Pascal's acquaintances, were perhaps indifferent to religion, but they were
not scoffers.

It was a period of financial difficulties. Far from leading
a gay and brilliant life, clattering in his coach across the
Paris cobbles, Pascal was almost in a state of financial em-
barrassment. Since his father's death, he had been forced to
abandon the family house in the rue de Touraine and to
content himself with rooms sublet to him in the house of a
financier in the rue Beaubourg. This explains his attitude
in the affair of Jacqueline's dowry; as Mother Angélique

recognized, he had not enough money to live in the style which his social rank demanded.

It was a period of business anxieties. To get on his feet again, the first thing Pascal had to do was gather in his inheritance and obtain from his father's debtors the repayment of their debts. When he had got this money together, he had to invest it; Pascal bought some shop premises in the Halle au Blé, which he could let at a good rent; he became involved in the scheme for draining the Poitou marshes, under the patronage of the Duc de Roannez. As a source of additional income, he continued to construct arithmetical machines, but he counted above all on a marriage which must primarily be "an advantageous marriage".

It was a period of scientific labours. Popularizing his discoveries through fashionable lectures, Pascal at the same time pursued his researches, especially during the exceptionally fertile months at the beginning of 1654. More than ever he felt himself possessed by a passion for science which, besides its intrinsic interest, conferred on him a kind of sovereignty in the intellectual world.

It was a period of inner development, whose precise range and limits, however, are rather difficult to determine. At the beginning of this period, Pascal no doubt already knew his Epictetus and his Montaigne, but had he thought much about "honesty", or had the knowledge of nature made him neglect the knowledge of man? If so, in contact with Méré and other men of that type, Pascal discovered the latter without forgetting the former.

Finally, it was a period to some extent of inner uncertainty and confusion. Pascal had not turned away from the practice of religion, he continued to see Jacqueline, but he no longer felt that ardour and that inner joy which for the disciples of Saint-Cyran are the signs of indwelling grace. Pascal was at first indifferent to this dry state of his soul; then it began to cause him suffering and this led to his second conversion.

III. *The Second Conversion*

In relation to this second conversion, we possess a document of extreme value, written by a witness to the conversion and a confidante of Pascal's, Jacqueline Pascal, who had now become Soeur de Sainte-Euphémie in religion. The document consists of letters sent to Gilberte to tell her the news. We must follow these letters closely, supplementing them where we can.

On 8th December, 1654, Jacqueline wrote that for more than a year Blaise had experienced "a great contempt for the world and a great distaste for the people who compose it. Even if this is an exaggeration, it forces us to date the new development in Pascal as far back as the early months of 1654. This was the period following the journey to Poitou, a period of great scientific activity and of prolonged visits to the Hôtel de Roannez. These outer appearances were deceptive; within himself, Pascal was in agony.

In another letter, of 25th January, 1655, Jacqueline gives more exact details. Towards the end of the previous September, she tells us, her brother had come to see her, and had confessed that in the midst of all his occupations and in spite of his real attachment to the world, he was feeling the greatest aversion for his mode of life at that time; but he did not feel in the least drawn towards God; seeking to recapture his former fervour, he had failed to do so. Such was his spiritual state in spring, 1654. And in the *Ecrit sur la Conversion du Pécheur*, of which Pascal is probably the author, disgust with the world without any attraction towards God is, in fact, described as the first stage in the convert's journey. Taking Jacqueline into his confidence was for Pascal a decisive step. Shortly afterwards, he left the rue Beaubourg to settle in the Faubourg Saint-Michel, near Porte Saint-Michel, and according to Gilberte this change of lodging marked a break with some of his habits and some of his acquaintances. His visits to Jacqueline grew more frequent.

But a new step had to be taken; Pascal had to agree to submit to a spiritual director and, at Port-Royal, this could only be Monsieur Singlin. Pascal, with a remnant of independence, resisted this proposal as long as he could, cunningly putting off both his sister and himself. Finally, however, he attained that fervour which he had not been able to feel and that spirit of submission which was still lacking in him. The change came in a single night, 23rd November, 1654, and was accompanied by a mystical ecstasy which has become famous. Pascal recorded the memory of this experience on a piece of parchment. In accordance with a pious custom of the seventeenth century, he always carried this piece of parchment with him, sewn inside the lining of his clothes. Nobody saw it while he was alive. This was Pascal's *Mémorial*, a famous text in which Pascal's deepest inner feelings, ranging from the most fervent exaltation to the most contrite humility, express themselves with spontaneous originality. The important part played by Biblical reminiscences shows that the *Mémorial* records the climax of a long period of solitary meditation.[1] The crisis has been reached and passed. The penitent has found peace and declares: "Total submission to Jesus Christ and my director." On 8th December Jacqueline was able to announce: "He has totally surrendered the guidance of his conduct to Monsieur Singlin."

What importance, however, are we to attribute in the bringing about of Pascal's "second conversion" to two events which have often been discussed, both in regard to their significance and in regard to whether, after all, they ever really took place? The first of these episodes is the accident at the Bridge of Neuilly, reported by an anonymous writer who claims to have heard the story from d'Arnoul de Saint-Victor, the parish priest of Chamboursy, who heard it from the Prior de Barillon, who heard it from Gilberte. Pascal "a few years before his death", was going, according to his habit, on a public holiday, for a drive to the Bridge of

[1] See appendix

L'an de grace 1654

Lundy 23 novembre jour de St Clement pape et martyr et autres

au Martirologe Veille de St Chrysogone martir et autres

Depuis environ dix heures et demy du soir jusques environ minuit et demy

FEU

Dieu d'Abraham, Dieu d'Isaac, Dieu de Jacob

non des philosophes et des savants

Certitude Certitude sentiment Joye

Dieu de Jesus Christ

Ton Dieu sera mon Dieu

Oubly du monde et de tout hormis Dieu

Il ne se trouve que par les voyes enseignées dans l'Evangile

Grandeur de l'ame humaine

Pere juste le monde ne t'a point connu mais je t'ay connu

Joye, Joye, Joye, pleurs de Joye

Je m'en suis separé

Dereliquerunt me fontem aquae vivae

Mon Dieu me quitterez vous

Que je n'en sois separé eternellement

Cette est la vie eternelle qu'ils te connoissent seul vray Dieu

et celuy que tu as envoyé Jesus Christ

Jesus Christ

Je m'en suis separé je l'ay fuy renoncé crucifié

Que je n'en sois jamais separé

Il ne se conserve que par les voyes enseignées dans l'Evangile

Renonciation totale et douce

Neuilly with some friends in a carriage with four or six horses. At the part of the bridge which had no protective barrier at the side the galloping horses got the bits in their teeth, leapt into the water, and would have dragged the coach after them if the reins had not broken. This accident, we are told, made "Monsieur Pascal resolve to give up his drives abroad and to live in total solitude".

Such is the original narrative, without a date, without names, and without any of the vivid details which subsequent writers have gratuitously added. A critical spirit might even almost lead us to question whether an event that rests on such solitary and belated testimony ever really happened. Without going so far as that—for such accidents, in seventeenth-century France, were an everyday matter—we should notice that the language used by the narrator does not allow us to date the episode in 1654: the accident took place only "a few years" before Pascal's death and Pascal's decision "to live in total solitude" was certainly not taken in 1654. Is the narrator not alluding to a later development, what might almost be called a "third conversion", which we can date around the winter of late 1658 and early 1659?

According to a second story, which we owe to Marguerite Périer, Pascal was converted by a sermon of Singlin's delivered at Port-Royal de Paris on the day of the Conception of Our Lady, 8th December, 1654. Marguerite's summary of this sermon does, in fact, correspond with a sermon of Singlin's on the Conception of the Virgin, published in 1671, but without any mention of the year of its original delivery. The sermon insists on the difficulty of working out one's salvation when caught up in the "commitments" of the world. It would have been easy for Pascal to relate this argument to his own situation. But has such a relationship not been merely imagined by Marguerite, after reading the printed sermon, and with the help of confused memories? For, as it stands, her story cannot be accepted. On that very day, 8th December, Jacqueline was speaking of her brother's conversion as an accomplished fact, and over the same period

Mother Angélique's letters confirm that Singlin, who was ill, was unable to preach. Some scholars have tried to date the sermon back to 21st November, the day of the Presentation of the Virgin. This hypothesis has no evidence to support it and seems in itself implausible.

In addition to all these objections, these two stories share the fault of making Pascal's conversion something abrupt, a sudden decision, while both Jacqueline's much more direct testimony and the *Ecrit sur la Conversion du Pécheur*, if that can be assumed to be Pascal's work, bear witness in a contrary sense.

Let us return to what followed on the writing of the *Mémorial*. Not every difficulty was yet cleared away. The new convert felt a great repugnance at the idea of revealing to his circle the change which had taken place in him. He thought at first of going to find Monsieur Singlin at Port-Royal des Champs under the pretext of wanting to discuss business. In this interim, the Duc de Roannez, who had come back from Poitou at the end of December, 1645, was the first to learn the secret: "with his consent, which was not given without tears", Pascal left on 7th January to make a retreat at Port-Royal des Champs. He passed a fortnight there, first at the Château de Vaumurier with the Duc de Luynes, and then at Granges, a hostel for the "solitaries" who had come to flee the cares of the world and seek this "desert". Here he met Monsieur de Saci, the confessor of the nuns, and had the famous conversation with him which the *Mémoires* of Fontaine, Saci's secretary, have preserved. In this conversation-piece, we can notice the narrator's sense of humour, the phlegm and mistrust of Monsieur de Saci himself, who was incapable of letting himself be carried away by Pascal's genius, and the vigour of Pascal's thought, expressed in a style which could belong to nobody but himself; for Fontaine's convenience he had to put the ideas he had expressed down in writing. The conversation deals with Pascal's reading; the two chief authors discussed are Epictetus and Montaigne. The Stoicism of Epictetus depicts man as capable through his own strength of carrying out his duties. Montaigne, a sceptic, shows the frailty of reason and its incapacity to attain philosophic, scientific, or moral truth: it follows, for Montaigne, that human conduct is regulated only by custom and convenience. Even though these two philosophers must be condemned from the point of view of the Christianity represented by Saint Augustine, it remains true that each of them understands very well a single aspect of human nature. Epictetus has recognized the traces of greatness in man that date back to his unfallen condition; Montaigne has depicted the present corruption of fallen man. The Gospel reconciles the two opposite opinions; weakness is natural to man, but his moments of greatness are bestowed by God's grace. Thus two natures are united in the person of the Man-God.

It is obvious that many of the leading ideas of the future *Apology* had already ripened in the mind of the new convert, as the fruit of his long secret meditations throughout the year 1654. The apologetic scope of such reflections, moreover, has already received definition at the end of this conversation, where Pascal shows how he will be able to use his reading to trouble unbelievers. Far from reacting against what the world had taught him, Pascal incorporated his worldly discoveries about human nature into his religious thought.

The *Mémorial* and the *Entretien avec Monsieur de Saci* express feelings and ideas that ripened during the last months of Pascal's "worldly period". On the other hand, the new convert, in spite of Monsieur de Saci's distrust, did not hesitate to make good use of his experience in the world. We ought not, therefore, to exaggerate the break marked by the second conversion. It would be inaccurate to say that Pascal now wholly withdrew from the world. He renounced marriage, he provisionally renounced the sciences, but he was in no sense the "fierce solitary of Port-Royal" of whom Tourneur, following on all the other biographers, speaks. He was neither fierce nor solitary. On 21st January, 1655,

Pascal left Port-Royal des Champs; he spent some days at Port-Royal de Paris, and then returned to his house in the Faubourg Saint-Michel. This was a small, unpretentious, but rather attractive house situated "between two tennis courts" and possessing a garden "laid out with flower-beds and with climbing fruit trees on the walls". As a house-keeper, Pascal employed Madame Pinel, the sister of Louise Default. She lived with him with her husband and two daughters; under her orders she had a footman and a female cook. In spite of some efforts in that direction, Pascal had not yet really adopted an ascetic mode of life. Jacqueline thought that he looked a little too "jovial" for a penitent.

But if he did not abandon the world, he sought to conquer it. In the spring of 1655 he was again staying with the Duc de Roannez and sought to convert the great nobleman in his turn. The Duke was won over, renounced the brilliant future that he was looking forward to and even the rich marriage with Mademoiselle de Mesmes which he had been coveting for so long. His plan of withdrawal from the world infuriated his great-uncle, the Comte d'Harcourt, to whom the Duke owed his splendid career. The Comte was so angry that he tried to have Pascal murdered. The latter owed his life to mere chance. The morning when the porter of the Hôtel de Roannez came in to stab him on his awakening he happened, contrary to his usual habits, to have got up very early.

He also kept up his contacts with Méré and Mitton. Méré gradually acquired the reputation of being one of those worldly wits who were drawn to Jansenism. A curious manuscript, which reports conversations at the Hôtel de Liancourt, declares that Mitton corrected *The Provincial Letters*.

Meanwhile, Pascal did not lose sight of Port-Royal and its solitaries. No writings of his can be plausibly dated from 1655, but Jacqueline tells us that during this year he invented a new method of teaching reading for use in the Port-Royal schools. In January, 1656, he went to make a short retreat at Port-Royal des Champs. There he saw Arnauld, who was sheltering at Port-Royal from his pursuers. This chance meeting led Pascal to play a leading part in the defence of Jansenist theology against the Sorbonne. Before the end of the month, the first *Provincial Letter* had appeared.

CHAPTER THREE

THE EVOLUTION OF "THE PROVINCIAL LETTERS"

IN spite of their admirable clarity and their formal per-fection, Pascal's *Provincial Letters* are a complex work. Critics have often neglected their depths. Their purely literary importance has certainly been fully grasped. Their moral and theological scope has been less firmly defined, and it might be said that critics have hardly thought at all of looking in them for Pascal's soul and the development of his inner life.

To unravel these various problems, we must transplant ourselves to the intellectual climate in which *The Provincial Letters* were born. They are merely the most important example of a whole class of works, a very abundant class, provoked by the debates between the Jesuits and the Jan-senists. This controversial literature is to-day little known and difficult of access, though it is still full of instruction for the philosopher and even for the cultivated general reader, the *honnête homme*. Yet for some scholars it is still a pas-sionately interesting subject of research; and though we have no guide to this topic as surefooted as M. Jean Orcibal on the origins of the Jansenist movement, we shall attempt to summarize the controversy in such a fashion as to avoid if not simplification, at least caricature.

I. *The Origins of the Debate*

The narrative of Pascal's conversations with M. de Rebours shows us that he had taken an interest in the controversies provoked by the rise of Jansenism. But in fact he devoted to these controversies a merely external attention. He was a devout Christian without much interest in pure theology, and with even less of a taste for polemics. He was sensitive above all to the inner religious impulse to which such a man as Guillebert bore witness. He wanted to lay the foundations of his life as a Christian on a sound spiritual doctrine. Such a doctrine, let us emphasize once more, Pascal found above all in Saint-Cyran, who is a very strong influence on all the writings of his youth. However, in 1656, Pascal, a novice in theology, flung himself, on Arnauld's suggestion, into the thick of the theological battle. What stage had the debate then reached?

The opposition between the Jesuits and the Jansenists ought not to be considered as one between two formally constituted bodies of doctrine. It was rather an opposition between two tendencies already ancient in the history of the Church which were capable of assuming new and various forms. The "Jansenists" did not always follow the doctrine of Jansenius with scrupulous exactitude; and the great theologians of Port-Royal, Arnauld, Nicole, Barcos, were sometimes profoundly at variance with each other as well as with their supposed master. On the other hand, if the Jesuits were the chief opponents of the Jansenists, they were not alone in the field; and among the Jesuits themselves some superior men had taken up theological positions which were much less unpalatable than what was thought of as the general Jesuit position to Port-Royal and its devotees of the Augustinian tradition. Bellarmine, in the sixteenth century, had been one of these, and quite recently Pétau. And broadly speaking both the tendency represented by Jansenism and that represented by the Jesuits can be considered as two aspects of that Counter-Reformation to which the progress of Protestantism had given rise.

The earlier of these two tendencies was that represented by the Jesuits. Moreover, the fundamental ideas underlying the Jesuit Counter-Reformation had much more novelty than those of the Jansenists. In fact, in the battle against

Protestantism, which claimed to go back to Christian origins and to link up with the purity of the ancient Church, the Jesuits adopted an attitude of intransigent modernism. Themselves a body of recent foundation, with an evangelical mission that forced them to keep in close touch with all the currents of their age, they had been deeply affected by the humanism of the Renaissance and sought to reconcile traditional doctrine with the demands of the new spirit of the age. With the Jesuits, what the lawyers call "constructive" arguments, based on abstract reason, played a great part in theology; they were conscious of putting forward novel opinions and did not feel any scruples about doing so. For them, no doubt, as for other theologians, it was the duty of the Christian to remain faithful to tradition; but tradition had to be thought of as something living that grew and developed with the passage of time. The doctrine of the Church, moreover, ought not to be identified with any of its transitory expressions, however much credit may have been given to such expressions at a particular time. The only criterion of truth is what the Church here and now believes. And the Christian must submit himself to the hierarchy of the Church, which imposes harsh and definite limits on his right to free examination of theological facts and arguments.

From the humanism of the Renaissance there can be derived an essentially optimistic conception of the nature of man. Is this humanist conception radically opposed to that of Christianity? Not if we adopt the views of such a thinker as Molina, a Spanish Jesuit who gave his name to the famous system of Molinism. No doubt, through original sin, man is a fallen creature, but Adam's fault deprived him only of the supernatural gifts which God had bestowed upon him. His nature remains unchanged. He still possesses "free will" or "free choice", that power of making a decision to act in one way or another without lying under the compulsion of any motive; consequently he possesses an equal power of doing good or doing evil.

However, to assist man to act well, God has granted him His grace. But grace is not an infallible assurance that a good, not a bad, choice will be made; for if it were, man's free will would be destroyed. God grants to man only "sufficient" graces, mere promptings towards the good, which the human will can accept or reject, render "efficacious" or otherwise. Man remains the sole shaper of his own fate.

Moreover, no man can ask for his sin to be excused on the grounds that he has not been granted grace. All men possess grace; the just so that they may persevere in holiness, sinners so that they may amend their lives, unbelievers so that they may be converted. No doubt the salvation of the elect is "predestined", but only in the sense that God foresees the merits which they will freely acquire and which will, so to say, earn them salvation.

In everyday life, since man is not fundamentally bad, he need not seek to change himself radically; it is enough for him to accomplish virtuous actions, to obey the commandments of God and the Church. But these commandments have been given in very general terms. To know how to apply them to each particular circumstance of life, we must have recourse to "casuistry" or the science of cases of conscience. In every particular case casuistry will be able to suggest to the penitent a new attitude that can be taken up without disturbing the tranquillity of the soul. Casuistry was already an ancient science, but it had been considerably developed by the Jesuits who, in order to encourage the diffusion of the Faith, sought to determine a "minimal" level of Christian living, sufficient to attain salvation. In the same way, a "minimum" of dispositions towards amendment made it permissible to receive the sacraments; it was sufficient for the sinner to regret his sins through the mere fear of Hell for him to receive a valid absolution, that would cause grace to abound in him. If perfection is desirable, it is not needful. Such a perfection, where it is achieved, will consist above all in an inner discipline, a hierarchical ordering of the faculties of the soul, above all in a scrupulous obedience to the Church.

The practices of poverty and of self-abnegation find their justification not in our concern to struggle against the corruption of our nature but in our desire to imitate our exemplar, who is Jesus Christ.

In reaction against this whole set of attitudes and in the hope of striking more deeply into the bulwarks of Protestantism, there developed, from the sixteenth century onwards, the other set of tendencies which were later to receive the name of "Jansenism". This set of tendencies was characterized above all by an impulse towards a return to Christian antiquity. We have already noted this impulse in the spiritual doctrine of Saint-Cyran and its development by Arnauld in his book, *On Frequent Communion*: both of these writers emphasize and glorify a conception of penitence, and of the use of the Eucharist and other sacraments, inspired by the customs of the primitive Church. But it was in the field of theology that this impulse of return towards primitive models was particularly notable. According to such thinkers as Saint-Cyran and Arnauld, the Christian of the seventeenth century ought not to acknowledge any dogmas other than those of the ancient Church. To define these the theologian ought to turn to the Scriptures and to the Fathers of the Church whose writings constitute tradition; his task consists simply and solely of defining the sense of these ancient writers. Truth, being immutable, cannot change or develop. Its authority is something that is imposed as firmly on Popes and Bishops as on the simplest believer; papal authority does not permit the Pope to introduce new dogmas. Among the ancient Fathers there is one who deserves special attention because of the support which the Church has always lent to his teachings. This is Saint Augustine. And among Saint Augustine's writings the Jansenists attached special weight to his polemics against the Pelagians. These heretics had denied original sin, and the Jansenists sometimes identified their doctrine with that of the Jesuits. But what doctrines about original sin, and what general attitudes, had they themselves discovered in Saint Augustine?

In the first place, in their whole doctrine there is a profound pessimism. Original sin has totally corrupted man. Adam, created for God, intended to love God only, made a bad use of the power of free choice which he possessed; he rebelled against God and preferred himself to his Creator. His sin, as a kind of habitual condition of human nature, was transmitted to his posterity. From the moment of Adam's fall, our "concupiscence" has led us to seek our happiness in created things and not in their Creator. "Self-love" makes us love ourselves instead of loving God. Our wills, perverted, can no longer lead us towards the good.

To the absolute liberty of man postulated by the Jesuits, the Jansenists therefore oppose an omnipotent divine grace. For them, the Molinist notion of "sufficient" grace is inconceivable: for to accept grace is already a good action and the human will, in itself, is incapable of any good action whatsoever. Do the Jansenists then conceive of divine grace as acting on the human will with a kind of mechanical compulsion, do they conceive of a "necessitating" grace? No, for that would be to fall into the heresy of Calvin. For the Jansenists, divine grace merely produces in the soul a kind of attraction towards the good which triumphs over the opposite attraction of concupiscence. Grace does not destroy man's freedom of choice, though the manner in which divine omnipotence and human freedom work together for the salvation of souls must remain an incomprehensible mystery.

Where the question of the distribution of grace is concerned, if the Jesuits envisage above all God's mercifulness, the Jansenists emphasize His Sovereign Majesty. Mankind being in a state of rebellion against Him, God could condemn all men to damnation, and it would be mere justice. But in His goodness, He has wished to save at least a part of mankind. For this purpose, He has given His only Son; the sacrifice of Christ was in its own nature sufficient to have redeemed all men, but in fact it has only redeemed those who have actually been saved. Who, then, will be saved? The man who has merited salvation? But all merit presupposes grace.

These only are the elect whom God, from all eternity, has predestined for salvation. At this point, are the Jansenists once more about to fall into the Calvinist heresy, as their opponents allege? No, for God does not act in a capricious fashion. The elect do not reach heaven except along the path of merits and of Christian virtues; no living man ought to think of himself as already rejected. Predestination is reasonable, though it is not for mere man to work out the reasons for it. Here, once more, we have a recognition of mystery, but one which should lead us to humility and not to fatalism.

With the Jansenists as with the Jesuits, the principles of a good life are deduced from a fundamental conception of human nature. Man being radically corrupt, it is not enough for him to carry out virtuous acts. His whole soul must be transformed, so that it passes from the state of sin to the state of grace. To hark back to the ideas of Saint-Cyran, if we wish to attain to the Christian life, we must bring about a total conversion of our interests, renouncing self-love for the love of God. To love God, moreover, does not mean to feel an affection for Him in the sensitive part of our natures but rather to seek to do His will in everything, to strive towards perfection. If they are to confer grace, also, the sacraments must be received by a soul pierced through and through by the love of God; thus absolution is not valid unless the penitent regrets his sins not only because of the fear of Hell but also because of the offence he has done to God. In the same manner, the Christian's own sense of the fervour of love for God in his soul must regulate the frequency with which he takes communion. To the ideal of order, of discipline, of submission which is represented by the Jesuit doctrine at its best there corresponds in Jansenism a concern for the inner life, for communion with God, for the quest of an ever higher perfection.

These two tendencies, then, had already come up violently against each other in the sixteenth century. The scene of the conflict was Louvain where the Faculty of Theology, passionately attached to the tradition of Saint Augustine, clashed with a powerful Jesuit college. In 1567, the Augustinian Balus suffered condemnation at Rome, though he got off rather lightly. Towards the end of the sixteenth century, the Molinists had been attacked by the Dominicans, disciples of Saint Thomas Aquinas, who defended, like their Master, a moderate Augustinianism; the Molinists were almost condemned in their turn, but the famous Congregations *de Auxiliis* (or Conferences about Grace) led to no positive result; the secret wish of Rome was to see all controversies about grace come to an end, since they were thought to do harm to the faithful. Finally, on several occasions, at the beginning of the seventeenth century, the relaxed moral code of the Jesuits had been censured.

All these quarrels sprang to life again in 1640 when there appeared, shortly after the death of its author, the famous *Augustinus* of Jansenius. This work restated, often in very moderate terms, the traditional standpoint of the University of Louvain. Controversy arose first at Louvain itself, and then spread to France. Jansenius, well known in France through his friendship with Saint-Cyran, was defended there by the disciples of the latter, notably Arnauld. Arnauld had himself, since the days of his earliest theses in the Sorbonne in 1635, put forward a similar interpretation of the thought of Saint Augustine. The ties which bound Saint-Cyran to his disciples at the monastery of Port-Royal explain why the latter place came to seem the stronghold of Jansenism. Given all these circumstances, the controversy was naturally a lively one.

It began in 1643, after the publication of Arnauld's work, *On Frequent Communion*. Provoked by the contrasting attitudes of the directors of two great ladies, the debate, by force and combination of circumstances, began to attract the attention of a wider public. Published in French, and notable for its exact reasoning, Arnauld's book was within the reach of any intelligent reader. It was completed, in 1644, by his *Moral Theology of the Jesuits*, a profound criticism, and one which had been approved by the Sorbonne, of the whole Jesuit system of casuistry.

In 1649, on the initiative of the Jesuits, Nicolas Cornet, a member of the Faculty of Theology at Paris, drew up a list of five propositions in which he claimed to have summed up the doctrine of Jansenius. He asked that these five propositions should be condemned. The propositions did not come under the immediate censure of the Sorbonne. They were sent to Rome, which condemned them in 1653. For Arnauld and his friends, there were two possible methods of self-defence. They could claim that the five propositions, in addition to their heretical meaning, were capable of bearing another meaning, which was the real meaning of Saint Augustine and also of Jansenius. Or, on the other hand, while acknowledging the heretical nature of the propositions, they could deny that they were to be found in Jansenius. Since the Pope had declared that the doctrine of efficacious grace was not affected by his condemnation of the propositions, Arnauld and his friends at first adopted the first method.

The controversy thereupon to some extent died down. But in 1655, one of the curates of Saint-Sulpice, the Abbé Picote, refused absolution to the Duc de Liancourt, under the pretext that he had too close an acquaintance with the Gentlemen of Port-Royal. This was treating all the friends of the Monastery as excommunicates. Arnauld replied on 24th February with his *Letter to a Person of Quality*. He condemned the five propositions and asserted that it was only to the doctrine of Saint Augustine himself that he was bound. In a reply, Father Annat, a Jesuit and the King's confessor, accused Arnauld of Calvinism.

On 10th July, Arnauld replied to Annat's attack in a *Second Letter to a Duke and Peer*, addressed to the Duc de Luynes, one of the friends of Port-Royal. A Commission of the Faculty of Theology extracted two sets of errors from this letter. There was a "question of fact": Arnauld, adopting the second of his two tactical possibilities, declared that the five propositions were not to be found in the *Augustinus* of Jansenius. There was a "question of right" or doctrinal correctness: Arnauld, at the risk of readopting the first of the five condemned propositions, claimed that Saint Peter, on the occasion when he denied his Master, was a "just person" to whom grace was lacking. On 14th January, 1656, Arnauld was condemned on the "question of fact". He was threatened with condemnation on the question of doctrine.

By writing these two letters, Arnauld brought this theological debate before the great public. But his style was heavy and inelegant, and promised him little success as a controversialist. He had the help for some time of Nicole, a young Bachelor of Theology, but neither had Nicole the required liveliness of talent. It was about this time that these two met Pascal at Port-Royal des Champs. "You, who are young," said Arnauld, "you must do something." And the first test of Pascal's powers was taken as conclusive proof of the soundness of Arnauld's choice.

Before analysing *The Provincial Letters* in detail, it is important to note some of their essential characteristics. (1) They were a *collective* work, springing from the collaboration of Pascal, Arnauld, and Nicole. These two provided Pascal with facts and quotations and sometimes sketched out the general plan he was to follow. Each letter, as soon as he had finished it, was submitted to their judgment. (2) They were an *anonymous* work, appearing in the first instance as separate letters, addressed "to a provincial by one of his friends" to keep him informed about the disputes in the Sorbonne. In the first collected edition, published in 1657, the author took the pseudonym of Louis de Montalte. In 1658, Nicole published a Latin translation accompanied by notes written under the pseudonym of Guillaume Wendrock. The veil of anonymity was not pierced till 1659. (3) They were a *clandestine* work, and they compelled Pascal to take multifarious precautions. He left his own apartments in the Faubourg Saint-Michel as often as possible, spent some time in an inn at the sign of the "Roi David", near the

Sorbonne, left the inn to stay with the Duc de Roannez, who had come back from Poitou towards May; and once or twice he betook himself to Port-Royal des Champs. The printing and the distribution of the letters were undertaken by friends of Port-Royal, Nicolas Vitart, the Intendant of the Duc de Luynes and a cousin of Racine's, and Baudry d'Asson, a nobleman from Bas-Poitou. Neither they nor Pascal were to suffer from the searches for the instigators of the letters undertaken by Chancellor Séguier. But the printers were more vulnerable; they were often harried and sometimes jailed. The courage and devotion of some of them, such a man as Savreux for instance, gives a touching quality to the story of *The Provincial Letters*.

II. *The Evolution of "The Provincial Letters"*

Thus *The Provincial Letters* were, in their origin, a work arising out of given circumstances. They underwent various changes, as one succeeded another, both in the topics dealt with and the tone assumed, according as new circumstances arose in the course of the controversy. It would be interesting also—but it would be an extremely delicate task—to try to trace in what ways the thought of Pascal and his collaborators grows more exact, more subtle, as it runs up against objections. Above all, it would be interesting to analyse those details which picture for us Pascal's spiritual evolution; finding himself so deeply engaged in theological controversy, the convert must necessarily have explored more deeply his own religious life.

For ease of approach, it is possible to group the letters into various broad classes, within each of which there is to be found the same inspiration or the same artistic method.

The first three letters already form such a group. Appearing in rapid succession on 23rd and 29th January, and then on 9th of February, their immediate object was the defence of Arnauld who was threatened with censure by the Sorbonne on the question of doctrinal incorrectness. There were many Doctors of the Sorbonne who defended Arnauld, but the passing of a vote of censure appeared certain because of the attitude taken up, under the direction of one of their regents, Father Nicolaï, by the Dominicans of Paris, or Jacobins. Though their doctrine, that of Saint Thomas Aquinas, was nearer to Jansenism than to Molinism, and though the Dominicans of Rome had taken the side of Jansenius, the Jacobins made common cause with the Molinists against Arnauld. Pascal makes fun of this attitude. Without entering into the depths of theology—he was not yet capable of doing so—he sought to establish the fact that, though the language of the Jacobins recalled that of the Molinists, their real doctrine was fundamentally that of Arnauld himself. Let us consider, for instance, the question of "proximate power". Both Molinists and Jacobins agreed that "the just" have always "the proximate power" of obeying the Commandments. But for the Molinists, once this proximate power is admitted, what is actually done will depend entirely on the human will; for the Jacobins, a supplementary grace from God is necessary if the commandments are really to be obeyed; and this was just Arnauld's own opinion. It was the same story in the matter of "sufficient grace"; this, both Molinists and Jacobins agreed, was granted to all men, but according to the Molinists it sufficed in itself for action, while according to the Jacobins it remained inoperative without the addition of "efficacious grace"; this really amounted to denying sufficient grace, which was what the Jansenists did. Only worldly interests could unite the Jesuits and the Jacobins, whose fundamental lack of agreement was masked under a verbal artifice. Did Pascal, however, really properly understand the doctrine of Father Nicolaï? It seems that, guided by Nicole, who was himself working on a refutation of the doctrine of sufficient grace, Pascal very much over-simplified; for Father Nicolaï "sufficient grace" was not merely an empty phrase; it is a first solicitation by God which the will must yield to before receiving efficacious grace. But we should also notice the care taken by the French Jansenists, in contrast to those of Louvain and to Jansenius himself, to establish their agreement with the doctrine of St. Thomas Aquinas.

In these first three letters, Pascal has perfected his controversial method. The author presents himself as a person of sincere and general intellectual curiosity, an *honnête homme*, not at all learned in theological matters. Through the medium of the provincial friend whom he is keeping in touch with the disputes in the Sorbonne, Pascal addresses a wide public. His appeal is in the first instance to the fashionable world, much less ignorant then than to-day about theological matters, but also more widely to all men of goodwill and notably to the general body of preachers and ecclesiastics. Such a public had to be both interested and amused.

To keep up interest, Pascal seeks for complete clarity. It is a clarity not only of individual sentences and paragraphs but of total composition. This clarity of composition, above all in the first of the letters, develops with a cunning and rigorous logical progress, and leads us back again and again to the key idea; the attack on Arnauld in the Sorbonne is a lot of fuss about nothing. There is a clarity, in the second place, of style; in *The Provincial Letters*, the sentence— and this marks a decisive point of progress in the evolution of French prose—abandons the mould of rhetoric and becomes lively and light. There is a clarity, in the third place, of expository method. In each case, Pascal seeks to confine the discussion to one particular point, at once precise and typical, in relation to which the attitudes of the parties opposing each other can be quite simply defined; and he explains all technical terms by expressive and picturesque comparisons. He felt that every simple Christian believer had a right to demand such clarity when a question of faith was at stake; and that theology itself could not despise such clarity without running the risk of debasing itself.

To give pleasure, to keep his readers amused, Pascal felt it necessary to add wit to clarity. Thus in *The Provincial*

Letters ideas are not linked together in abstract argument. Each is represented by one of its defenders, sometimes by a whole chorus. Thus there is a living background to the argument—a background never to be more perfectly evoked than in the very first letter. The narrator, all on fire to discover the reason for the disputes in the Sorbonne, hurries from a Doctor of Navarre to a Jansenist and back, then dashes off to see a Molinist, and then to the Monastery of the Jacobins; and to each journey there corresponds a forward leap of the argument. The narrator's feverish desire to get at the truth communicates itself to the reader. The logical demonstration has become a human drama. The skill of the composition is completed by the lightness and delicacy of the smallest details; here is an unexpected comparison, there an attitude sketched from life. Above all, arising from premises that are above criticism, there are the most pungent conclusions. "Sufficient grace" does not, in fact, suffice. It seems absolutely necessary to be "either odd, or heretical, or a Jansenist". "It is not the opinions of Monsieur Arnauld that are heretical, it is his person." Pascal's wit, however, does not exclude a deep seriousness. In passing, he reminds us that two conceptions of human nature are at issue in this dispute. His tone grows loftier when he wishes to reproach the Jacobins for having let fall the torch handed down from the Fathers to Saint Thomas. Though they are addressed to the great world, *The Provincial Letters* never lose their note of religious sincerity.

These first three letters could not prevent the condemnation of Arnauld, but they had a great success with the general public. As a preliminary to the third letter, Pascal published tributes from a member of the Academy, possibly Chapelain, and from a great lady, possibly Mademoiselle de Scudéry. The enemies of Port-Royal were able to put up only a rather clumsy defence. They repeated their accusations of heresy. They made use of their position at Court to have the printers suspected of publishing the letters jailed. There were constant rumours of schemes of persecution.

It was in such an atmosphere of tension and expectation that the fourth letter appeared. This has a unique position in the whole design of the work. Mere defence of Arnauld had become useless, and Pascal instead begins to attack. He attacks his chief opponents, the Jesuits, who had been so far kept out of the argument since they did not sit at the Sorbonne and therefore were not directly concerned in Arnauld's condemnation. Pascal here abandons the rather superficial tactics of his first letters to treat the problem of grace in all its implications. Speaking both as a theologian and a moralist, he puts forward a whole theory of human nature.

In this letter, a conversation takes place between Pascal, accompanied by a Jansenist friend—who has the task of putting forward those more expert and technical arguments that could not plausibly be put in the mouth of an *honnête homme*—and a Jesuit Father. The discussion concerns "actual grace", or grace as actually operative on a given occasion. According to the Jesuit, "an action cannot be imputed to sin if God does not give us, before we commit it, a knowledge of the evil that there is in it, and an inspiration which moves us to avoid it." This knowledge and this inspiration constitute what the Jesuit calls actual grace; and according to him it is given to all men. But for the Jansenist, God does not always give actual grace, and a sin committed without actual grace is none the less a sin.

The Jesuit produces his proofs, which are all quite modern: Jesuit authors like Father Bauny and Father Annat and their disciples, like Dr. le Moyne. After a few brisk expressions of ironic surprise, Pascal proceeds to his refutation of the Jesuit thesis, a refutation which is precise and pitiless. First of all there is the refutation by the *honnête homme*, the ordinary man of honour, intelligence, and some experience of the world. In this role, Pascal denounces the logical absurdity of the Molinist theory of actual grace. According to this theory the sinfulness of an act depends on one's attention being directed to the evil in it which one ought to avoid. Therefore the less one thinks of avoiding evil, that is, the more one sins habitually and thoughtlessly, the less risk one runs of falling into sin. Then Pascal, still in his role as *honnête homme*, points out that the theory contradicts everyday experience. Men do not, in fact, always experience remorse before committing an evil act; and no theoretical argument of theology ought to go against admitted facts. It is now time for a refutation by a man of learning. The Jansenist speaks. Reason and Scripture condemn Molinism, first as applying to sinners, secondly as applying to "the just", and thirdly in its whole general application. For, though it is true that an action can only be blameworthy if it is voluntary, an action can be voluntary without the actor's having discerned all the good and all the evil in it; such was the opinion of Saint Augustine, as also of Aristotle.

This debate has a theological scope; it seeks to define the action of God within man. It has also a moral scope; it centres upon the problem of human responsibility. And, finally, it has a psychological scope; it opposes two conceptions of human personality. For the Jesuit, the essential nature of a man expresses itself in his transitory acts; for the Jansenist, that essential nature is to be identified with a man's deep and intimate selfhood, a selfhood corrupted by original sin and whose fundamental perversity is not always conscious of itself. The psychology of the Jesuit is undeniably a summary and artificial one; that of the Jansenist is curiously in agreement with the analyses of Bergson and William James and indeed with certain even more modern conceptions of "the unconscious".

In the fourth letter, then, Pascal's thought goes deeper; and his art becomes more refined. In spite of the importance of the ideas at stake, and the extreme concentration of the thought, the conversation between Pascal, the Jansenist, and the Jesuit retains an air of suppleness and ease. The cunningly calculated progress of the argument can be followed, without any strain, beneath its outward disguise of a spontaneous exchange of opinions. The discussion, skilfully built up round a few quotations whose whole inner meaning is gradually drawn out, remains at once lively and exact. But Pascal's most decisive progress in his art is to be seen in his portrait of the Jesuit. In the first of the letters, the speakers were identified with their views, and had no clearly defined personal character. Here, the Jesuit is a real hero of comedy, at once complex and natural. He is a simple and sincere man, gentle and obliging, always eager to satisfy the curiosity of his visitors, always quite placid when exposed to their objections or to their raillery. We guess him to be a pious and serious person, in spite of his connections with "the great world". His only defects are an incredible simplemindedness and a blind admiration for all Jesuit authors; he is a man who has abdicated his right of personal judgment and made a gift of it to his superiors. Out of all this, Pascal extracts the most delicate comedy. Yet his tone sometimes becomes loftier and more urgent, as when he sketches the corrupt life of the habitual libertine and the dangers to which a bad theology exposes the faith. Already, Pascal was thinking of his *Apology*.

At the end of the fourth letter, Pascal announced his intention of deflecting his attack on to the morality of the Jesuits. Was this change of front suggested by his fashionable friends, by Méré perhaps? There are credible documents that might lead us to suppose so. But one can also explain this new tactical change by profounder arguments; questions about morality, while they still kept the theological problem of grace in view, were likely to interest a wider public than questions of pure theology; above all, since the Jesuits had already been condemned for the laxness of their casuistry, they were especially vulnerable on this flank. The struggle between Jansenists and Jesuits was becoming fiercer, above all after 24th March, when there took place what came to be known as the Miracle of the Holy Thorn. Marguerite Périer, Pascal's niece, who suffered from a weeping fistula judged to be incurable, was in fact cured on being touched with a thorn from Christ's crown worn on the cross, exposed to the veneration of the faithful in the chapel of Port-Royal de Paris. This miracle looked like a sign that God favoured Port-Royal and it gave Pascal new confidence to carry on with his struggle.

Letters five to nine, published between 20th March and 3rd July, have a striking unity. There is a unity of subject-matter—the morality of the Jesuits, founded on casuistry. There is a unity of background; the narrator continues to relate his visits to the Jesuit Father. The latter has become an indefatigable collector of cases of conscience. The solutions proposed for these in Jesuit manuals of casuistry fill the good man with admiration, however unwarrantable they may be. For they are always extremely ingenious, and moreover they are the work of Jesuit authors. There is a unity of method; Pascal pretends to be an ignorant man anxious for information and leaves it to the Jesuit Father to define the doctrine of the casuists, without seeking to refute him. The comedy arises from the quotations from the casuists themselves, and has to do with both their choice and their arrangement. Sometimes, however, Pascal, in the reported conversations, allows himself to express his own deeper feelings through an ironic raillery. The Jesuit Father is nearly always deceived by this, and fails either to notice or resent the irony.

Two elements are mingled in this series of letters: on the one hand, the exposition of the general moral principles of the Jesuits; on the other, the analysis of a few particular cases. Both elements were extracted by Pascal from the works of casuists, of whom many but not all belonged to the Society of Jesus; their decisions are summarized in the *Moral Theology* of Escobar, a Spanish Jesuit, whom Pascal used as his principal source.

What, then, are the essential principles of this morality? The Jesuits, anxious to extend their influence, which they considered as a measure of the extent of the Kingdom of God on earth, wished to adapt themselves to the most various types of conscience. They did not despise or under-estimate the severity in Christianity and they presented that severity, in all its harshness, to souls desirous of an austere life; but to the weaker brethren they offered easier paths to salvation. Thus they made use of the doctrine of "probability"; to decide whether an action is good or malicious; for instance, we need not have recourse to the testimony of our own consciences, it is sufficient to consult "grave" authors, such as the Jesuit casuists. When an opinion is supported by one of these authors, it becomes a probable opinion and can be followed with a secure conscience, even if the opposite opinion is supported by another doctor, and even if the opposite opinion is more probable. And in choosing between several probable opinions, we have merely to follow our own pleasure or interest. There is another convenient method of the casuists, that of "the direction of intention"; we can will an action which is bad in itself if we consider it merely as a means to a good end; thus we may provoke an enemy to a duel, not in order to kill him, but in order to defend our honour or our fortune. And, finally, everybody had heard of the Jesuit doctrines of "equivocation" and of statements that may be made "with a mental reservation".

In regard to the particular application of these principles, Pascal gives many examples of awkward cases of conscience for which the casuists have found facile and generous solutions. He is aiming, in this set of letters, at variety of illustration rather than at pursuing a rigorous train of argument. In one letter, he will continue with the examination of a case which he brought up in the last. He analyses in succession the cases of conscience which apply specially to heirs, to priests, to monks, to servants, to noblemen, to judges, to merchants. For the end of each letter, he knows how to save up some typical and if possible ironic detail; a comic enumeration of casuists whose names, mostly Spanish, had, when strung together, for French ears a ludicrous effect; the story of Jean d'Alba, a servant at the College of Clermont, his conscience set at ease by a reading of Father Bauny, made up his inadequate wages by stealing a pewter plate; the unexpected conclusion of the admirable seventh letter, on homicide, where, after the justification of murders of many kinds, there comes the question: "Is it possible to know whether the Jesuits may lawfully kill the Jansenists?" The answer is: "No, they may not." And the reason? "It is not in the power of the Jansenists to injure our reputation."

In spite of the apparently passive attitude which he has imposed on himself, Pascal from time to time outlines important objections. Would it not be better to follow Holy Writ and the Fathers rather than modern casuists? Does not our reason tell us to follow, not *a* probable opinion, but *the most* probable opinion? Can all the external practices of devotion really be a substitute for the giving of oneself to God? But Pascal was not really to define his own position till the tenth letter, which, like the fourth, has a central importance.

This letter, dated 2nd August, 1656, differs from its immediate predecessors in two ways; Pascal has now been made familiar with the doctrine of the casuists and he seeks to refute it; and irony now ceases to be his essential weapon, and often gives way to indignation. The letter ends with a passage of vehement eloquence, and the narrator declares that he will pay no more visits to the Jesuit Father.

The conversation turns on the sacrament of penitence. Many people find it difficult to go to confession; they feel shame in confessing certain sins, they cannot resolve not to sin any more, above all they cannot succeed in genuinely regretting their wrong-doing. This need not deter them! The Jesuits have found ways of getting round these difficulties, notably the last one: "attrition", that is, regretting one's wrong-doing because of a fear of Hell, is a sufficing condition for valid absolution. To this doctrine of the sufficiency of attrition, Pascal strongly opposes that of the necessity of "contrition", that is, of a regret for one's wrong-doing founded on the love of God. The love of God—from which the casuists sought to deliver men, as from a painful obligation—contains for Pascal all the law and the prophets. Where this love is not present, confession is merely an insignificant rite; for a heart which remains immersed in the love of created things will never be able to receive the supernatural grace of absolution. Here, again, man's inner being is everything; without a preliminary "conversion", the sacrament will not act in an efficacious manner; no authentic moral and religious life will be possible.

Letters eleven to fourteen—dated from 18th August to 23rd October—are still taken up with the moral philosophy of the Jesuits. But it is without much propriety that they still retain the title of *Provincial Letters*. Pascal now abandons the fiction, of which he had made such a happy use, of writing to a friend in the provinces. He speaks in his own person and addresses himself directly to the Jesuits. His tone becomes more bitter, and his irony almost completely disappears, to be replaced by an indignant eloquence. Finally, instead of attacking, Pascal now has to defend himself.

At first almost struck dumb, the enemies of Port-Royal had after a time decided to publish some answers to Pascal. These are wretched libels, but they contain the substance of the accusations that will always be directed against *The Provincial Letters*. These are the work of a heretic, of a Calvinist, of a slanderer without originality. They are a piece of pamphleteering buffoonery which rashly makes public problems that ought to be reserved for theologians and confessors. They attribute to the Jesuits as a body the opinions of a few writers among them, and attitudes and methods that are not theirs. After the eleventh letter, Father Nouet, who had already come into the field against Arnauld, was to publish a violent answer. He would reply in the same fashion to each subsequent letter, denouncing the "impostures" of the Jansenists. Thus to the long-range attack of the earliest letters there succeeded "a strange and prolonged campaign".

The accusation that touched Pascal most keenly—no doubt because it had been repeated to him by people he respected, Singlin or Mother Angélique—was that of having "made a jest of holy things". He replies to this accusation in his eleventh letter. Can one really call the works of the casuists holy things? Does not God, in the Bible, mock sinners? Do not Tertullian and Saint Bernard use ridicule as a weapon in controversy? Is it not rather the Jesuits themselves who make a jest of holy things, like Father le Moyne, who indulges his facetious wit in his *Devotion Made Easy* and his *Moral Pictures.*

As for the accusations of imposture made by Father Nouet —the accusations that Pascal had misrepresented the authors whose views he quoted or summarized—we have only to turn to the passages under debate to dismiss all Nouet's objection. Let us take the case of homicide. To kill someone who has struck me, says Lessius, is permissible in theory but not in practice. Certainly, but why not in practice? . . . Because there would be too many killings, it would be the ruin of the State. What a delightful argument! And do we not read later on in Lessius that one may "follow in practice opinions that are probable in theory". Thus the distinction between speculative and practical moral theology which Pascal's opponents are attempting to establish loses all meaning. No doubt some other casuist, like Vasquez, disagrees with Lessius on this particular topic of a life for a blow. But the general doctrine of probability permits anybody to follow Lessius with a safe conscience.

Thus while all divine and human laws rigorously prescribe homicide (except in the cases of self-defence, military operations, and legal executions), the Jesuits admit killing to be permissible if a man has been slapped on the face or insulted. The greatest criminal, from the point of view of the laws of the State, is assured that he is acting justly.[1] According to Lessius, I may kill another man who has robbed me of a ducat or an apple if I think that my honour is at stake.

There was an increasing violence in the tone of the Jesuit polemics against Pascal. One reason for this was that the enemies of Port-Royal were making progress. The Assembly of the Clergy had drawn up on 1st September the draft of a

---

[1] Pascal makes the point that while the King and Richelieu had been making the most stringent efforts to stamp out duelling in France, the Jesuits were palliating it.—*Translator.*

"formula", condemning the five propositions of Jansenius; there was talk of forcing every clergyman to sign it. On 16th October, Pope Alexander VII once more condemned the five propositions, expressly declaring that they *were* extracted from Jansenius's book and that they were condemnable in the sense which Jansenius himself attached to him. It was some time before news of this Bull reached France, but already there were symptoms of the beginnings of a scheme of persecution there.

It was in this atmosphere of high tension that Pascal rapidly composed the fifteenth and sixteenth letters, which appeared on 25th November and 14th December. Pascal was now defending not merely his own letters but all Port-Royal, now threatened with persecution. He sought to refute all the accusations that had been made against the Monastery. He tried to show that these accusations all sprang from the same secret source, the theory of the Jesuits regarding calumny.

Pious souls would find it hard to believe that any religious organization could deliberately employ calumny, or slanderous or libellous misrepresentation of its opponents. According to Lessius and Caramuel, however, calumny is merely a venial sin, when one makes use of it to defend one's honour. *A fortiori*, it would be almost less than venial, when made use of to defend the honour of the Jesuits: which the Jesuits themselves tended to confuse with the honour of the Church. That, according to Pascal, was why the Jesuits allowed themselves to make attacks, even from the pulpit, on the honesty or good faith of pious persons; being quite ready, if conditions should change, to have such attacks publicly disowned by their own superiors. This was the explanation of all the falsehoods in the replies to *The Provincial Letters*, of the vague and general accusations that implied the worst, and to which it was enough for Pascal to reply: "*Mentiris impudentissime*, you lie without shame."

This principle of the Jesuits in regard to calumny explained, according to Pascal, the slanders and libels on Port-Royal, its priests, its monks, and its nuns: the accusations of Calvinism, of contempt for the Eucharist (though it was part of the rule of the nuns at Port-Royal that the Holy Sacrament should be continuously adored, night and day); and all the other accusations. If, by their theory that calumny was in certain circumstances justifiable, the Jesuits had managed to quiet their own consciences, at the same time they had betrayed their tactics to their opponents. Henceforth, it would be impossible for anyone to believe anything they said.

Thus, gradually and without being consciously aware of it, Pascal was coming back to the central theme of the debate: the problem of grace and the five condemned propositions. With the seventeenth and eighteenth *Provincial Letters*, Pascal once more handles the topics of the earliest group, but in a much more profound fashion. These letters are no longer addressed to the body of the Jesuits but to one of their spokesmen, Father Annat, who had just been violently accusing the Jansenists of heresy. In these letters, Pascal adopts a quite new and singularly conciliatory tone. Official raids on the bookshops to confiscate copies of *The Provincial Letters* were becoming more and more frequent. The question of the formula, condemning the five propositions, to be imposed on every clergyman in France, was becoming more and more urgent, following the official dispatch to France of the Pope's Bull. Nevertheless, the supporters of Port-Royal were hoping to achieve something through negotiation. Pascal and his friends were now showing themselves more than merely conciliatory; they held back the publication of these two last letters for a long time, in the hope that an agreement might be reached.

In these two letters, Pascal seeks to defend the Jansenists against the accusation of heresy. The Jansenists, too, he says, readily and sincerely condemn these five propositions. But they refuse to affirm that the propositions are those of Jansenius. Has the Pope asserted the contrary? But on "questions of fact", as distinct from questions of doctrine or principle, the Pope is capable of falling into error; that is the admission even of Cardinal Bellarmine, himself a Jesuit. The condemnation of Galileo was not able to prevent the earth from turning. There are truths which are worthy of being revealed to us by God, and others which are not so. Why were the Jesuits so eager to make this question of fact—whether or not five given propositions were in Jansenius's work, or whether, if they were, the sense attached to them by Jansenius was their condemnable sense—a matter in which their own opinion was to be imposed on the faithful? Was it because they hoped that, once they had achieved the condemnation of Jansenius, they would be able to show that, with Jansenius, Saint Augustine's doctrine of efficacious grace had also been condemned? Molinism would then triumph.

Might it not be said, however, that there are two conceptions of efficacious grace? Calvin's, which is heretical, and that of St. Thomas, which is Catholic? But, if that were so, in what sense could the Jansenists, who though they were the champions of efficacious grace detested Calvin's doctrine, be described as heretical? They admitted that the human will can resist the weaker graces, the weaker promptings to good which God bestows on us. They admitted that efficacious grace itself never mechanically compels the will; God changes our hearts by wakening in them a desire for what is good; if in fact our wills never *do* resist a desire thus powerfully excited, in principle they always *can*. Such is Augustine's doctrine, such also is that of Saint Thomas. The whole dispute within the Church about grace, which has made so much noise in the world, has no solid foundation.

Is there a doctrinal difference between these last letters and the earliest ones? It has been claimed that there is, and that Pascal's adherence to Saint Thomas is a kind of recantation. But any doctrinal difference, that we can define, between the earliest and the last letters is of the slightest and least significant sort. It is important not to be misled by differences of tone and method. The method of the first letters was

that of a skirmisher, the method of the last that of an ex-
positor of dogma. But the doctrine that has become explicit
at the end of the letters was implicit from the beginning.
The earliest letters show the same respect for Saint Thomas;
his disciples, the Jacobins, are attacked only for not being
loyal to their own doctrine. Moreover, the collaboration of
Arnauld and Nicole is more obvious in these last letters than
in any of the others. So there is no possibility of their representing a merely personal development.

Why, however, were there no more letters? Did Pascal
break with his friends? A balanced interpretation of the
final letters and of Pascal's subsequent career makes non-
sense of that hypothesis. Did he yield to scruples of conscience, to the advice of Singlin and Mother Angélique, who
felt that the best weapons were silence and prayer? That is
not improbable; but what is certain is that Pascal *did* prepare
a nineteenth letter, of which a fragment remains. And he
did not give up the struggle, he continued it in another
field. To explain the cessation of the series, we must look
above all, for reasons based on expediency. There was a
threat of persecution; Port-Royal and its friends needed
some means of defence more effective than even the most
brilliant literary polemic. The Jesuits, too, felt this so
keenly that they did not bother to reply to Pascal's final
letter.

III. *The Scope and Impact of "The Provincial Letters"*

There can be no question in this section of touching on all
the problems that *The Provincial Letters* raise. Such a task
would demand a completely new and comprehensive
investigation of that masterpiece. We shall leave on one
side, in particular, purely literary questions: the influence
of *The Provincial Letters* on such contrasting writers as
Molière and Bossuet has often been analysed: and their
importance as a model, at the outset of the classical age in
French literature, is recognized by everybody. On the other

hand, there have always been lively disagreements about the scope and impact of the work, from a philosophic and human point of view; about the originality and sincerity of its author; about its value for Christian doctrine; and about its historical consequences.

What, then, do Pascal's "little letters" teach us? And first of all, what is there specifically Pascalian about this collective work of Port-Royal? Nicole and Arnauld, as we know, supplied Pascal with his facts and quotations, with his leading ideas; and yet the work, in its very essence, remains incontestably that of Pascal. It is, of course, the very note of the classical tradition in art to achieve its originality not by creating its own subject-matter, but by bringing a given subject-matter to formal perfection. Also, there is hardly a detail in *The Provincial Letters* that does not reveal to us the personality of Pascal. We find, for instance, Pascal, the physical scientist; anxious to define his problems clearly, to appeal to experience whenever a theory can be verified by facts. We see the religious apologist, disturbed over the spiritual health of sinners, dreaming of their conversion, already sketching out his method by showing the correspondence that exists between two great facts: the content of Christian doctrine as it has been handed down, and human nature as we know it. Finally, and above all in the last letters, we see the mystic, displaying, even in the midst of a fierce polemic, the results of his deep and passionate meditations on the Bible.

Nevertheless *The Provincial Letters* do remain an eagerly polemical work. As a polemical writer, is Pascal always faithful to the facts as he sees them and to his own feelings? Is he always sincere? "A slanderer who had genius"—that was Chateaubriand's verdict: nobody would repeat it to-day. Nobody any longer claims, now that Pascal's sources, especially Escobar, are better known, that he falsified his quotations from the casuists or distorted the sense of passages he quoted. But there is a further objection. Pascal insists on the laxer decisions of the casuists and ignores the more

severe ones. This objection has been dealt with in advance
in *The Provincial Letters* themselves: severe decisions do
not balance lax ones since the doctrine of probability allows
us to follow, in every doubtful case, the laxer decision.

Was Pascal unjustly biased against the Jesuits? In fact,
for a long time, both in the Faculty of Theology, and in
cultivated circles in the fashionable world, the morality of
the Jesuit casuists and a lax morality had been considered—
and not without reason—as being one and the same thing.
Pascal is also accused of gratuitously accusing the Jesuits of
plotting and conspiring to make sure that they would
dominate the consciences of the faithful. That accusation
would not have been a novel one, but it is not to be found in
The Provincial Letters; Pascal readily admits that the Jesuits
are acting in good faith and sincerely desire the good
of religion; what he denounces are some bad tendencies in
the Society of Jesus: its tendency to confuse its own interests
with those of the Church as a whole; its eagerness to adapt
itself to all kinds of consciences; its excessively developed
"team spirit". The great fault of the Jesuit Father who
figures in *The Provincial Letters* is precisely his unaware-
ness; he does not foresee the sinister practical consequences
of his own doctrine. In this, he resembles Escobar. Escobar
himself might have admitted that it was Pascal who, by a
stroke of genius, had revived interest in, and found new
readers for, his *Moral Theology*. A visitor to Valladolid was
to find Escobar a genial and placid old man, surprised by
the noise his name was making in the world, and excusing
his casuistical maxims on the ground that there were other
Doctors even laxer than himself. In a preface to a new
edition of his book in 1659, Escobar ingenuously confessed
that, when he gave lax opinions, it was not because he
shared them personally; he wanted merely to make things
easier for confessors and penitents. The Jesuit in *The Provincial Letters* had already said much the same thing. There
is, nevertheless, perhaps one matter about which we can
slightly reproach Pascal; when he shifted the debate from

the theological to the moral plane, he was inspired by
tactical insight rather than deep conviction. He had heard
that the Jesuit casuists were peculiarly vulnerable. But as
soon as he opened the books of the casuists, and read them
for himself, he felt he had a mission to fulfil. One might even
say that Pascal's indignation as a Christian sometimes got
the better of his skill as a polemist.

Finally, there is the most serious accusation. Was Pascal
lying when he declared, "I do not belong to Port-Royal,"
and, "I am alone, one man against thirty thousand." The
belief that he was lying can be supported only by a double
legend: that of Pascal as "the solitary of Port-Royal",
which we have already exploded, and the equally histori-
cally inaccurate notion of the Jansenists as an organized
sectarian body. Mere chance, as we have seen, made Pascal
the author of *The Provincial Letters*. And when he wrote,
"I am alone" he had in mind less the numbers of pam-
phleteers writing against him than of government agents
seeking for him. He was warning these agents that, if they
arrested the solitaries of Port-Royal, they would be on the
wrong track. But he was very far from ever denying that he
belonged to what might be called a *moral* or *ideal* Port-Royal;
he declares that his heart is with these solitaries and these
nuns, as were the hearts of many other friends of the Monastery, whose activities were quite independent of his own.
There have, in fact, been few polemical writers with anything like Pascal's complete loyalty to truth.

But was Pascal as charitable as he was loyal to truth?
We know already about the reservations of Singlin and
Mother Angélique: and these retain their value. Though
fighting perfectly fairly, Pascal can hardly be said to have
respected the Gospel precepts on charity. But he was himself
faced with a real problem in casuistry—and we have seen
that, much as he disliked lax solutions, he did not ignore the
existence of such problems. He had to choose between silence
or an ineffective "brotherly correction", on the one hand,
and speaking out and denouncing a hidden danger on the

other. An imperious sense of duty forced him to speak out. Let us acknowledge, also, that Pascal had not reached this moral height at the beginning of *The Provincial Letters*; and that the letters seem to bear witness to a progressive refinement of his religious sense; to a rather external irony there succeeds, gradually, a healthier laughter, expressing the spontaneous reaction of an honest mind; then laughter gradually gives way to moral indignation, and finally that indignation is itself appeased; Pascal's tone once more becomes serene; and it was to remain so even in those polemical writings that followed *The Provincial Letters*. The letters, in fact, echo Pascal's inner life for us, and they cover more than a year of it.

But if we think of *The Provincial Letters* objectively, or in abstraction from their author, what is the value of their theological and moral doctrine?

On the theological level, what remains valid in the criticisms addressed to Pascal by his contemporary opponents? These were, in the first instance, the Thomists or rather the neo-Thomists, of the school of Father Nicolaï. Pascal, under the influence of Nicole, had arrived at a rather over-simplified idea of their way of conceiving "sufficient grace". But Father Nicolaï had departed strikingly in many fields from traditional Thomism, and at a first reading Nicole had failed to understand the originality of his thought.

In order to estimate the value of Pascal's attacks on Molinism, certain distinctions have to be held in mind. There was a popular, superficial Molinism, that of which we gave a sketch earlier in this chapter, and that, also, which Pascal found taught by contemporary Doctors, like le Moyne. Molinism, so conceived, reduced the role of grace to insignificance and, thus rendering Redemption unnecessary, ran the risk of degenerating into Deism; it was against such a Molinism, with its attendant dangers, that Pascal struck. But there was also the Molinism of Molina himself. Molina's own doctrine and also, and especially, the doctrine of Bellarmine are more complex and profound; they remain partly unaffected by Pascal's criticisms. In fact, they are much nearer to Jansenist doctrine than to the popularizations of le Moyne; a theologian like Arnauld could have fully accepted the ideas of Bellarmine on predestination. This is the most promising field, in our own opinion, for deeper research into the theological background of the letters.

Pascal's positive doctrine, as distinguished from his criticism of the doctrine of others, was no different from that of Arnauld and Nicole. To deal with it thoroughly, we should have to touch on all the problems connected with Jansenism. We shall confine ourselves to outlining a few key ideas.

The Jansenist heresy, if there were one, would consist essentially in denying that the human will is free; the gist of the five condemned propositions comes down to that. But Pascal, like Arnauld and Jansenius, acknowledges at once the omnipotence of divine grace and man's complete freedom; for him, Catholic truth is to be deduced from the mysterious union of these opposites. Jansenism is vulnerable to the degree in which this opposition, or this polarity, between grace or freedom runs the risk of appearing merely a verbally embodied self-contradiction. From this point of view, we can find a certain equivocation in some passages of Arnauld and Jansenius and also, if we are being stringent in the earliest *Provincial Letters*. But there is just as much equivocation in Saint Augustine himself. And in the last *Provincial Letters* such equivocation has certainly completely disappeared.

How valid, then, were the defence-tactics adopted by Arnauld and his friends in relation to the five propositions? Monsignor Calvet, who cannot be suspected of any excessive sympathy for Jansenism, to-day acknowledges that only the first of them is really to be found in Jansenius's *Augustinus*. But Arnauld's tactics were none the less clumsy. They were not, however, new; at all times it has been permissible to give a legalistic interpretation of a papal condemnation. But when Pascal refused to accept the decision of the Pope on the question of fact—were the propositions, in the condemnable sense, to be found in Jansenius?—did he not, by so doing, separate himself from the Church? To claim that this is so, is to commit a double blunder. First, the claim involves a serious anachronism: the doctrine of papal infallibility was not, in Pascal's time, acknowledged in France. When Pascal learned that *The Provincial Letters* had been put on the Papal Index of Prohibited Books—a step which was taken, however, solely because they were written in a living language—he cried out: "Ad tuum, Domine Jesu, tribunal appello!" He was repeating, word for word, the phrase used by Saint Bernard in similar circumstances. Secondly, even since the decision of the Vatican Council that the Pope is infallible when speaking *ex cathedra* on matters of faith and morals, he is seldom considered as being infallible about matters of fact.

The attitude of Pascal and his friends can by no means, therefore, be considered a heretical one, even if some of their doctrines are questionable. A librarian of the seventeenth century, drawing up a library catalogue, would never have dreamt of classifying Jansenist works with heretical works. If we keep this point in mind, we shall find it easier to avoid certain errors in our examination of Pascal's later life.

In the moral field, there have always been vigorous attacks on Pascal. Till the end of the nineteenth century, however, these were always on his fairness as a controversialist. When the results of objective research no longer made such attacks permissible, Pascal's adversaries, of whom the most important in this century has been the Abbé Baudin, turned their offensive against the very basis of his moral doctrine and attempted to rehabilitate the casuistry and the probabilism of the seventeenth-century Jesuits in the teeth of Pascal's arguments. Such a criticism of Pascal is extremely interesting but to us it seems to lack real importance. For one thing, critics like the Abbé Baudin have not a sufficient grasp of the given historical situation; they define both casuistry and probabilism in their ideal forms, forms that have little in common with the facts that Pascal had before him; for another thing, on the purely theological plane, the Abbé Baudin's work had been refuted before it appeared by the article "Probabilisme" in the *Diction-naire de Théologie Catholique*. This article was written by Father Demain and is remarkably well documented. Finally, the Abbé Baudin's attack rests, it must be recognized, on a rather inaccurate interpretation of Pascal's own moral doctrine.

Let us, however, consider some of the points of detail raised by the Abbé's arguments. Casuistry, according to the Abbé Baudin, is an eternal science, rendered necessary by the doubt about what is a right course of action that inevitably arises in the human conscience. It consists either in adapting general rules to particular cases or in resolving apparent conflicts of duty. But Pascal, after all, does not attack the casuists of his time for doing these things. He attacks them for attempting to reconcile duty with self-interest. And he invents nothing; let us recall, for instance, the satisfaction shown by Escobar in noting that the multiplicity of "probable opinions" on questions of casuistry rendered "the yoke of the Lord more easy and gentle". That was the true spirit of seventeenth-century casuistry. And Pascal does not attack, let us repeat, the type of casuistry of which the Abbé Baudin speaks; in fact he rarely speaks merely of "casuists" as such, he mentions rather "lax casuists", "casuists of the Society (of Jesus)" or "the new casuists". Pascal is no more unaware that there is a healthy casuistry than were the Fathers of the Church or the directors of Port-Royal. But for the solving of cases of conscience he demanded that man should depend not on his corrupted reason but on "Holy Scripture, Canon Law and the Holy Fathers" who were considered as the only real "grave" doctors by casuists of Jansenist inspiration such as the author of the *Théologie Morale* published in 1677 under the auspices of the Bishop of Grenoble, the future Cardinal le Camus. Reason, however, even for the Jansenist casuists, had still a certain part to play: that of interpreting tradition and solving such new cases of conscience as might arise from time to time in the spirit of the Fathers.

Again, by a "probable opinion", as the casuists of the seventeenth century whom Pascal was attacking used that term, ought we really to understand, as the Abbé Baudin does, an *approximation* to moral truth, in the cases where absolute moral truth eludes us? To do so is to imagine the "moral probabilism" of the seventeenth century as modelled on our modern "scientific probabilism". In fact, as used by seventeenth-century casuists, the word "probable" retained the sense, deriving from its Latin root, of "worthy of approbation"; and the "probabilists" of the seventeenth century denied the very existence of a "moral truth" on all fours with "scientific truth". The Abbé Baudin, moreover, is forgetting that it is of the very essence of the idea of moral probabilism that one has the right to follow a *less* probable opinion, knowing that a *more* probable opinion exists. Even defined in this way, of course, moral probabilism would be by no means an indefensible theory, provided that the opinions called "probable" really were so. However, even before the seventeenth century, probabilism had become confused in practice with "laxism", an attitude which consisted in showing oneself very easy-going in establishing probability. It was currently acknowledged in Pascal's time that one had kept one's conscience safe and sound by following a "probably probable" opinion and that one might choose between the various probable opinions put forward by "grave authors", letting one's interest, and that alone, be the deciding factor. The opposition between "probabilism" and "laxism", the hinge of the Abbé Baudin's argument, was not really clarified till after Pascal's time and under Pascal's influence. Pascal's own moral doctrine does not, in fact, seem to exclude a "probabilism" that has scientific foundations. Pascal's doctrine is often thought of as a "tutiorism" (doctrine of the safer path) or a "rigorism" (doctrine of following very severe rules exactly) that obliges the Christian always to make the hardest of several morally possible decisions; but it is more accurate to think of the doctrine as being founded on "moral truth", defined apart from any idea of compulsion. If such truth cannot be finally reached, we should, Pascal thinks, "at least demand a sincere quest for truth". That was the point which the "probabilists" of Pascal's own time did not take into account.

There is a criticism of Pascal's attitude to Christian morals, however, that goes a great deal deeper. Did not Pascal, confusing the "precepts" and the "counsels" of the Gospel—we might say to-day, its commands and its advice—wrongly demand of each Christian "perfection"? Here again we must make clear what the question implies. In distinguishing "precepts" from "counsels" do Pascal's critics merely mean that the Gospel is not meant always to be followed literally, that not every Christian, for instance, is obliged to live in actual poverty? Pascal would not have disagreed; he acknowledges that each man has his "vocation", that he lives in the style of the social rank to which he has been called. Pascal did so himself. He even acknowledged that one man may kill another in legitimate self-defence. Or, on the contrary, do Pascal's critics mean that perfection is not necessary to salvation, that it is enough to keep the commandments, without falling short or going beyond? A distinction of this sort between precepts and counsels is purely scholastic, corresponding to nothing real or living in the soul. As an eminent Jesuit, Father de Montcheuil, has said: "Not to wish to make further progress is enough in itself to constitute sin." Whoever wishes merely neither to fall short of the law nor to go beyond it is on the point of breaking it. Not to wish to make further progress was, for Pascal, to leave out the one thing needful: "the sincere search for truth", or, in other words, the love of God.

We have seen that when the Jesuits of the seventeenth century were aiming at a moral ideal, that could be defined as an absence of uneasiness, a perfect sense of balance within the conscience, and a complete self-mastery under the dominion of the will. Pascal, for his part, demanded a certain healthy disquiet in the soul, an always unfinished quest for moral truth, and an aspiration after the infinite. Thus in Pascal and the Jesuits of the seventeenth century we can see two eternal tendencies of the Church in tension with each other: the Roman sense of order, and the spiritual ferment of the Gospels.

We shall pass rapidly over the historical consequences of *The Provincial Letters*, for most of the common conclusions that have been reached in this field seem to us very much open to question.

Thus, what was the influence of *The Provincial Letters* on the fate of the Society of Jesus? Pascal, it has been said, excited the prejudice against the Jesuits which still persists; he created the Jesuit of legend. It is also said that he halted the advance, broke the attack, of the society of Jesus, which was henceforth incapable of attaining that predominant position at which it aimed. These assertions are much too broad and sweeping, and need qualification. Pascal's attacks were not the earliest ones, nor the only ones, nor the most violent ones which the Society of Jesus had undergone. All one can say is that Pascal's literary genius had intensified the effect of earlier attacks. It would be a wild exaggeration, for instance, to consider the suppression of the Jesuits in 1764 as a belated consequence of *The Provincial Letters*; we should remember that they had already been expelled from France in 1594. We should notice also that Pascal did not find among the Jesuits of his time any opponent of his own moral and intellectual stature; it is this crisis in the history of the Society in the seventeenth century, its failure to attract or produce really great men, rather than Pascal's attack on it, that explains its subsequent decline. It is even permissible to maintain that Pascal's attacks, in the long run, had a healthy effect on the internal development of the Society.

More widely, what was the influence of *The Provincial Letters* on the general life of the Church? They provoked a widespread reaction against a lax moral theology, which led in the end to the official condemnation of "laxism". But were they a dangerous impediment to the progress of moral theology? On the contrary, it seems to us that they helped it to progress along a safer path. But did they hinder the Church from adapting itself to the modern world, as the Abbé Baudin claims? It is necessary, I am afraid, to point out that the very men who were so gaily "adapting" the morality of the Gospels to the needs of the world around them found great difficulty in sacrificing such principles—principles without any religious bearing whatsoever—as those that the earth does not move or that Nature abhors a vacuum. This pretended "adaptation" of the Gospel was a mere concession to the worldly spirit. Pascal's own religious sense was a far more firm and solid one.

What was the influence of *The Provincial Letters* on the "freethinkers"? By making such men, already on the edge of unbelief, condemn the morality of the Jesuits, did Pascal, as Sainte-Beuve thinks, hasten the flowering of their own merely secular morality, the morality of the *honnête homme*? Possibly so, but this morality of the cultivated gentleman, which grants to outer social appearances everything that the Jesuits granted to the inner secret intention, has nothing in common with the morality preached by Pascal. It would have come into existence without him. But by demanding of men of goodwill that they should aim at a religious ideal beyond their reach, did Pascal discourage them? Here, again, we must not exaggerate Pascal's "rigorism", and for that matter would a religion which did *not* demand of man an effort to transcend himself have the least attraction for unbelievers? But by giving wide publicity to theological controversies, did Pascal disturb men of simple faith? These controversies, long before *The Provincial Letters*, were already known to a wide public. Did Pascal's irony pave the way for that of Voltaire? Possibly, but Voltaire had also behind him a long tradition of anti-religious irony. Nobody denies that *The Provincial Letters* played a very great part in the subsequent cultural history of France; when we try to go into detail about this, we are hampered, even to-day, by the lack of close and accurate researches in this field.

CHAPTER FOUR

THE LAST YEARS

THIS is a confused period. But we are helped through it, both by the testimony of Gilberte Périer and by documents from many other sources. During the winter of late 1658 and early 1659, Pascal fell seriously ill. From 1654 to 1658, his relatively satisfactory state of health had permitted him to work with intense concentration; after his illness, he remained weak and languid and was virtually forced to give up all his work. The last few months of this final period demand separate attention because of the complexity of the problems which they raise.

I. *The Period of Activity*

Between 1656 and 1658 Pascal composed those works which are the heart of his achievement. *The Provincial Letters* were the most finished of these. He also accumulated materials for his projected *Apology* for Christianity directed against unbelievers. We shall confine ourselves in this section, however, to dealing with less important works, the letters to Mademoiselle de Roannez, the new polemical writings, the *Ecrits sur la Grâce*, the educational works and the scientific treatises.

We possess nine letters written by Pascal to the sister of the Duc de Roannez. They are, in fact, rather nine fragments of letters, difficult to date with precision, and kept by their recipient, according to the habit of the time, for the sake of their edifying character and the widely general scope of their themes. As what they are, they remain one of the most attractive of the more fragmentary portions of Pascal's work.

We know how this correspondence arose through the notes,

as usual extremely imprecise, of Marguerite Périer, but even more through a few very exact and detailed pages of the *Mémoires* of a Jansenist of the second rank, Godefroi Hermant.

Mademoiselle de Roannez, as we have already learned, had known Pascal and his family since her childhood. She was now twenty-three years old. She had no wish to imitate her brother in his life of religious retirement, but was pondering marriage. She was very pious, however, and in August, 1656, hoping to cure an ophthalmic illness, she went into retreat for nine days at Port-Royal de Paris. On the last day, she felt a very strong desire to become a nun. Singlin, whom she consulted, advised her to wait and test herself. Possibly the Duke also doubted his sister's vocation. In any case, he decided to take her into Poitou for some time. They left Paris towards the middle of August, accompanied by their mother, who had not been informed about her daughter's project of becoming a nun, but who nevertheless always had her suspicions about it. It was during Mademoiselle de Roannez' stay in the country that the correspondence with Pascal took place of which fragments have been preserved.

Gilberte Périer tells us that her brother often used to receive visits from fashionable people, who came to consult him about their religious problems. The letters to Mademoiselle de Roannez reveal to us this role of Pascal's as a spiritual guide, which furnished him with much detailed experience for use in his projected *Apology*. Pascal here reveals himself as a complete disciple of Saint-Cyran. In the first place, the idea of a lay director of conscience was quite familiar to Saint-Cyran, though of course he insisted that such a lay director should never replace the priest, the only real director, the only master of such decisions as might have to be made; in fact Pascal left all the initiative to Singlin, who was carrying on a parallel correspondence with his penitent. On the other hand, also according to Saint-Cyran, no spiritual guide ought to impose his own will on the penitent; he should leave God's grace to act, confining himself to clearing away obstacles to its operation. Thus in these letters Pascal, very discreetly, avoids giving concrete and definite advice. He encourages the sense of vocation which has just been born in Mademoiselle de Roannez, but without the least peremptoriness. In our opinion, critics have exaggerated the harshness of the tone of some of the letters; when Pascal, sensing in the young woman a certain disquiet at the thought of parting from the world, reminds her that suffering is inevitable, that every conversion entails the ruin of the old Adam, that the soul is pulled in two directions at once by concupiscence and grace, and that this struggle ends only with death, he is, in the last analysis, merely expressing ideas that are familiar to every soul that has felt the call to a life of religious retirement, and he is certainly remembering his own experiences. But even in the most austere letters, Pascal's tone remains one of placation; he seeks above all to conduct an excessively tormented soul towards a state of calmness, peace, and joy, and this tendency is even more marked in the final letters, which can be dated around Christmas, 1656.

But very often in these letters, also, Pascal the spiritual director disappears; we find instead Pascal the man, the friend, expressing himself spontaneously and familiarly. We find him, having finished one of the "Provincial Letters" and being about to start on another, asserting his horror of a lax morality, his fears of the persecution that threatens him and his friends, his attachment to the unity of the Church and the person of the Pope. He describes his meditations on some passage in the daily office, some chapter of the Bible. These meditations expand into magnificent images and noble spiritual ideas, like that of God as hidden, mysteriously present under the veil of material things, but visible only to the pure in heart. The didactic tone of the letters of 1648 has completely disappeared, and nevertheless these modest and friendly pages give out a supreme impression of authority.

Mademoiselle de Roannez' fate was not a happy one. Her

reception into Port-Royal in 1657 was a great triumph for the convent, which had few supporters among the aristocracy. Therefore the Jesuits sought to snatch her back into the world and succeeded, thanks to the support they received from her mother, who was violently opposed to her daughter's project. Nevertheless Mademoiselle de Roannez had taken the vow of chastity and remained faithful to it so long as she was upheld by the presence of those who had been her spiritual directors. After the deaths of Singlin and Pascal, she had herself released from her vows and in 1667 married the Duc de la Feuillade. She soon repented of her decision and saw the hand of God in the many unhappy experiences she underwent. Both physically and morally she had little balance, suffering from perpetual disquiet and inner instability, but it may be that the life of the cloister would have given her peace.

A little after the last letter to Mademoiselle de Roannez, the eighteenth "Provincial Letter" appeared. Pascal's polemical task, however, was not yet completed. But it was necessary to take into consideration the latest developments of events. The Bull of Pope Alexander VII, condemning the five propositions in the sense in which Jansenius was deemed to have upheld them, had been officially received by the King. The Assembly of the Clergy had also accepted it and had drawn up a new "formula" condemning "the five propositions of Cornelius Jansenius, contained in the book called *Augustinus*". Every priest would have to sign it, and it completely destroyed the distinction between "the question of right", or principle, and "the question of fact". There was only one way out for the friends of Port-Royal; Parliament would have to record the Bull before it became applicable in France. But the Parliamentarians, much attached to the liberties of the Gallican Church and hostile to any too pointed and forceful intervention of the Papacy in the affairs of France, were able effectively to bar the road to persecution. On their behalf there was published on the 1st June, 1657, the *Lettre d'un Avocat au Parlement*, in which

Pascal collaborated, but which was given its definitive form by the lawyer, Antoine de Maistre. Of only mediocre literary value, it had nevertheless a certain practical effect. Though Parliament might still yield to the insistence of the King and have the Bull transcribed in its records, that gesture from the anti-Jansenist point of view was a vain one, since Parliament also prevented the establishment of an Inquisition. The signing of the formula was not demanded; and a relative peace reigned until 1661.

On the level of dogmatic theology, the battle was thus provisionally at an end. It continued, however, to be waged against the moral philosophy of the Jesuits. But the direction of this campaign was now in the hands of the parish priests of Paris, Rouen, and certain other large cities. Their clerical assemblies, greatly moved by the campaign against casuistry conducted in *The Provincial Letters*, had demanded the official censure of lax casuistical maxims. However, in December, 1657, there suddenly appeared a violent *Apology for the Casuists*. This anonymous work of Father Pirot, a friend of Father Annat clumsily defended some of the decisions of the casuists most open to criticism: for instance, those on homicide. The book created a scandal; the parish priests of Paris decided to seek its condemnation both by Parliament and by the Faculty of Theology at the Sorbonne. To put their case to the judges, they printed, as the custom was, a "Factum", or summary memorandum of their case, which was published in February, 1658. Contemporary testimonies attribute it to Pascal, and also attribute to him a *Second Ecrit des Curés de Paris* which appeared about this time.

Following a third and fourth manifesto on behalf of the Paris priests, which are attributed respectively to Arnauld and Nicole, Pascal gave definitive form, in June, 1658, to a *Cinquième Ecrit des Curés de Paris* which he himself considered, if we are to believe Marguerite Périer, his best work. In fact in these extraordinarily packed pages we can recognize at once the fighter, the apologist, and the theologian.

This work postulates very clearly the principle of two opposite errors, those of the Calvinists and the Jesuits. The Calvinists use the moral philosophy of the Jesuit casuists as a weapon against the Church; they pretend to believe that this lax system is the only morality of Catholics. On their own side, the Jesuits make every effort to justify the Calvinists by attempting to base the lax system on tradition. How many souls have been lost through listening to such insidious arguments! But the real doctrine of the Church, that of the Fathers, supported by the bishops and the parish priests, condemns equally the error of the Calvinists and that of the Jesuits. However, schism is the greatest of evils and the Calvinists are more to blame than the Jesuits, who have at least not broken away from the Church. Thus the doctrinal strictness of Pascal's pamphlet does not exclude a certain moderation of tone.

The campaign of the parish priests soon met with signal success. Bishops censured the *Apologie pour les Casuistes*. A *Projet de Mandement*, drawn up by Pascal, was no doubt intended for one of them. Condemned by the Faculty of Theology, the *Apologie* was disowned by the Jesuits themselves. Pascal again participated in the battle by composing a *Sixième Ecrit des Curés de Paris*, dated 24th July, 1658, and perhaps a *Factum des Curés de Nevers*. The whole business came to an end in 1659 with the condemnation of the *Apologie* in Rome.

It is to this period also that we must attribute the *Ecrits sur la Grâce*, if we trust certain hints of Nicole's, confirmed by the evident close relationship of these writings with the *Cinquième Ecrit des Curés de Paris*. Of these writings on grace, which are little studied and which are nevertheless one of the keys to Pascal's whole work, the original manuscripts were still in existence at the end of the seventeenth century, but we now only possess copies. As a whole, this uncompleted work takes the form of fifteen fragments which can be divided under two headings; on the one, general reflections on the problem of grace; on the other, an examination of a particular question, whether "the just" can always obey the commandments.

The spirit of Pascal's *Ecrits sur la Grâce* has been clearly defined by Nicole: Pascal shows himself as inflexible as ever in defending the doctrine of efficacious grace, but seeks to "deprive that doctrine of an air of fierceness which people give to it". This is, in fact, the dual impression which we derive from a reading of the work.

More original in certain ways than *The Provincial Letters* —Pascal is now better informed about theological questions and can elaborate a personal doctrine—the *Ecrits sur la Grâce* are the expression of a very strict Jansenism, sometimes stricter than that of Arnauld. One might guess this even by means of considering Pascal's sources; he does not forget Aquinas, but makes a particular use of the more rigid doctors of the school of Louvain, such as Conrius and Sinnich. We should notice also a more precise development of the theory of "proximate power" than is to be found in the early "Provincial Letters", a development closer to that of Jansenius: the just—that is, those who are in a state of grace—cannot persevere in goodness without a renewed grace, which God may at any moment refuse them, efficacious grace is therefore indispensable to the just if they are to obey the commandments. God's action always precedes that of man.

How is Pascal going to free this doctrine from its "air of fierceness"? Solely through his method of exposition.

The first step in this method of exposition consists in detaching points on which there is agreement from disputed points, and putting a special emphasis on them. All the theological schools acknowledge that some men may be damned and some men are saved, and that the will of man and the will of God are concurrent in bringing about both damnation and salvation. Disagreement arises only when we seek to know whether the will of man or that of God plays a more powerful part in the process. Pascal does not cease to rely solely on authority and tradition, but his presentation of the doctrine has a completely logical pattern, and in the sequel he is not afraid to make frequent appeals to common-sense.

The second step in the method of exposition, less specifically characteristic of Pascal's personal approach, consists in presenting the doctrine of Saint Augustine as an essentially comprehensive one, equally distant from the opposite errors of Calvin and Pelagius, which it transcends and reconciles. Thus, for instance, according to Pascal, all the Molinist propositions about grace are true, if we admit that the complementary propositions are true, also. The Molinists are right in saying that salvation is acquired through human merit, but we have to add at the same time that this merit is the gratuitous gift of God. In fact, human merits are the secondary cause of salvation, but they are themselves caused by God's will, the primary cause of everything that is good.

Going into more detail, Pascal seeks to clear away the ambiguities and misunderstandings that are inseparable from the Augustinian doctrine of grace. He makes it clear that each man has the duty of considering himself as one of the number of the elect, that while life remains no man ought to consider himself in a state of final reprobation; he makes it clear also that if the just have no guarantee that they will persevere in grace, still it is in fact very rarely that God withdraws his grace from them. Finally, since man owes his salvation to his merits, the Augustinian theory of grace does not relieve him from moral effort; in practice, it is just as if he were acting alone.

We should notice also the skill with which Pascal analyses and comments on his texts. The quotations chosen at once clarify and justify the doctrine. These quotations are borrowed not only from Scripture and the early Fathers, but also from the more recent tradition of Aquinas and the Council of Trent, with the purpose of showing that the doctrine of efficacious grace expresses the constant teaching of the Church.

Like *The Provincial Letters*, but in a very different fashion, the *Ecrits sur la Grâce* thus constitute a very original effort to make certain extremely dry theological problems accessible and interesting to a wide audience.

We have seen what help Pascal gave to Port-Royal as a controversialist and a populariser of doctrine. He also rendered Port-Royal service as an educational theorist. On behalf of the "little schools" where the solitaries of Port-Royal taught children, he had already suggested a new method of teaching reading. In 1657 or 1658, Arnauld asked him to put into shape the Port-Royal *Elements of Geometry*; but the Doctor found the result confused and reshaped Pascal's work in what Pascal himself recognized to be a clearer fashion. Nothing remains of Pascal's *Elements of Geometry* therefore, except perhaps two projects for a preface, if the two important fragments published in the next century as *De l'Esprit Géometrique* and *De L'Art de Persuader* can be considered as such.

The first of these fundamentally important texts begins by describing the rules of geometrical method: no term is to be employed for which a preliminary definition has not been given, no preposition is to be sustained which cannot be demonstrated by truths already familiar, and, in any demonstration, we should mentally substitute the definition for the thing to be defined. But, Pascal adds, it is absolutely necessary, at the very beginning of our reasoning, to allow the use of certain terms for which we have no definition, such as space, time, and movement, and also to accept certain undemonstrable principles. In these cases, clearness is the only test of truth. Among these principles which could not be demonstrated, Pascal particularly emphasized the idea of infinity, both the infinity of greatness and that of littleness. Given space, time, number and movement, we can always conceive a larger or a smaller without ever reaching either infinity or nothingness. Every magnitude, of whatever sort, is equally distant from these two extremes. This undemonstrable truth constitutes the very foundation of geometry. Replying to the objections of Méré who could not accept the idea of space as infinitely divisible, Pascal showed that the idea of "the indivisible" is inconceivable, or at least that no accumulation of indivisibles could ever make up a finite extension. An indivisible is a magnitude of another *kind* than an extension. And here Pascal added the conclusions of one of his treatises of 1654: the point is an indivisible in relation to the line (no number of points put together can "make" a line), the line in relation to the plane surface, and the plane surface in relation to the solid body. These different magnitudes are radically discontinuous, they are different *orders*. All these ideas were to be largely exploited in the *Apology*.

In the fragment *De l'Art de Persuader*, Pascal is writing from a more practical point of view. He is dealing with the problem of belief. There are two channels by which opinions are received into the soul, the understanding and the will. The understanding infallibly accepts every proposition correctly deduced from premises previously accepted; these premises may be universal or particular, true or false, but in accepting conclusions drawn from them all that matters is that they themselves should have been accepted. The will, on its side, accepts only that which satisfies its aspiration towards happiness. In order to persuade, we have at the same time to convince the understanding and please the will. This is a difficult task: the understanding and the will often pull the soul in opposite directions and moreover one never knows exactly either what any given man acknowledges to be true or what he turns to as a source of pleasure: for men are all different and even as individuals are not self-consistent. But if the *principles* of truth and pleasure are known, there are rules which can be easily followed in a process of demonstration. And Pascal here repeats, with even more firmness and clarity, the rules elaborated at the beginning of the *Esprit Géometrique*. The fragment terminates with a magnificent tribute to the spirit of geometry, superior to the rules of the ancient logic and of universal application. It is in the light of these admirable pages that we must interpret the famous fragments about the spirit of geometry and the spirit of *finesse*—of tact, of delicacy—whose composition certainly also belongs to this period.

The year 1658, finally, was also marked by an important resumption by Pascal of his purely scientific activities. These had never been completely interrupted. On his conversion, Pascal had left several scientific works in an unfinished state, and had even renounced the publication of completed treatises, but he had kept in touch with the scientific world, with Roberval, Carcavi, and Mylon, and had sometimes received visits from them. In 1657, Pascal had entered into correspondence with Sluse, a canon of Liège Cathedral, one of the soundest mathematicians of the period. Together they sought to solve certain problems relating to the geometry of curves.

Towards the middle of 1658, in rather curious circumstances, Pascal became once again rather more directly involved with science. The narratives of Gilberte and Marguerite Périer, confirmed as they are by independent sources, can in this case hardly be questioned. One evening Pascal had gone to bed with a raging toothache. To forget his pain, he set himself to reflect on a difficult problem, not completely solved even to-day, that of the curve then called in France the "roulette" and later more generally known as the cycloid. It is a curve traced by a point on the radius of a circle within, on, or outside its circumference, as the circle rolls along a straight line. By dint of concentrated reflection, Pascal solved his problem and also cured his toothache.

Pascal did not intend to publish his solution. But the Duc de Roannez pointed out to him the advantage he would gain, in his campaign against unbelievers, by the prestige of a great scientific discovery. People would see that, though Pascal demanded that reason should abase itself before the mysteries of faith, this was because he had an exact knowledge of the scope and limits of reason. In order to give the discovery more publicity, the Duke even proposed that a challenge should be issued to other scientists and that there should be a competition with a prize for the best solution. Pascal agreed. In June, an anonymous circular letter was addressed to the scientists of Europe, stating six problems whose solution was to reach Carcavi, the president of the jury by 1st October.

The history of this competition is a very complex one. Pascal soon perceived that the first four problems had already been solved by Roberval, and decided to judge the competitors only on the basis of their solutions for the last two problems. Some confusion resulted from this decision; and on the other hand, in his *Histoire de la Roulette* Pascal attributed to Mersenne and Roberval—the latter collaborated with Pascal in the writing of the treatise, and is responsible for the error—discoveries for which the credit really went back as far as Galileo and Torricelli. This error gave rise to lively polemics. Finally, the competitors showed much dissatisfaction with the decisions of the jury, and yet it is hard to feel that they had a legitimate grievance. Sluse, Huygens, and Wren did not officially take part in the competition. Only two answers were received, from an English mathematician, Wallis, and from a Jesuit of Toulouse, Father Lalouère. Wallis had undoubtedly made serious errors both in his calculations and in his general method, but he complained of the conditions of the competition, and especially of the spectacular form that it had taken, as discouraging to foreign mathematicians; he claimed that Pascal had deliberately under-estimated the value of his (Wallis's) work and that Pascal had been able to arrive at his own solution by making use of various memoranda he had received in connection with the competition. As for Lalouère, he very soon sent in solutions to the first three problems, and later to the fourth. But soon, in circumstances of which we know little, his exchanges with Pascal became rancorous. The Jesuit had discovered some errors in his own calculations, and therefore he renounced his claim to the prize; but at the same time he declared that he now possessed the solutions to the two final problems, while refusing to produce them. Obviously, he thought that he had solved them, but lacked confidence in himself. When he finally consented to make his solutions public, Pascal discovered serious errors in them and pitilessly rallied the unfortunate Jesuit. Lalouère's resentment was no less lively than that of Wallis.

In December, 1658, Pascal published his own solutions to the problems in a letter to Carcavi, under the pseudonym, Amos Dettonville. This letter was followed by two others, addressed to Sluse and Huygens. In this remarkable collection of letters Pascal laid the foundations for the integral calculus.

Some of Pascal's attitudes in this affair do, however, lay him open to severe criticism. We should not take the accusations of Wallis and Lalouère too seriously, but there is no doubt that Pascal's return to the sciences also involved a return, in some degree, to a "worldly" spirit. As during the period of his controversy with Father Noël, he now also showed himself ready to glory in his own superiority, skilful in claiming his due, pitiless towards opponents, and without indulgence for their weaknesses. This was only a transitory state of mind, but it warns Pascal's biographers to avoid excessively simplifying the story of his "inner life". There is a sense in which Pascal's conversion was a process in which he was always having to start again at the beginning.

Thus the description which Gilberte Périer has given us of her brother's life during this period needs certain qualifications. No doubt we can agree with her that Pascal spent a great part of his time reading the Holy Scriptures, that this was "as it were the centre of his heart", that he "found his joy in it": in fact both *The Provincial Letters* and the letters to Mademoiselle de Roannez bear witness to Pascal's close and fervent knowledge of the Bible. But when Gilberte adds, "He had exempted himself from a superfluity of visits and did not even want to see anybody", many witnesses contradict her. As for the dual resolution which she attributes to her brother, to renounce every kind of pleasure and every kind of superfluity, we must be careful not to interpret this too literally and it seems very improbable that Pascal made such a resolution immediately after his second conversion: all the examples by which Gilberte illustrates this resolution are obviously taken from the last years of Pascal's life, the only period of her own adult life in which Gilberte, who had by that time established herself in Paris, knew her brother closely. In our own opinion—and Gilberte's own narrative, in several particulars, bears this hypothesis out— one can observe an effort on Pascal's part to achieve "sanctity" only after his serious illness, which forbade him almost every kind of intellectual effort, had set the bearings of his life more clearly and firmly towards mysticism and the practice of charity.

II. *The Years of Sickness*

It is important therefore to discover precisely when Pascal fell seriously ill. If we are to believe Gilberte, it was towards the end of his thirty-fifth year, that is to say, towards June, 1658: she says that the illness began with the raging toothache which led to the solution of the problem of the cycloid. This assertion is undoubtedly excessive; Pascal was never so active as in the months following June, 1658; it is the period of the *Ecrits des Curés de Paris* and also of the treatises on the cycloid. We get more reliable information from the correspondence of the scientists of the time, Carcavi, Huygens, Boulliau, Sluse. In February, 1659, for the first time, Carcavi told Huygens that Pascal's state of health was very unsatisfactory. However, at the end of the month, there appeared the *Lettre de Dettonville à Huygens*. It was only at the beginning of March that, as a result of the overstrain to which he had been subjecting himself, Pascal fell into a state of exhaustion which made any effort of attention unbearable to him. From then on, there are many successive testimonies about the illness. Boulliau, in June, speaks of a kind of languor into which Pascal had fallen and which the doctors tried to alleviate with the aid of strong soups and ass's milk. In August, Pascal himself admitted that he had been unable to read a pamphlet which Sluse had sent him. Later, Boulliau sent Huygens similar news. The year 1660 was marked by a relative improvement of Pascal's condition, but he still felt very weak. He confessed to Fermat that he still found reading and writing a painful effort. This evidence, and the very few writings of Pascal's own that we can date with certainty between 1659 and 1662 allow us to accept, without too many qualifications, Gilberte's statement: "During the four more years of life that still remained to him—if one call the state of pitiable exhaustion in which he spent them, life—he was unable to work at anything at all."

What kind of life, then, did Pascal lead during these years of sickness? Here we can accept Gilberte's account, which is often confirmed in a very moving fashion by the intimate notes contained in the manuscript of the *Pensées*.

It is certain that the care of the poor became one of Pascal's chief occupations. He thus followed the example of a few friends from Port-Royal who had devoted their lives to works of charity, such as Charles Maignart de Bernières. In the battle against the frightful social miseries of the period of the Fronde, the latter had already become the chief assistant of St. Vincent de Paul. He continued the good work in subsequent years, both in Paris and in the provinces, thanks to a series of agents who determined the needs of each locality. It was no doubt through Bernières' organization that Pascal, in the winter of late 1661 and early 1662, learned of the distress of the poor in Blois and sought to alleviate it. He had close ties with Monsieur de Bernières, whose family he had known in Rouen. In 1660, he procured important subsidies for Bernières' work. But, while collaborating in these great charitable enterprises, Pascal also wished "to serve the poor in poverty of spirit", to visit them in their homes and draw near to their wretchedness, so that he might learn lessons from it for the conduct of his own life and steel himself to do without any kind of superfluity.

Another aspect of Pascal's "sanctity" has been emphasized

by Gilberte in her description of how her brother thought of affection and friendship. "He had an extreme tenderness for his friends", but, far above the tenderness of sensibility, which is often selfish, he placed that rational tenderness that makes us desire the good of those we love and that fulfils itself in charity; for charity, coming from God, clarifies our understanding of that in which our neighbour's true interest lies. In his friendships, Pascal avoided both "attachment" and "frivolity", demanding of others that they should act towards him, in this respect, as he acted towards them. He also used to reprove the signs of the affection, too much confined to the feelings and the senses, that existed between Gilberte and her children. God being the end set before all things, it was our duty to love all things in God and for God. But if Pascal's ideas about affection and friendship transcended mere sensibility, they did not destroy it. We are wrong moreover to consider, as we sometimes do, Pascal's conception of the ties of family and friendship as narrowly Jansenist; in its basis, it rests on a psychology which is very close to that of Descartes and Corneille and which can also be discovered, expounded more gently no doubt, but not in fundamentally different terms, in St. François de Sales.

Throughout her narrative, Gilberte depicts Pascal to us as an austere Christian, hard on himself and hard on others, but finding in prayer, in his Bible readings, and in his devotional practices a real and deep inner joy. Such also is the impression given to us by what Pascal himself wrote in his last years.

There is a curious fragment of a letter in which it is Pascal's austerity that chiefly comes out. In 1659, the Périers had been planning a rich marriage for their daughter Jacqueline, then fifteen years old and a pupil at Port-Royal. The directors of the convent, when consulted on the marriage formally advised against it. It was Pascal who brought his sister and his brother-in-law their answer; he delivered it in extremely vigorous terms, declaring that marriage was "the most dangerous and the lowest of the conditions of life per-

mitted to a Christian". Such a passage may appear excessively harsh in tone, but in the particular case of Jacqueline Périer, whose parents proposed to marry her off without
consulting her and without inquiring about her vocation,
Pascal's austere advice coincided, in its practical outcome,
with what would have been the advice of ordinary good
sense.

Pascal's *Prière pour Demander à Dieu le Bon Usage de ses
Maladies* can be dated about the same period. We are
accepting, here, the formal testimony of Gilberte Périer;
the editors of the *Pensées*, for their part, used to consider
the prayer as contemporary with Pascal's first conversion.
Their error can easily be explained by the content of the
prayer itself. Pascal there asks God for the grace of "conversion"; he has made a bad use of his health, has exploited
it to enjoy the pleasures of life; he prays that his illness may
bring him back to himself, may make him regret his faults,
and that, by uniting him to the sufferings of Jesus Christ,
it may make him pleasing to God and worthy of God's
grace, the only true source of consolation. The prayer ends
with a motion of self-abandonment to the will of God: "I
ask from You neither health nor sickness, neither life nor
death, but that You shall dispose of my health, and my
sickness, of my life and my death, for Your glory, for my
salvation, and for the service of the Church and Your
Saints. . . ." There is a strange sweetness under the austerity
of the thought. There is no need, however, to attach this
prayer to any precise event in Pascal's life, for the conversion
of a Christian is never completed; and in any case the notion
of a new "conversion", a third one, at the beginning of the
years of sickness in 1659 seems to us quite justified by our
preceding analysis. Moreover, two other reasons induce us
to attribute to the composition of the prayer this comparatively late date: first, the strength and richness of the
doctrine, quite on a level with that of the *Pensées*; and
secondly, the lyricism of the style, the poetic fascination of a
text in which the successive movement, in which there recur

what can almost be described as refrains, are comparable to stanzas of magnificent rhythmic control. The style of the younger Pascal has never this impassioned note.

There is nevertheless an aspect of Pascal's life which Gilberte has left completely on one side: his relationships, in these last years, with "the great world". There are, however, other important documents which throw some light on the subject.

What a change of atmosphere there is when we pass from Gilberte's narrative to the wonderful letter to Fermat which Pascal wrote on 10th August, 1660, while staying at Clermont. Fermat, who lived in Toulouse, wished to take advantage of this visit to meet his old correspondent and proposed an interview half-way between their two places of residence. Pascal was unable to accept the invitation: "I am so feeble," he wrote, "that I cannot walk without a stick or hold myself erect on horseback." In his answer to Fermat, which has a wonderful distinction and charm, he draws a parallel between science and *honnêteté*. Geometry is "the noblest exercise of the human mind", but it remains "useless"; it is "the finest craft in the world, but in the end only a craft"; it is "good to try ourselves out on, but not to use up our strength". Its whole value consists in teaching us to reason well, but its subject, in itself, is a futile one. Pascal no doubt, by a discreet allusion to the life of retirement he is leading, lets Fermat understand that other reasons have led him to lose his interest in geometry, but it is clear that, on the road that leads us from the letter to Christina of Sweden to the letter to Fermat, Pascal has been guided not only by Saint-Cyran, but also by Méré.

We have further evidence that Pascal had not abandoned the "great world" in a letter which, towards the end of 1660, he addressed to Madame de Sablé; Pascal thanks her for having procured for him the acquaintance of a Protestant doctor of medicine, Menjot. The Marquise, who had close ties with Mother Agnès, had occupied since 1656 a house near the church of Port-Royal de Paris. It was there that she received her friends. Pascal was one of the dearest of them and she felt his death acutely.

Finally, we know that Pascal would have liked to devote himself to the education of a prince. He wrote—towards, according to Monsieur Lafuma, the end of 1660—three *Discourses on the Condition of the Great.* Intended for the Duc de Chevreuse, the son of the Duc de Luynes and a pupil of Lancelot's, these discourses were preserved by Nicole. In these three discourses, Pascal denounces certain faults to which noble birth particularly disposes men. In the first place, noblemen tend to consider their goods and their honours as legitimately theirs, though they owe them merely to the chance of birth and to a legal status which has nothing absolute about it. They should not renounce these contingent advantages, but they should realize that in their essential nature they are no different from other men. Secondly, noblemen often confuse natural greatness, based on a man's real gifts, with their own conventional greatness, based on their position in the social hierarchy. High rank gives a man the right to be treated with outward deference, but it is only virtue that we can really respect. "I do not have to respect you because you are a duke, but merely to greet you respectfully." Thus noble birth and high rank do not free a man from the necessity of acquiring virtues. The third discourse distinguishes three stages on the path to true kingship: the king who rules by force, the king who rules by desire, the king who rules by charity. To attach them to himself, the king who rules by force makes his subjects submit by frightening them; the king who rules by desire caters to their pleasures, is of service to them; but the king who rules by charity, who models himself on God, makes his subjects aspire towards the practice of charity. If a nobleman wishes to be at least an *honnête homme* he must act like the king who rules by desire, not like the king who rules by fear, but if he wishes to show that he is a true Christian, he must force himself to imitate the king who rules by charity. Thus, at the foundation of what is rather imprecisely called Pascal's "politics", there lies a respect for social conventions, conditional on their being recognized *as* conventions. We shall find similar ideas in the *Pensées*.

We need not, therefore, imagine Pascal's life during his last years as that of a frigid ascetic fleeing from human society. His exact, fervent, and scrupulous piety did not prevent him from mingling in the world and giving a very high place to the world's ideal of *honnêteté*, as the first stage on the path to charity.

III. *The Dispute About the Formula, and the Death of Pascal*

In relation to the year 1661, when the enemies of Port-Royal resumed their persecutions, much more complex problems confront Pascal's biographers. The vagueness and sometimes the inconsistency of the records have excited lively controversies among scholars. What is certain is that, in regard to these persecutions, a serious difference of opinion divided Pascal from Arnauld and Nicole. But discussion still rages round three points: the date of this difference of opinion, its nature, and its consequences.

On the first of these three points, however, there is no longer really any possible room for doubt. Let us recall the facts. We have seen that, thanks to the Parliament, the formula of 17th March, 1657, had been laid aside. But in 1660 the influence of certain bishops, and above all the personal action of Louis XIV, who was resolved to exterminate Jansenism, put an end to the calm. On 1st February, 1661, the Assembly of the Clergy decided that every ecclesiastic and every schoolmaster should be forced to sign the formula. The Council of State ratified this measure on 13th April; severe penalties were decreed against those who refused to sign. At the same time the "little schools" were dispersed; Port-Royal was forbidden to recruit new female devotees; and Singlin, and Maignart de Bernières, had to remove themselves.

Arnauld and his friends were not in a mood to reject any compromise at all. But, before consenting to sign the formula—which, let us remember, formally attributed the five condemned propositions to Jansenius—they demanded that, in some fashion or another, the old distinction between "the question of right" and "the question of fact" should be re-established, and that they should not be asked to submit on "the question of fact". Thus on 8th June, 1661, under their inspiration, there was published a "charge" from the Grand-Vicars of the Cardinal de Retz, who was then a political fugitive. This charge defined the sense which was to be attributed to the signing of the formula: submission on "the question of right", respectful silence on "the question of fact". Arnauld now saw no further difficulty in signing the formula. But he was resisted by some of his friends; thus Le Roy, the Abbot of Haute-Fontaine, demanded that the signature should be followed by an express restriction, since after all the charge issued by the Grand-Vicars did not in any way alter the text of the formula. For the same reason, the nuns of Port-Royal felt serious scruples, for they considered that signing the formula was equivalent to acknowledging the presence of the five condemned propositions in a book in which they had not seen them. They did sign, however, with certain reservations, but for some of them the drama of conscience had been so violent that it shook their health. Jacqueline Pascal was the most deeply affected; she died on 4th October, 1661.

What, then, was Pascal's attitude? It did not differ from that of Arnauld. Trustworthy documents, confirmed by an allusion in a letter of Jacqueline's, even attribute to him the composition of the charge issued by the Grand-Vicars. The difference between Pascal and Arnauld and Nicole came to the surface, however, on the occasion of the issue by the Grand-Vicars of a *second* charge.

In fact, the first charge, attacked by the enemies of Port-Royal, was suppressed by the Royal Council on 14th July, and condemned at Rome on 1st August. On 31st October, the Grand-Vicars were forced to sign a second charge, in which the whole distinction between the question of right and the question of fact was abolished.

What attitude should the defenders of Port-Royal now adopt? Two parties, in fact, formed themselves: on the one side Arnauld and Nicole: on the other Pascal, transformed by Jacqueline's death, inheriting his sister's unyielding spirit, and supported by his compatriot, the great lawyer, Domat, and by the Duc de Roannez. Arnauld's point of view is known to us through a great many documents; Pascal's is defined in, unfortunately, an extremely short *Ecrit Sur La Signature*. Another, more important, piece of his on the subject has disappeared.

There were a certain number of points about which Arnauld and Pascal were obviously in agreement. Thus, no disagreement about doctrine separated them; their divergences related only to the most effective way of protecting the reputation of Jansenius and the doctrine of efficacious grace. Moreover Pascal, like Arnauld, would have signed a formula which did not involve "the question of fact". Finally, neither Arnauld nor Pascal were willing to sign the formula without making certain reservations. But what would these reservations consist in?

For Arnauld, since submission was demanded both in relation to "the question of right" and "the question of fact", it was necessary, when signing, explicitly to exclude "the question of fact": thus he thought that the friends of Port-Royal should declare that they submitted "so far as the Faith was concerned", that is so far as "the question of right" was concerned. Pascal, without rejecting the distinction between "the question of right" and "the question of fact", considered that the terms of the formula itself made the distinction, in this context, an illusory one. In fact, given a formula of the following sort: "I condemn the five propositions in the sense of Jansenius", is it not the sense in which Jansenius is stated to have held these propositions, that is, "the question of fact", which determines the nature of the doctrine to be condemned, that is, the "question of right", law, or principle? "The question of right" is subordinate to "the question of fact": to submit on "the question of right" is *a fortiori* to submit on "the question of fact". Such a formula flatly condemns Jansenius, that is to say, according to Pascal, it condemns "efficacious grace, Saint Augustine, and Saint Paul". Whoever wished to save efficacious grace, therefore, according to Pascal, would, while signing the formula, have to except the general doctrine of Jansenius from condemnation "in formal terms".

To all this Arnauld and Nicole replied that since the Pope and the Bishops had always defended the doctrine of efficacious grace, the expression in the formula about condemning the five propositions "in the sense of Jansenius" referred, in their opinion, to some completely different doctrine, no doubt a completely imaginary doctrine, but the only one whose condemnation was involved. The error of the formula, according to Pascal and Nicole, lay in attributing to Jansenius this completely imaginary doctrine. Thus in the very nature of the case "the question of right" and "the question of fact" remained separate; and a submission "so far as the Faith was concerned" was perfectly explicit.

Critics have often contrasted the sturdy straightforwardness of Pascal, his love of truth, with the equivocations and timidities of Arnauld and Nicole. Let it be so. But Arnauld was a man who knew how to bear persecution bravely when the true doctrine seemed to him really in danger. And, however much we may admire Pascal's unyielding spirit, we may wonder whether in this case he really had strict logic on his side. There are a great many inconsistencies in the *Ecrit sur de Signature*. In the first place, Pascal bases his whole argument on a garbled quotation from the formula. The real text is: "I condemn ... the doctrine of the five propositions of Cornelius Jansenius, contained in his book called *Augustinus*." That statement juxtaposes "the question of right" ("I condemn the doctrine") and "the question of fact" ("contained in the book"), without subordinating one to the other. On the other hand, if Pascal's garbled version of this text, "I condemn the five propositions in the sense of Jansenius" is equivalent to a condemnation of efficacious grace, the reason must be that these five propositions themselves express this doctrine of efficacious grace, and are therefore orthodox. Pascal is mingling the two strategies which have been defined in relation to the Bull of 1653; without forgetting the distinction between "the question of right" and "the question of fact", he is implicitly claiming that the five propositions, in addition to their heretical meaning, have also an orthodox meaning, and that this is the meaning which Jansenius attributed to them. Thus the reservation proposed by Pascal amounts to accusing the Pope and the Bishops of making a blunder, and a blunder not only about the question of fact, but, since the two things are linked, about "the question of right", about principle, about doctrine. He considers that the Church, under the influence of the Jesuits, is on the point of condemning "efficacious grace", that is, on the point of denying and betraying itself. The duty of every simple faithful Christian was to assert the truth, even against the Pope and the Bishops. It is certain that, in acting in this way, Pascal did not feel that he was lacking in respect for the hierarchy, still less that he was withdrawing himself from the unity of the Church; as Jacqueline had said to him some months earlier, "Nobody can be cut away from the Church against his will." Such a position, which had a basis of justification in some passages of Saint Bernard's work, was not at that time an untenable one, in spite of the development of the Church's inner structure. But on this whole matter Pascal is certainly much bolder than Saint-Cyran; not to mention Jansenius, whose sentiments were probably ultramontane.

What were the consequences of this difference of opinion? There are critics who, with a fine contempt for logic, wish to assume that after separating himself from Arnauld and

Nicole through an excess of the Jansenist spirit, Pascal then renounced Jansenism. We shall see what their arguments amount to. In any case, the immediate consequence was a certain coldness, which we ought not however to exaggerate, in his relations with Arnauld and Nicole. Above all, since his advice had not been taken by the partisans of Port-Royal, Pascal decided to withdraw from any further controversy and to devote his life, even more than in the past, to works of charity and piety. Thus the end of the year 1661 was marked by a new "conversion".

However, the fact that Pascal was still playing a part in the world is made clear by the affair of the "carriages at five sol fares". In the course of their conversations, Pascal and the Duc de Roannez had the idea of establishing in Paris regular carriage services, going from one district to another and carrying passengers for a small fare. It was the germ of the idea of the omnibus. A company was formed to finance the undertaking, and the first "route", which led from Porte Saint-Antoine to the Luxembourg, was opened on 18th March, 1662. A picturesque account of this opening ceremony is to be found in a letter addressed to Arnauld by Pomponne, one of the shareholders in the company; the actual writer is not Pomponne, but Gilberte Périer, writing on behalf of her brother who was too ill to hold a pen. Other "routes" were soon also established. We can recognize in the whole episode that taste for workable ideas which was one of Pascal's essential characteristics.

With his profits from this undertaking, Pascal hoped to be able to aid the poor of Blois. Another charitable deed, related by Gilberte Périer, can be dated about the same period. Coming back from attending Mass at Saint-Sulpice, Pascal met a girl of fifteen who was begging. Her father was dead, her mother had just entered the hospital of the Hôtel-Dieu. Understanding the dangers she was running, Pascal handed her over to the care of a priest at Saint-Sulpice, furnished him with money for her support, and

later saw that she was established "in an honourable condition". The priest wished to know the name of the girl's benefactor but could not succeed in discovering it.

Shortly after this episode, Pascal's illness grew worse. However, he had taken a poor family into his house and one of the children had got the smallpox. Gilberte, who was in the habit of visiting Pascal to nurse him, was afraid that she might carry back infection to her own children. Pascal, rather than cast the family whom he was protecting out of his house, decided himself to remove to his sister's house. He went there on 29th June, 1662. The house was in the Faubourg Saint-Marcel, in the parish of Saint-Etienne-du-Mont.

Some days after his arrival, Pascal had to take to his bed. Violent pains, colics and headaches assailed him. He made confession to Father Beurrier, the priest of Saint-Etienne-du-Mont. He felt an ardent desire to have the Viaticum, but the doctors, thinking that he was not in any acute danger, were against this, as too likely to excite him. The last few weeks of the dying man were little but a long waiting for the moment when he might receive communion. In the intervals of his sufferings, he received visits from friends, from Sainte-Marthe, one of the confessors at Port-Royal, and from Arnauld himself, who was now forced to live in hiding. He conversed often with Father Beurrier, and renewed his confession. On 3rd August, he drew up his will; of his share in the carriage service company, which constituted the greater part of his fortune, the poor were to receive half. On 17th August, his pains grew even worse. During the night, he was seized by such violent convulsions that Father Beurrier, summoned in haste, gave him communion. "He received the Holy Viaticum and Extreme Unction with such tender feelings," Gilberte relates, "that he was moved to tears." Then he said: "May God never abandon me!" These were his last words. He died twenty-four hours later, on 19th August, 1662, at one o'clock in the morning.

After such a moving narrative it is sad, but it is necessary to return once more to the examination of controversies. There are still scholars who think that Pascal, before dying, had cut himself away from Port-Royal, and had "retracted" his Jansenism. Some rumours to this effect were current even in the seventeenth century, shortly after Pascal's death; Fénelon allowed himself to echo them. Long forgotten, this thesis was revived and vigorously defended by Ernest Jovy in 1910. Of Jovy's many arguments, we shall consider here only those which still appear to have some possible validity.

With Jovy, the narrative of Pascal's last months takes on a quite new significance. Pascal's charity to the poor young girl? Pascal met the girl on his way back from attending Mass at Saint-Sulpice, and assisted her with the help of one of the priests at Saint-Sulpice. But Saint-Sulpice was one of the centres of Anti-Jansenism. Therefore Pascal had separated himself from his friends. . . . Here again we have the notion of two parties in the Church, excommunicating each other and refusing to know each other. Is it worth our trouble to defend Pascal, as a Jansenist, from the accusation of displaying such narrowness of spirit?

Pascal's transference to his sister's house? This, according to Jovy, was a scheme of Gilberte's to withdraw Pascal from the influence of Saint-Sulpice. Jovy attempts to adapt to his thesis, as well as he can, the statements of Rapin, according to which the Périers were anxious to avoid the last sacraments being refused to the author of *The Provincial Letters* by the priests of Saint-Sulpice, The parish priest of Saint-Etienne-du-Mont, on the other hand, was rather pro-Jansenist. Legal documents, however, enable us to answer Jovy's thesis decisively. Pascal was a parishioner, not of Saint-Sulpice, but of Saint-Côme, whose parish priest had signed the *Ecrit des Curés de Paris*. Moreover, in the month of July, Gilberte rented a house almost next door to that which her brother had just left: she was therefore counting on taking him back to his own house as soon as possible.

Let us come, however, to the only important point in

Jovy's case. Towards the end of 1664, there was a rumour that Pascal had died without receiving the last sacraments. Beurrier, summoned by the Archbishop of Paris, Hardouin de Péréfixe, defended the memory of his penitent and even signed a declaration on the subject of the state of Pascal's opinions at his death, in so far as Beurrier could judge them from his several conversations with Pascal. Three important assertions emerge from Beurrier's declaration. First, Pascal for two years—which is to say, since 1661—had broken with the theologians of Port-Royal because "they were going too far in the matter of grace and it seemed they were showing less submission than they ought to to Our Holy Father the Pope". Secondly, for two years Pascal had been solely preoccupied with "things that concerned his salvation". Thirdly, Pascal had finally died as a good Catholic "in perfect submission to the Church and to Our Holy Father the Pope".

What is the scope of these three assertions? The second of them is perfectly accurate, but tells us nothing new. We might say as much of the third, for Pascal had always upheld the principle of the unity of the Church and the pre-eminence of the Pope; as we can see if we consult, for instance, his letters to Mademoiselle de Roannez. This does not mean that Pascal acknowledged either papal infallibility or the superiority of the Pope over General Councils; his attitude resembled that of Arnauld and Bossuet. But, as for the first of Beurrier's assertions, it rests on a complete misunderstanding, since Pascal had parted from his friends at Port-Royal not because of a reaction against their Jansenism, but because of the excessive and unyielding quality of his own. So Gilberte Périer protested to Beurrier, asking him if he had not misinterpreted her brother's words. Beurrier acknowledged that in fact he must have been mistaken.

The question, therefore, could be considered as solved, if Jovy had not produced a new document, the unpublished *Mémoires* of Beurrier. One chapter in this book is devoted

to the death of Pascal. What new light does it throw? None
on Beurrier's third assertion in his declaration. Very little
on his second: for two years, Beurrier says, Pascal had
withdrawn himself from the disputes about grace and papal
authority, because he saw both that they were very difficult
and that they gave rise to dissensions among the faithful;
he leant on the authority of the Church and remained in
submission to the Pope. These are very vague statements,
and by no means imply an abandonment by Pascal of his
Jansenism. Finally, in relation to the first assertion in his
declaration, Beurrier remembers the disputes to which it
has given rise and makes an effort to please everybody;
without disavowing what he has signed, he allows that it
can be interpreted in all sorts of ways. Thus the *Mémoires*
offer us nothing decisive. But what are they worth as a
whole? Beurrier's book has been much discussed but very
little read. It should be read carefully, and read *as a whole*:
how many anachronisms it contains, how many inconsistencies, how many narratives which are purely conventional and obviously fictitious! Beurrier has one central
purpose, that of edification; in comparison to that purpose,
facts are a matter of minor importance to him. Like all the
more sympathetic characters in the *Mémoires*, Pascal is
visibly idealized or rather made to conform to Beurrier's
own ideal of the Christian life, which can be summed
up in two words, simplicity and submission. These *Mémoires*
are incontestably the work of a holy man, but as history
they have no value whatsoever.

In any case, there is no document which authorizes us
to speak of a "retractation" by Pascal. Such an act was
never demanded of him. Besides, what is it that people
wished him to retract? Being a layman, he was not
asked to sign the formula. Should he have disavowed *The
Provincial Letters*? On the contrary, Beurrier depicts him
as still very hostile to a lax moral theology. Should he
have recognized the infallibility of the Pope? Neither he
nor any other Catholic at that date was obliged to do so.

Should he have renounced the doctrine of Jansenius? He had always considered it as a Catholic doctrine. Should he have become a Molinist? No notion could be more absurd.

For the idea of a retractation to have even a meaning, we must first suppose that Pascal had fallen into heresy; but it is just this supposition that a strictly historical examination of the facts obliges us to reject. Here, therefore, we shall merely insist on those facts which establish Pascal's loyal self-consistency. These include the attitude of his dearest friends, the Duc de Roannez and Domat, who were always unyielding on the question of the formula (to Domat, moreover, Pascal bequeathed a substantial legacy) and above all the last words of the dying man which are words we should expect from the author of the *Ecrits sur la Grâce*: "May God never abandon me!" There is nothing in the story of these last months in which we can trace a development of thought that would, in addition to all the other arguments against it, have certainly led Pascal to disavow his whole past life and past achievement.

CHAPTER FIVE

THE "PENSEES"

ON his death, Pascal left behind him a great many manuscripts. These included scientific works, dating back to 1654, many of them unfinished, but some ready for the printer, like the treatises on the equilibrium of liquids and on the arithmetical triangle. They included also drafts for the *Ecrits sur la Grâce* and an abridgment of the life of Christ which was not printed till 1845. But the most important part of these manuscripts was an accumulation of notes, chiefly intended for the work of Christian apologetic that Pascal was known to have been pondering for a long time. It was to these notes that the first editors gave the title, *Pensées*.

The *Pensées* therefore present themselves to us in a thousand fragments. Sometimes, as it were, a thought is caught flying and sometimes a portion of argument is already fully elaborated. The unfinished state of the *Pensées* makes us feel very close to Pascal, and gives the work a unique and singularly attractive character, but it does favour an arbitrary approach on the part of editors, whether seeking to establish a sound text (we had to wait till 1845 for an edition really representing the original manuscripts) or faced with the dual problem of separating the fragments out under various subject-headings and then arranging them logically within these groups. It favours an arbitrary approach, also, on the part of critics, when they strive to interpret vague thoughts and apparent self-contradictions, when they seek to reconstruct Pascal's philosophical and religious "system", and finally when they seek to determine the principles of his art. However, we can to some degree safeguard ourselves against this dual arbitrariness; an accurate study of the manuscripts will enable us to reach the most objective solution of the editorial problem, and to see Pascal's design as a whole; a detailed consideration of the intellectual influences to which Pascal was exposed will make the interpretation of obscure passages notably easier, and enable us to determine the degree of originality in Pascal's work in its relation to the climate of his age.

I. *The Manuscripts and the Editions*

The problem of how to edit the *Pensées* has taken on an entirely new shape since the decisive labours of Monsieur Louis Lafuma. After two centuries of forgetfulness and one century of research, we find ourselves to-day once again in the privileged position of Pascal's relations and friends when at his death they acquired possession of his papers. To trace the history of these manuscrupts and of the successive editions of the *Pensées* is to demonstrate that the first editors possessed if they had realized it, very precise indications of how to establish both a sound text and a correct arrangement of the material. These indications were neglected by the first editors, forgotten, and gradually rediscovered, thanks to a series of victories for scholarship and the critical spirit. It is by no means superfluous to go over this story in detail; first, because the story teaches us just in what sense the generations that succeeded Pascal have really known the man as he expressed himself in the *Pensées*; and second, because the recent discoveries are based on an accurate interpretation of the history of the manuscripts and the early editions. The chief merit of Monsieur Lafuma appears to us to consist in having finally clarified that history.

It was in 1670 that there appeared in print for the first time the *Pensées de M. Pascal sur la Religion et sur Quelques Autres Sujets*. The text of this first edition was preceded by a preface, written by Etienne Périer, Pascal's nephew. In spite of certain errors which it contains, and which have been repeated by subsequent editors, this preface is a document of capital importance, which we must analyse with care.

We ought not, however, to look in it for much originality. The last few pages of the preface are taken almost word for word from Gilberte's life of her brother. The beginning of the preface is merely a summary of a *Discours sur les Pensées de M. Pascal*, the work of a friend of the Duc de Roannez, Filleau de la Chaise. Etienne Périer, like Filleau de la Chaise, claims to be summarizing a lecture, given no doubt at Port-Royal, in which Pascal explained the plan of his projected apology for Christianity. In 1667, Filleau de la Chaise dates this lecture more than eight years back; in 1669 Etienne Périer dates it back ten or a dozen years. It is all very vague. Fortunately, Etienne Périer adds that the delivery of the lecture shortly preceded Pascal's last illness. This illness, as we have seen, did not really display itself till March, 1659, but Gilberte dates its first symptoms in June, 1658. Gilberte's son would certainly follow his mother's account of the matter, thus we can date the delivery of the lecture somewhere around May, 1658. Here we are at issue with Monsieur Lafuma, who, interpreting Gilberte's text differently, assigns the lecture to October or November, 1658.

Let us turn, however, to the central portion of Etienne's preface, the most interesting portion in our present context. This is, as it were, a first history of the *Pensées*, a history of their composition. Here, Etienne Périer, ill-informed, accumulates error. It is basing themselves on him that so many critics have assigned the composition of the *Pensées* to the period of Pascal's last illness; it is Etienne who invented the theme, which was to make such a great appeal to subsequent critics, of the sick Pascal snatching a thought in one convulsive movement and hastily transcribing it on the first handy scrap of paper. We shall see later why Etienne made this mistake.

When he tells the story of this first edition, however,

Étienne Périer has a more direct acquaintance with what he is talking about. We owe to him two very valuable details; Pascal's papers were found "all together, threaded together in various batches", and "the first thing that we did was to have them copied just as they were, and in the same disorder in which we found them". What does that mean? It is only recently that we have understood.

How were these fragments going to be edited? Let us still follow Etienne's preface, supplementing it, however, by other contemporary documents. There were, we are told, three ways of considering the task of the editors, and each of these had its partisans within the "editorial committee". The first plan was that of reproducing the fragments just as they stood, and in their initial disorder; this was the attitude of the Périer family, who considered Pascal's papers as relics that ought not to be disturbed. The Duc de Roannez, on the other hand, with a self-assurance which he owed to having received Pascal's confidences, claimed that he was in a position to reconstitute the work as it had been originally planned by completing the unfinished fragments and arranging them according to the scheme Pascal had in mind; the Duke was going to enlist the help of two friends from Poitou, Filleau de la Chaise and Goibaud du Bois. Finally, a third group proposed to publish only those fragments which were in a relatively clear and completed state, and to group them in a logical order, without bothering about Pascal's original plan. This was the scheme of Arnauld and Nicole, supported by two rather odd characters; a wit and man about town, recently "converted", the Comte de Tréville, and a young Secretary of State who had recently entered the Oratory, Loménie de Brienne.

The Périer family resisted the scheme of the Duc de Roannez. "That would not be giving Monsieur Pascal's work to the world, but giving something quite different." However, the "objective" edition, which the family hoped for, also still remained an impossibility, and for two reasons. One was a reason of expediency: the first edition of the *Pensées*, already delayed by the violent persecutions to which Port-Royal was exposed between 1661 and 1668, was going to appear at the moment when "the peace of the Church" was at last achieved. It was necessary, therefore, to be careful not to awake old quarrels by publishing those reflections of Pascal's which were excessively Jansenist or even merely excessively daring. The second reason was of a literary sort; the French classical period aspired too strongly to perfection of form really to appreciate an often obscure sketch of a work, a sketch with no obvious order, and lacking that finish so indispensable to a work of art. It was, therefore, the third group in the committee, that of Arnauld and Nicole, that prevailed, but, even so, it was impossible, in spite of the protests of Gilberte, to print even the texts selected for publication exactly as they stood in the first copy of the manuscript; respect for the "peace of the Church", respect for a certain artistic ideal, imposed a number of modifications and dilutions. All the audacities of Pascal's thought and style disappeared from what is called the Port-Royal edition of the *Pensées*. Presented in this fashion, Pascal's projected apology for Christianity became a work of piety, perfectly orthodox, and perfectly adapted to the narrowest neo-classical taste. Let us avoid, however, being too severe on the editors of 1670. Nothing, certainly, seemed more permissible to them than the modification of a text which the author would certainly never have allowed to appear as it stood. They gave the *Pensées* the form best calculated, at a given period, to make their reading easy and to assure their success. Moreover, the knowledge they possessed of Pascal's deeper intentions perhaps even to-day allows us to derive more profit from their work than we suspect.

It remains true, however, that they respected neither Pascal's text nor his plan. However, even if the last survivors of the Périer family carried away many secrets to the tomb, they did leave behind them a mass of manuscripts which would in time enable these secrets to be rediscovered. But in spite of the existence of these manuscripts, the Port-Royal edition, slightly augmented in 1678, held the field till 1776, and the editors of the last quarter of the eighteenth century profited little from the manuscripts at their disposal.

The Pascal papers, which had been transported to Clermont in 1664, belonged at the beginning of the eighteenth century to Louis Périer, a canon in the cathedral there. The latter deposited in 1711 in the library of Saint-Germain-des-Prés in Paris a certain number of these manuscripts, including the original of the *Pensées*. Before doing so he had them copied, along with some minor works, so as the possess within the covers of one small volume his uncle's essential achievement. He died shortly afterwards. His heir, Marguerite Périer, towards 1715 gave one of her relations, Dom Jean Guerrier, a Benedictine of Saint-Jean-d'Angély, a manuscript copy of the *Pensées* and also Pascal's library. The manuscript copy of the *Pensées* was sent to Saint-Germain-des-Prés in 1731, to facilitate to reading of the original manuscript, which, as we have seen, that library already possessed. On her death in 1733, Marguerite Périer left the rest of the papers in her possession partly to the Oratory at Clermont, partly to Pierre Guerrier, a nephew of Jean Guerrier, who had just entered that order. Into the hands of Pierre Guerrier there thus came, in particular, a second manuscript copy of the original *Pensées*. The latter was later made available by Guerrier de Bezance, Master of Requests, to the Abbé Bossut. It ended up, shortly afterwards, along with the first copy in the Bibliothèque du Roi which, during the French Revolution, had inherited the possessions of the library of Saint-Germain-des-Prés.

The eighteenth-century editors were not ignorant of the existence of the original manuscripts and the two copies made from them. But they did not dream of exploiting their knowledge. Nevertheless, a few unpublished fragments saw the light of day, taken perhaps from Abbé Périer's copy, perhaps from copies which have to-day disappeared.

In 1727, Colbert de Croissy, the Jansenist bishop of Montpellier, published the *Pensées sur les Miracles*. In 1728 Father Desmoulets published some minor works and also the famous fragment on self-esteem. In 1740, the "Recueil d'Utrecht" published the *Mémorial*.

A few unpublished reflections figured in Condorcet's edition of 1776. This was the first edition to break away from the classifications established by Port-Royal. Full of contempt for the merely edifying reflections (many of which he suppressed) and anxious to edit Pascal "philosophically", Condorcet simply divided the fragments into two large groups: philosophical thoughts, and religious thoughts.

A similar scheme was proposed in 1779 by the Abbé Bossut, though fortunately a more comprehensive one in its approach to Pascal. Bossut did not suppress anything. But, merely textually, his edition does not mark any advance; he contented himself with returning to the text of 1670 and adding the unpublished material that had appeared since. Though he had in his hands both Abbé Périer's manuscript and the copy communicated by Guerrier de Bezance, he made no attempt at all to restore the fragments, as altered by the Port-Royal editors, to their original state. Bossut's critical sense was not such a remarkable one as some scholars have claimed.

It was not till 1842 that Victor Cousin, in a report to the French Academy, proclaimed "the need for a new edition of Pascal's *Pensées*". In the Bibliothèque du Roi, he had *discovered*—it is the only appropriate word for it—the manuscripts of the *Pensées*. He made no attempt to decipher the originals, now bound together in an album collection, but a reading of the copies was sufficient to reveal to him how unfaithful to the text all the editions were. The problem of a sound text was thus clearly raised. About the problem of arrangement of the material, Cousin had no such precise suggestions to make. He proposed merely to distinguish the fragments connected with the projected *Apology* from other fragments that had clearly nothing to do with it.

The programme outlined by Cousin was carried out in 1844 by Faugère. The latter carefully deciphered the "collected originals", which from now on were to be considered as the basic source of every edition. In his classification of the material, he separated the reflections foreign to the *Apology* from the *Apology* properly so-called. He arranged the material for the latter bearing in mind the scheme described in Pascal's lecture at Port-Royal as sketched by Filleau de la Chaise and Etienne Périer. This was the first modern edition of the *Pensées*; and for a century, no further real progress was to be made.

This is not to say that Pascal's work did not become better and better known. But in 1852, Havet contented himself with adapting Faugère's text to Bossut's arrangement of the material, though accompanying his edition with a remarkable commentary. In 1877, Molnier returned to the decipherment of the original manuscript and notably improved the text as far as detailed accuracy went. In 1896, Michaut, publishing the first "objective" edition, merely adopted the order of the "collected originals", in which, however, he discovered about a dozen unpublished fragments.

In 1897, Brunschvicg's edition profited from all the progress that had been made in relation to knowledge of the actual text. Following, however, the examples of Port-Royal and Bossut, Brunschvicg renounced the attempt to reconstruct Pascal's plan, renounced even the attempt to distinguish fragments intended for the *Apology* from others, and contented himself with grouping the reflections as logically as possible, to make the reading of them easy and pleasant. He succeeded magnificently but his classification of the reflections, both in his large groupings, and in his arrangement of thoughts within these groupings, remains extremely arbitrary.

The beginning of the twentieth century saw other editorial attempts—Monsieur Chevalier once again attempted to reconstruct Pascal's original plan with the help of Filleau

de la Chaise—but they did not succeed in eclipsing the success of the Brunschvicg edition, to which, in any case, they owed a great deal.

The nineteenth-century editors, notably Brunschvicg, have left us fairly exact descriptions of the manuscripts of the *Pensées*. They liked emphasizing the disorder of the "collected originals"; they attributed the pasting up of the fragments to some illiterate handyman, who had scattered in various parts of the album sheets which originally formed a single argument, who had cut other sheets into an infinity of small strips and who had amused himself by pasting the greatest possible number of these on a single page. As for the "copies"—but let us consider here only the first copy, since the second is practically identical—Brunschvicg had noticed their curious mode of arrangement. In the first part of the copies, the fragments are grouped in chapters —there are twenty-seven of these, not twenty-six as is often said—each with a title; the second part of the copies contains the remaining fragments in almost complete disorder. Both Michaut and Brunschvicg considered that the arrangement of the material in the copies was a first sketch of the Port-Royal edition; neither of them saw any editorial use in the copies except that of facilitating the reading of the "collected originals".

But from 1935 onwards there was a new editorial revolution. It was started off by the work of a modest scholar, Z. Tourneur. The latter first of all studied the "collected originals" much more attentively than any of his predecessors; he established a much more certain text, and carefully emphasized variant readings. On the other hand, in his presentation of the text, he adopted in principle the classifications of the "copy", which correspond, in his opinion, to a first grouping of the material by Pascal himself. The decisive first step had been taken, but Tourneur's work remains in the end inadequate. He had formulated hypotheses without demonstrating them and, in all his labours, profound intuitions run parallel with obvious

errors. Finally, he was quite unable to present his material in a manner in which it could be assimilated by the general cultivated public. His palaeographic edition of the *Pensées* is sometimes more difficult to read than the original manuscripts.

But it only needed a little reflection for that principle, which in an obscure way had guided M. Tourneur, to be clearly formulated by other scholars. The credit goes to two learned men, Monsieur Lafuma and Monsieur P. L. Couchoud. We have learned already from Etienne Périer that Pascal's papers, on his death, were "threaded together in batches"; they were thus *already* classified and, according to the usual method of the time, held together in groups by a thread passed through the hole made by a needle; many of the fragments still visibly bear the hole through which the needle was passed. But Etienne Périer adds that the fragments were copied out in the very order in which they were found, that is, in the order of the threaded batches. How, therefore, can we avoid establishing a relationship between the order of the batches and the order of the material in our first "copy". That "copy" is the very copy of which Etienne Périer speaks; the chapters which it distinguishes must correspond to the various threaded batches; therefore the copy restores to us Pascal's original plan of composition.

Having reached this point, Monsieur Couchoud launches out into a number of more doubtful hypotheses. Among the fragments of the *Pensées*, he notes, there are some very short ones, appearing on little scraps of paper, and other more extended ones, written on long sheets. May the passages on long sheets not have formed a complete work, which was originally independent? In fact, if we assemble these long sheets so as to obtain a more or less continuous text, we find ourselves faced with a kind of "Discourse on the Condition of Man". This would be the first, and as far as it went completed, form of the *Apology*, basing its argument for religion purely on the analysis of human nature and ending with the famous argument of the wager. At Port-Royal, this discourse must have been sharply criticized because it took no account of the traditional evidences for religion. Pascal would therefore have reshaped his work and divided out the fragments of this original continuous discourse between the various chapters of a longer and more comprehensive *Apology*. Thus the manuscripts enable us to reconstruct two successive plans for the great work which Pascal was projecting.

The whole historical part of this theory smacks of fantasy. Even the hypothesis of an original "Discourse on the Condition of Man" does not really rest on any evidence that would satisfy a scientific scholar. Thus, arguing that the long sheets originally constituted a continuous whole, Monsieur Couchoud points out that some of them seem to stop short in the course of an argument and others, on the other hand, to begin in the middle of one; this suggests to him that there has been cutting of the pages. But this abruptness is also a marked quality of the shorter fragments which nobody considers as having formed part of an original continuous essay. Is it not probable that, in revising his notes, Pascal often stopped short when he had made the general line of his proposed argument sufficiently clear to himself? More broadly speaking, we have no valid reason for grouping the more polished fragments of the *Pensées* apart from the others; we find fragments representing every stage of composition from a first rough draft to an apparently final revision. On this whole topic, therefore, we are still waiting for more solidly based arguments; and for the moment we shall leave Monsieur Couchoud's hypothesis on one side.

Let us follow, rather, Monsieur Lafuma, and follow him on safer ground. And let us begin by trying to determine, as precisely as we can, the editorial value of the first "copy". Let us look at the various evidence. Let us compare the arrangement of the material in the "copy" with that in the Port-Royal edition. There is no relationship between the two arrangements; therefore the arrangement of the material in the copy is not due to the first editors. Now let us compare the arrangement of the material in the "copy" with that in the "collected originals". There are numerous correspondences. Whoever pasted up the album followed as far as he could the order of the threaded batches, which had not yet been seriously disordered; no doubt he was working under the direction of Louis Périer in 1711. The actual disorder of the threaded originals must be attributed rather to somebody who re-bound the album much later, and confused the original order of the pasted up sheets he was binding. Here, again, we have evidence that Pascal himself had originally grouped his papers and that the first "copy" restores to us this original grouping.

Let us attempt now mentally to rearrange the originals in the order of the "copy". Let us remember that the first part of the copy consists of a classified portion, divided into twenty-seven chapters. The corresponding originals, with a few easily explained exceptions, consist of fragments of paper cut down to the dimensions of the text that is written on them, and each fragment contains only a single text. On the contrary, however, the second and unclassified portion of the "copy" is represented in the "collected originals" sometimes by uncut papers, sometimes by long sheets containing several fragments. What conclusions are we to draw? Pascal, it seems, did not write on scraps of paper but on long sheets; at a given moment, he cut up these long sheets, dividing the scraps thus obtained under various headings, and threading the material thus grouped together into batches. The cutting of the sheets is not the work of some clumsy person who pasted up the album, but of Pascal himself. Pascal's arrangement of his material was, however, interrupted by his illness of the winter of 1658 and 1659. Thus the first portion of the "copy" represents a logically arranged sketch of Pascal's plan for the *Apology*; the second portion of the "copy" contains fragments intended for the *Apology* but left on one side by Pascal pending classification, fragments that have nothing to do with the *Apology*, and fragments written after 1658.

We can see only one slight objection that can be brought against this argument of Monsieur Lafuma's. No doubt illness considerably slowed down Pascal's intellectual activity. But could Pascal's illness have sufficed to interrupt this almost mechanical task of grouping papers, a task which could have been completed in a very short time? And why should Pascal have set himself to group his papers together? Was it with the purpose of revising and completing his work? In our opinion, it was much more probably with his lecture at Port-Royal in view. This hypothesis appears to us confirmed by the presence among the threaded batches of fragments headed "A Port-Royal". All these are, as it were, the hinges of various arguments. They seemed intended to fill in gaps in a spoken argument and to rub in points. It is thus that we can explain the resemblances, which had already struck Tourneur, between the classified portion of the "copy" and a published *Discours* by Filleau de la Chaise. We agree with Monsieur Lafuma that Filleau de la Chaise must have drawn a great deal of his inspiration from the "copy".

How, then, does the editorial problem now stand? It would be unreasonable not to take account of the grouping and arrangement of the material that had already been commenced by Pascal himself: the more so, as there is no evidence that he ever, after his illness, thought of modifying it. But since the second half of the "copy" has no sort of order at all—apart from some material on miracles, the sketch of a kind of "Provincial Letter" which was to have dealt with the miracle of the Holy Thorn—editors are not obliged to retain the sequence of the material in the manuscript. Monsieur Lafuma divides the unclassified material into two portions: on the one hand, material foreign to the projected *Apology*, notes for other projected works or personal meditations like the famous *Mystery of Jesus*: on the other hand, fragments intended for the *Apology*. The latter M. Lafuma distributes, according to their subject, among the various classified portions. Subjective judgment thus continues to a play its part in the editorial task, but a minor part, and future researches may even further diminish its role.

Monsieur Lafuma's labours are thus comparable in importance to those of Victor Cousin and Faugère. They help to bridge the inevitable gap between writer and reader. But this is not to say all research is at an end. The manuscripts of the *Pensées* have not yet given up all their secrets. We must attempt to date the fragments. And we must still carefully study the second part of the "copy". In the actual matter of editorial presentation, moreover, it still remains necessary to reconcile the scholar's demand for objectivity with the general reader's demand for a pleasant clarity. The method of presentation suggested by Monsieur Lafuma is interesting; but one can think of others. What we must refuse to agree is that there is a fundamental contradiction between the needs of the scholar and the cultivated general reader; the most learned edition can and should be at the same time the most perfectly elegant.

II. *The Dialectic of the "Apology"*

Let us now attempt to disengage the main lines of argument in the *Apology*. For this purpose, let us follow the arrangement of the first portion of the "copy", since that is Pascal's own arrangement. Let us, however, bear the unclassified passages in mind, to clarify, where necessary, the classified passages. Let us also make use of the *Discours* of Filleau de la Chaise.

What a sense of astonishment we now feel! How very different is this new text from that presented to us by generations of editors! What we rediscover is, of course, broadly speaking the plan of Filleau de la Chaise; but then Filleau's own *Discours* now seems to us extremely insipid. He did not grasp the depth of Pascal's thought; he glided over the essential arguments and elaborated secondary points. But the difference is most striking, perhaps in the arrangement of material *within* the chapters. The fragment on the two infinites is juxtaposed with that on man as a thinking reed; we ought to have guessed this earlier since both these fragments, and a third, are preceded, in Pascal's handwriting, with the same sign, the letter H. And these fragments are to be found, not in a chapter on the wretchedness and greatness of man, as we had expected, but in another called "Transition de la Connaissance de l'Homme à Dieu". Thus they take on a quite unexpected meaning. The traditional commentaries on the thought of the *Pensées* will have to be entirely replaced. Our astonishment yields to actual wonder.

Speaking very generally, the fragments which early editors had tended to group together round a few central ideas, the wretchedness of man, *Deus absconditus*, and so on, are now found widely scattered throughout the work and lending support to a rich variety of particular arguments. Instead of a rigid and systematic classification, we find a cunning interweaving of themes, a subtle, almost musical mode of composition, and an athletic and balanced mode of argument, though always a rigorously logical one. No doubt this impression of a subtle, interweaving argument owes something to the unfinished state of the work—some fragments transcend the framework of the chapter in which they are grouped and only partly fit into it—but undoubtedly the completed work would have left a not fundamentally dissimilar impression. We can now understand what Pascal meant, in his remarks on the theory of literary composition, by "the order of the heart", the order of emotional persuasion, "which consists chiefly of digressing on each point that is connected with the general purpose, so as to keep that purpose always in view."

Given these facts, it is our critical duty to attempt to understand Pascal's classification and the development of his argument. We do not claim that, in a first attempt, we shall succeed in doing so: we offer only an essay in interpretation.

The plan suggested by Filleau de la Chaise and Etienne Périer as being Pascal's plan for the *Apology* falls into two parts: the first part putting the unbeliever in a frame of mind in which he would be willing to accept the faith; the second part then demonstrating the truth of religion. This is the very plan which Pascal sketches in the fragment which—a revealing detail—was the first to be fitted in his first threaded batch: "Men have a contempt for religion; they hate religion and are frightened lest it may be true. To cure this condition of mind, we must first show that religion is not opposed to reason; we must show that it is venerable, arouse a respect for it; then show that it deserves love, and make good men wish that it might be true; and then show that it *is* true." (Chapter I.) In our opinion, the division between these two parts occurs at the end of Chapter XI of the "copy".

The end of the fragment cited above defines the two themes of the first part: "To be venerated, since it has a real knowledge of human nature: deserving love, since it promises what is truly good." Six chapters raise the problem of man; three, that of the sovereign good; a final chapter forms the conclusion.

In man, according to Pascal, we find two opposite characteristics, wretchedness and greatness.

How much evidence there is for the wretchedness of man! A mere nothing suffices to distort his judgment, the veering of a weathercock, "too much or too little wine". A mere nothing starts him off on mad adventures: "a little cowl arms 25,000 monks". Above all, reason is perpetually misled by the play of "deceptive appearances". "Custom" prejudices our understandings and transforms accidental associations into necessary links. Our "imagination", without our being aware of it, substitutes its own fantasies for the reality of things. What good are all the riches in the world to the man who imagines himself poor? If the preacher

has not shaved properly, can the gravest judge listen to the
most edifying sermon without a secret inclination to laugh?
Thus imagination is the queen of this world; her laws
insidiously substitute themselves for the laws of reason.
Our judges and doctors who offer us only an "imaginary"
justice and science inspire respect only by striking the
"imagination", the judges by their red ermined robes, the
doctors by their square bonnets. Even if what we imagine
sometimes does correspond with the reality, how are we
to prove it? Finally our *amour-propre*, our self-love or self-
esteem, does not merely estrange us from reality, it makes
us hate the real. We cannot help seeing our own faults and
yet we wish men to esteem us; therefore we love those who
flatter us, knowing all the time that we are being deceived.
Human relations are founded on the lie. Thus the powers
of deception oppose to man's rational nature a second nature
wholly inclined towards error. (Chapter II.)

Incapable as he is of attaining to truth, can man attain
to the good, under its three forms of virtue, justice, and
happiness? To this single good there are opposed both the
infinite diversity of individual temperaments and social
customs and also the warring opinions of the philosophers.
How can we speak of an absolute virtue and justice, when
virtue and justice change from one country to the next?
There is no real virtue or justice in the world, there is only
custom and, given the impossibility of defining the true
justice, the best thing that men can do is to conform to
custom, to obey the laws of the State, however arbitrary
they may be. The only thing to be condemned in government is "tyranny" which consists of wanting to dominate
"out of one's proper field"; as if one wanted to be loved
because one was strong, or feared because one was beautiful;
for it is only beauty that can command love, and only
strength that can command fear. Such is the feeble justice
with which we must content ourselves. As for happiness,
human inconsistency and lack of perseverance makes it
perpetually vanish away. Yet if man is incapable of attaining

to the good, he still perpetually aspires towards it. (Chapter III.)

Let us return to the problem of happiness. Man in a state of repose cannot help feeling his *nothingness*, his dependence in regard to everything; he falls into weariness and despair. In fact, to his real dependence there opposes itself a desire for independence, which creates *need*. Man is thus hurried into a state of agitation which procures him an illusory happiness and which makes him feel his dependence all the more cruelly when he returns to his first state. It is the lot of man to be for ever tossed between repose and agitation, between weariness and illusion. (Chapter IV.)

In a digression of a different kind, Pascal attacks human arrogance on another flank. "The common people," he writes, "have very sane opinions." In other words, every effort of ours to raise ourselves above our condition, once it has reached its conclusion, brings us back to where we started from. The common people are ignorant; the learned man is able to note his own ignorance. The common people seek happiness in illusions; the wise man notes the impossibility for mankind of attaining to happiness except through illusion. It is only the half-learned, the half-wise who believe themselves to possess true knowledge and true happiness. It is in relation to the idea of justice especially that Pascal prolongs this analysis, using a dialectical pattern which is quite usual in his thinking. Thesis: the common people honour great men, they respect the laws because they think them just. Antithesis: the common people are deceived by appearances, for noble birth does not by itself bestow any merit on the ruling classes, it therefore gives them no rights and the laws have only a deceptive justice. Synthesis: in spite of everything, the attitude of the common people is the sensible one: true justice being inaccessible, or, at least, always open to debate, the only human justice is that of an established order, an order established by force— and kept up at once by force and by custom—and thus if force did not create justice, no social order would be

possible. The wise man, like the common people, must
conform to the laws of his country; but he has this superiority over the common people that, in accepting a social
order, he also understands its madness, he knows the
"reason of effects", that is, the rationality of an imperfect
system that bases itself on the facts of social life. Higher
synthesis: the people are still wrong; they see true justice
where there is only justice legitimated by force. But we
must take care not to show them their error, for if we did
they would rebel in order to institute the reign of true
justice, without seeing that they were merely replacing one
false justice by another, and that at the price of that civil
war which is the greatest of evils. Our wretchedness is such
that the highest effort of the human understanding only
ends in our becoming aware of that wretchedness. (Chapter
V.)

But our awareness of our own wretchedness is a proof of
our greatness. Our analysis of human nature has revealed
man's essential duality: subject to error, he aspires towards
truth; deprived of the true good and of justice, he aspires
to possesss them; dependent, he aspires to independence.
Wretched, he knows that he is wretched, and therefore he
is great. The animals have the same weaknesses as man,
but they do not suffer because of them, the weaknesses are
their nature; but "what we call their nature in the animals,
we call his wretchedness in man". If man suffers because he
possesses only a nature like that of the animals it is because
"he has fallen away from a higher nature, which was
formerly his". "For who would be unhappy not to be a
king except a king who had been dispossessed?" "Thought
makes man's greatness." Ought we not to conclude that he
possesses an immortal soul? In any case, we can attain
to a portion of truth. If we cannot demonstrate what our
feeble reason is that does not mean that we ought to renounce all knowledge. The "heart", a sort of instinct for
the truth, reveals to us the first principles of knowledge, and
from these principles reason can deduce multiple con-

sequences. Pyrrhonism, or radical scepticism, cannot therefore be a final attitude. (Chapter VI.)

Let us sum up about man. Man is a mere tissue of contradictions, an inseparable compound of baseness and grandeur, worthy at once of contempt and love. Always at war with himself, if he wants to be guided by reason he will soon feel the force of his passions, and yet if he wants to abandon himself to his passions, his reason will soon point out their baseness. The Pyrrhonists and the dogmatists have each seen only one aspect of man; these two doctrines, apparently opposite, really reinforce one another, for greater the man is the more wretched he is, and always most great when he knows himself most wretched. How can one get out of this vicious circle? Can one declare oneself neutral between Pyrrhonism and dogmatism? To do so, is to choose Pyrrhonism, whose essential nature consists of putting choice aside. Can one consciously hold to one or other of the two doctrines, Pyrrhonism or dogmatism? Neither is tenable. Can the Pyrrhonist really doubt "whether he is awake, whether he is being pinched, whether he is being burned"? Can the dogmatist prove that he "certainly possesses the truth"? Man cannot escape from his dual nature, of which reason cannot render an account. Only Christianity can explain that nature. Man has known a state of primitive greatness from which he has fallen through his own fault. If he had never been corrupted, he would possess truth and happiness; if he were merely corrupt, he would have no notion of truth or blessedness. Therefore "without this mystery, the most incomprehensible of all, we are incomprehensible to ourselves". (Chapter VII.)

Christianity therefore explains the secret of man's nature. Can it also nourish our desire for the sovereign good—that is, in a word, for happiness? Man is naturally unhappy and his awareness of his own greatness augments his unhappiness. How can he fill up the void that he feels in himself and that aches to be filled up? What do most men do? Do they really seek happiness? They seek, rather, to forget their wretchedness; they "distract" themselves. The repose which leaves them face to face with themselves is insupportable to them; action gives them the means of seeking distraction so that they need not think of themselves. Even a king, if he did not divert himself, would be overshadowed by sorrow, would be haunted by the idea of unhappiness. All human activity can be explained by this principle; it is to distract themselves that men engage in business, that they hunt, play, and dance. In all this bustle what they are looking for is not the thing they seem to be pursuing, the hare that they are hunting, but the very effort and fatigue that prevent them from thinking of themselves. If they achieve their aim, they also achieve repose and with it, weariness. Nevertheless, in all our bustle we feel the lack of an object, for we feel confusedly, through something that remains to us of our unfallen nature, that happiness is to be found only in a state of rest; yet, though aspiring towards rest, we find real pleasure only in bustle. But, it may be asked, is not this distraction itself the true happiness? No, for it rests on an illusion and, above all, because, coming from without, it can be perpetually disturbed by sickness, accidents, and afflictions. "This is all that men have been able to invent to make themselves happy." (Chapter VIII.)

What solution, now, have the philosophers to offer us? The problem of human nature divides Pyrrhonists from dogmatists; the problem of the sovereign good divides Epicureans from Stoics. The Epicureans place their happiness outside themselves, work the idea of "distraction" up into a moral system and offer us no aim in life but a happiness which is illusory. The Stoics make us seek happiness within ourselves and make us lift up our souls towards God but, believing themselves capable of loving God through their own merely human strength, they have put themselves in the place of God, forgetting their human weakness. Based on an incomplete knowledge of man, neither of these moralities can procure our happiness.

A true morality would take account at once of our wretchedness and our greatness. (Chapter IX.)

Of what does the sovereign good consist? Let us notice that, though all men seek happiness, nobody, who has not had the faith, has ever possessed happiness. What does this imply if not that we cannot attain to happiness through our own efforts? How can we explain our greed and our impotence in the pursuit of happiness if there was not formerly within man a real happiness, whose loss has left a hollowness which we try in vain to stop up with the most various objects, not realizing that this infinite gulf cannot be filled up except by the infinite, that is to say, by God Himself? Only the grace of God, humbly sought for, can give the soul its true delectation. (Chapter X).

In the light of such an investigation, what characteristics ought a true religion to possess? It ought to account for the contradictions in our nature, for our wretchedness and greatness. It ought to lay before us the soveriegn good as necessarily consisting only of the love of God; it ought to explain to us why we are opposed to God, that is, to our own highest interest; it ought to teach us what are the remedies for our powerlessness in the pursuit of happiness, and where these remedies are to be found. Let us make these demands of all the philosophers and all the religions. Only the Christian religion satisfies all these requirements. It explains the duality of human nature by original sin. It leads us towards the sovereign good by two paths: penance, imposed on our vileness, makes us fight against the passions which lead us towards false goods; grace restores our original greatness and unites us to God, the only real good. But is all this at once incomprehensible and unbelievable? The second part of the *Apology*, of which Pascal is now going to sketch some of the arguments, will answer that question. (Chapter XI).

If the second part of the *Apology* begins, in our opinion, at Chapter XII—which for that matter has the title "Commencement"—the historical evidences for the truth of the Christian religion are not expounded till Chapter XIX.

From Chapter XII to XIX we have a complex pattern of arguments, whose proper interpretation raises very delicate problems. This part of the *Apology* corresponds, in our opinion, to a variety of concurrent intentions on the author's part. In the first place, Pascal, having led the unbeliever to the very verge of belief, wants to show him the necessity of continuing his investigations. Secondly, he wants to define the spirit of such an investigation, to bring to birth in the soul of the unbeliever those inner dispositions which are necessary if the power of the actual evidences of the truth of Christianity is going to operate effectively; at the same time, Pascal is making clear to himself the rules of his own method. Finally, completing the work done by his preliminary arguments, he continues to demonstrate that the Christian religion is the only one "worthy of love", that is, the only one that suits human nature. This argument, by itself, appeared to him adequate to the conversion of certain kinds of souls. As Filleau de la Chaise said, Pascal had invincible evidence of the truth of the Christian religion "whether one considered it from the factual aspect, or whether one examined its foundations and its beauties".

At the beginning of this second part, Pascal has grouped the fragments that have an obvious relationship with the argument of the wager. That, therefore, has its place here. Its purpose is to constrain the unbeliever to commit himself more deeply. "Through sheer self-interest, you ought to take the trouble to seek out the truth."

It must be conceded to atheists that religion is not perfectly clear. But is their own doctrine any clearer? They refuse to accept mystery, but they cannot eliminate it from the universe. Religion, on the contrary, admits that it is full of obscurities; it is therefore self-consistent. Atheism is not.

We have thus arrived at a point where the odds are equal for and against the Christian religion. Religion cannot offer us a proof that God exists of the sort that will constrain all minds; but neither is it possible to discover a proof, of the sort that will constrain all minds, that God does *not* exist. Let us pause here provisionally. Must we renounce all further investigation? But life imposes a choice on us: we have got to "bet" for or against the existence of God. To abstain from making a choice is really betting against God. And since reason cannot determine our choice here, what, at least, does our interest suggest that we should do? Let us put our money on God: let us sacrifice earthly goods. If God does exist, we have gained heavenly goods, infinite in extent and duration. If God does not exist, we have lost earthly goods, that is, finite goods. The odds for and against God's existence being equal, we have a chance of gaining the infinite and a chance of losing the finite. Even if there is only one chance of gaining the infinite and several chances of losing the finite, our loss will still be a finite one. Our possible gain is therefore infinitely superior to our possible loss; in the presence of the infinite, the finite is mere nothingness. Our reason therefore commands us to bet on the existence of God. "But," the free-thinker may say, "for all that I cannot succeed in believing." It is because his passions prevent him from seeing his own truest interest. We must conquer the resistance of the body, its habituation to evil; we must "stupefy ourselves", which means, not that we should renounce reason, but that, since we now recognize at least the usefulness of religion, we should provisionally conform our attitudes to its precepts; even before we properly believe we should make the gestures of belief, and replace a bad habit of life by one generally recognized to be good, so as to suppress the obstacles to the working of grace. For that matter, when one renounces corrupt pleasures, one soon recognizes that one has lost nothing. (Chapter XII).

We must therefore continue our investigation, and pursue our quest. Is it necessary to make a sacrifice of the faculty of reason? No, true Christianity consists of "submission and the employment of reason". A religion which came into conflict with the principles of rational thought would be absurd and ridiculous; but a religion which explained itself in a wholly rational manner would have nothing of the supernatural about it. However, the Christian religion avoids these two excesses: to exclude reason is to leave the realm of piety for that of superstition; to admit only reason is to fall into deism or even into total unbelief. The fact that religion transcends reason does not mean that it contradicts it, for reason, in its own natural development, ought to recognize that there are an infinity of things that transcend it; thus reason cannot explain human nature. But reason ought to submit itself knowing well what it is doing and man is in the right in demanding of God that He should manifest Himself by signs, such as prophecies and miracles. (Chapter XIII.)

But man should not use his reason in attempts to demonstrate the existence of God. It is not possible to prove God's existence directly and it would not be a good thing if it were possible; man would feel too much pride at possessing such a proof. Just as Jesus Christ came to earth as a Mediator to reveal God to us, so it is by way of this Mediator that we must go to God. Now there is evidence for the sacredness of Christ's mission; there are the prophecies; and in knowing Jesus Christ, the Man-God, we avoid pride because in Him we know at once God and our own wretchedness. We find a living God, corresponding to all the aspirations of man, and at one stroke we demonstrate both the whole of Christian doctrine and the whole of Christian morals. (Chapter XIV.)

But if the Mediation of Jesus Christ opens for us the path towards God, what are the relationships between man and God going to be? Man, in his finitude, would not know how to communicate in any way with the infinite. His body is lost in the infinity of nature, equally at a distance from the infinitely great and the infinitely little, both similarly inaccessible to him. His mind knows only the things that have some proportion with his own nature; he is just as incapable of climbing up towards first principles as of descending to embrace the totality of created things.

Finally, man is both mind and body; he cannot know the simple substances, those that are merely body and mind; still less can he understand how it is that body and mind can be united in himself. Man therefore can neither know God, nor know himself. Yet his thought, in which his whole dignity lies, aspires to this double knowledge: "The natural order of thought begins with one's self and one's Author and one's end." The Christian religion permits man to resolve this contradiction; it allows him to know at once God and himself. But it is not the finite which grasps at the infinite, it is the infinite which communicates itself to the finite by grace. Grace, won for us by Jesus Christ, withdraws man from his wretchedness by opening the channels of communication with God. Man must expect nothing of himself and must expect everything of God. (Chapter XV.)

It is now possible to demonstrate the "falsity of other religions". Any religion will be clearly false that does not know man's nature and does not simultaneously explain his greatness and his wretchedness; at the same time, since there is a single principle of all things and a single end set before them, the true religion must teach us to adore and love only that principle and end. On the other hand, every religion will also be false that cannot produce historical evidence of its own truth. With these two criteria in mind, Pascal compares Christ and Mahomet, the Bible and the Koran. On the one hand, prophecies that have been fulfilled, on the other, no prophecy. On the one hand a completely saintly life, on the other the violence of a despot. On the one side, finally, an "admirable" doctrine and on the other a "ridiculous" religious ideal. (Chapter XVI.)

There follows a new parallel between Jews, pagans, and Christians. Jews, pagans, and Christians have the same miseries, but which of their religions offers a remedy? The pagans do not even hope for a Redeemer. The Jews hope for one, but in vain; the "carnal" Messiah whom they are waiting for would not bring them the real remedy. "There is no Redeemer except for the Christians." But Jesus Christ came for the sake of all of us and whoever sincerely seeks out the remedy for his wretchedness will find the Redeemer. The "true pagans" and the "true Jews" have come to Jesus Christ. On the other hand, any modern Christian who does not make a break with the spirit of the world does not know his Redeemer and is not "a true Christian". This sincere search for truth and for the true good constitutes for Pascal the essence of the religious spirit. (Chapter XVII.)

From here on Pascal is going to give a preponderant place to factual evidence, to the signs by which God makes Himself known to us. But we need to get a clear notion of the actual scope for Pascal of this evidence or these "proofs". The very essence of religion as such forbids the evidence for the truth of religion having an absolute clarity; for if Jesus Christ had revealed Himself manifestly to men, He would have been favouring pride and laziness; He would have been rendering useless that perpetual search for God which is the very life of the Christian soul. But if Jesus Christ had remained, on the other hand, completely obscure, unbelievers could be excused for not knowing Him. Thus the very proofs of religion have themselves a mingled clarity and obscurity. Only sincere souls pierce the veil of obscurity and reach God, or, what comes to the same thing, every good disposition of the soul comes from God. God makes the way clear for some and blinds others. This obscurity of religion should shock us less in that Holy Scripture itself warns us of it. Thus all objections are refuted; if the Christian religion is often considered as merely one of many religions, that is because only sincere souls recognize the true religion, as only they, also distinguish the Eucharist from ordinary bread. (Chapter XVIII.)

This mixture of clarity and obscurity is particularly noticeable in the Old Testament. Pascal makes a great effort to show that the Old Testament is wholly "figurative". In fact, what does this book contain? First of all a story, a narrative of events in which we first see God bestowing on

the Jewish people great "material" benefits: He saves them
from the Flood, He gets them across the Red Sea, He leads
them into the Promised Land. Then a religion is described
that again concentrates on "material" rites and sacrifices.
Finally, there are prophecies that announce a glorious
Messiah, who will bring to His people "material" goods.
But does the letter of the text contain its real meaning?
No—and for several reasons. Do we admit that the Old
Testament is a Divine Book? If so, it would be unworthy
of God to grant and promise only material goods, to demand
only material sacrifices; if we interpret it literally, the
Old Testament cannot satisfy a truly religious spirit. Are
we then to consider Holy Scripture as a merely human
document? But the prophets themselves say that the meaning
of their words is veiled and will not be understood; finally,
the purely material content of the rites and the prophecies
is contradicted by other Old Testament texts which define
religion as essentially a thing of the spirit. To reconcile these
contradictions, we must interpret all the material details
"figuratively"; these must be considered as "figures" or as
"figurative", that is, as concrete representations of spiritual
realities, signs which the soul must interpret. Thus the
temporal goods which God bestowed upon the Jewish
people prefigure the spiritual goods which the Messiah
was going to bestow on the Christians; the material rites
of the Jewish religion prefigure the spiritual sacrifice of the
Christian religion; finally, when the prophets announce a
Messiah who will bring material benefits, they also express
themselves figuratively. Let us notice that, in the case of
the prophecies, the "spiritual meaning" destroys the
"literal meaning", which is a mere veil; in other cases, the
spiritual and the literal meanings are simply different
layers which do not destroy each other. But what is the
reason for all these figurative expressions and events? To
blind some men, Pascal replies, and to make the way clear
for others. To blind the "carnal" Jews, who, caring only
for carnal goods, stop at the letter of the rites and the

prophecies, without seeing what gives them their real meaning. To make the way clear for the "spiritual" Jews, who penetrate to the spirit, who understand that their own history and religion have no meaning except as a pre-figuration of the history of the Redemption and of a more perfect religion; and who understand also that the Messiah predicted by the prophets was to be a humble Messiah and a bearer of spiritual goods. To blind the unbelievers, who do not understand that the prophecies have been fulfilled; and to make the way clear for Christians whom the fulfilment of the prophecies confirms in their faith. In fact the figurative theory enables Pascal to establish a strict correspondence between the Old and New Testaments. However, these two books came into existence quite in-dependently of each other; it is even the case that the Jews, to whom the Old Testament was granted, repudiate Christ, who is the centre of the New; there is no reason to suspect, therefore, the testimony which their sacred book, the Old Testament, gives in favour of the New Testament. Thus, the correspondence between the Old and the New Testa-ments is miraculous; and the whole Bible is a sacred book. (Chapter XIX.)

Armed with this great principle of figurative interpreta-tion, Pascal goes all through the Bible pointing out the facts that establish the truth of Christianity.

First of all, however, making use of the work of the old Jewish Rabbis, he seeks in the Talmud the distant source of the Christian religion, notably of the belief in original sin. (Chapter XX.)

Thus the important argument of *perpetuity* is introduced. The Christian faith, which can be summed up in the two ideas of the Fall and the Redemption, has always existed. The Old Testament, correctly interpreted, has exactly the same meaning as the New. At all times there have been spiritual Jews who pierced the figurative veil and thus knew the true religion. Following on Adam, following on the patriarchs, Noah, Abraham, Moses, who handed down the truth from generation to generation, following on the prophets who announced Christ's coming, Christ did Himself come, and His Church will last for ever. Other religions, on the contrary, have been revealed at a given moment of time and then have disappeared. However, there were two reasons why this true religion, which has always existed, should have been promptly stifled: men have always fought against it; and it sets up a moral system which is opposed to the passions of men. Its endurance, therefore, is miraculous. (Chapter XXI.)

The following chapter, dealing with Moses, is a mere sketch. Taking Moses to be the author of the Pentateuch, the most ancient part of the Bible, which includes Genesis, Pascal takes pains to establish the fact that Moses must have been well informed about the events which he was relating. His proof of this is the long life of the earliest patriarchs, which reduces the gap separating Moses from the creation of the world to a comparatively few generations. Pascal also attacks the "fable of Esdras" according to which the Holy Scriptures, destroyed in a fire, were reconstituted by Esdras at the direct dictation of God. Pascal's arguments here are very weak, but he has divined some of the very difficulties about the value and authenticity of the Pentateuch which Spinoza and Richard Simon were going to raise. (Chapter XXII.)

It is with a kind of mystical ardour that Pascal now enters on the great topic of "the proofs of Jesus Christ". He does not neglect the facts which prove Christ's divinity; Jesus Christ made Himself recognized by His miracles; He fulfilled prophecies which, though obscure in many particulars, did predict exactly the time of His coming; He has the testimony in His favour of the Jews themselves, who have been scattered and wretched since they denied them; the irrefutable testimony of the apostles and the evangelists; the testimony also of certain pagans, like Macrobius, who have alluded to Him; finally the testimony of certain heretics. But above all Pascal bases the divinity of Jesus on the perfect holiness of His life and doctrine, a holiness visible only to the pure in heart. There are three *orders* of reality, body, mind, and charity, with no communication between them, and incommensurable with each other. The greatest material wealth does not bestow the least intelligence on its possessor. The most extreme wordly greatness and the most extreme intellectual greatness cannot produce the smallest movement of charity. The greatness of Archimedes owes nothing to his princely rank. The splendour of Jesus could not be more shining if He had been a King or a genius. His greatness is of the order of charity: invisible to carnal concupiscence and to merely intellectual curiosity it bursts brilliantly forth "in the heart's eyes, that see wisdom". (Chapter XXIII.)

In the following chapter, Pascal makes a new use of the argument from prophecy which he has already handled several times. Skilfully, he has refrained from insisting on the fulfilment of the Old Testament prophecies in the person of Jesus Christ, foreseeing the obvious objection that the evangelists may have attempted to square their narrative with the predictions of the prophets. It is in the state of the Church and the World after the coming of Jesus Christ that Pascal finds the perfect fulfilment of the prophecies. The ruin of the Jews and the Pagans, the establishment of a new religion in Jerusalem and Rome, and at the same time the impulse of sanctity that would uphold the primitive Church, all these had been foretold, and in books that for centuries had been spread abroad about the earth. The accomplishment of the prophecies is like a "persisting miracle" which proves the truth of Christianity for ever. (Chapter XXIV.)

Then Pascal decides to examine the case of certain "concrete prefigurations", that is of cases in which facts or events related in the Old Testament prefigure the realities of the life of the Church. Such events with a figurative value are like facts instead of words prophesying. (Chapter XXV.)

What sort of life must the convert now lead? It will be

the life of a member of the Mystical Body of Jesus Christ; just as each member of the human body would perish if it loved itself instead of loving the soul that makes the whole body live, so the Christian must conform his whole will to the will of God: to love God, and to hate his own will, such is man's true good. The Christian life will be one lived as far from despair as from presumption for the wretchedness of man is always relieved by God. As for the outer formalities of religion, one should observe them humbly, but avoid putting all one's hope in them; it is a long way from devotion to real goodness. Finally, the Christian's life will be a happy life, for desire, the source of all evil, will be destroyed in him. (Chapter XXVI.)

And Pascal draws to a conclusion. Proofs, even the most obvious proofs, are not enough. We must humble ourselves before God and humbly await His Grace. It is useless to know God without loving Him. Those who believe without proofs, because they know their own wretchedness and have sought out a remedy for it, are none the less in possession of a sure and certain faith. It is always God who inclines the heart to believe. (Chapter XXVII.)

It is very obvious that this grouping into chapters, based on the arrangement of the "copy", enables us to characterize both Pascal's thought and his art with much more precision than formerly. Let us take two examples.

As to Pascal's thought, first, we remember the thesis, defended particularly by Victor Cousin, of Pascal's "scepticism". This thesis has now been abandoned by scholars, but the disorder of the fragments still left it in the state of being at least partly defensible. But the arrangement of the material in the "copy" throws a great light on Pascal's real attitude. At the beginning of the *Apology*, the chapter "Vanité" might seem full of scepticism, but it marks a provisional attitude and Pascal paves the way for future developments by bringing forward the idea of man's dual nature. With the chapter "Grandeur" he firmly establishes the possibility of attaining to truths of a certain sort. Further on, the chapter "Soumission et Usage de la Raison" elaborates a positive solution; reason has its part to play even in relation to faith, but it must submit itself to what transcends it, and what transcends it, we learn a little later, is the infinite. Suitably grouped, the texts take on all sorts of fine shades of meaning.

In what relates to Pascal's literary art, the arrangement of the "copy" enables us to recognize the essentially *dramatic* nature of Pascal's apologetic; it is an "apology" *in action*. But we wish to emphasize another point. The arrangement of the "copy" brings to the surface a very skilful mixture of rational demonstrations with arguments intended to touch "the heart". Before coming to his proofs, Pascal seeks to awaken in the free-thinker a religious sense; and it is even more notable that in his exposition of the proofs themselves he always strives to awaken that inner ardour without which any proofs will merely glide over the soul without leading to faith. It would be tempting to compare the part played in the dialectic of the *Apology* by this appeal to the religious sense with the principles of the art of pleasing expounded in *De L'Art de Persuader*. From a merely aesthetic point of view, the comparison is valuable, but there its value ends; between the realm of "the art of pleasing" and that of the religious sense, there is the same distance as between concupiscence and grace. It would be a moral contradiction to lead men to faith through the medium of their concupiscence. One may encourage belief by flattering men's self-esteem; but God alone bestows faith, and the apologist cannot arouse in the free-thinker the love of what is truly good without His express assistance. Thus Pascal's aesthetics are based on a theology of faith which we now must attempt to define.

III. *Pascal's Sources and His Originality*

We wish now to take a broader view and to attempt briefly to characterize the philosophic and religious doctrine of the *Pensées*. It is important to compare that doctrine, in this connection, with the great movements of thought of Pascal's time, so as to give their due to those who influenced him and determine his own originality. This is a very delicate task. The intellectual atmosphere of the first half of the seventeenth century is becoming better and better known, but there are very few detailed studies of Pascal's actual sources, religious and profane. Here, however, are the conclusions that seem to emerge from the most recent researches on this topic.

We should ask ourselves first of all how much Pascal knew about these "libertines" or free-thinkers whom he was setting out to oppose. Now the freethinker of whom we catch a glimpse all through the *Apology* and who sometimes even enters into a kind of dialogue with Pascal seems to us somebody who differs rather from the *esprit fort*, the hardy scoffer, who had inherited the naturalistic philosophy of the Renaissance, and also from the Italian freethinker of the time, as Monsieur Pintard, for instance, has described these two figures. No doubt we could establish some textual relationships. Monsieur Jasinski has proved the influence of Gassendi on the fragment on the two infinites. Monsieur Chinard has shown what odd resemblances there are between Pascal and Hobbes. But, without even asking ourselves how important these influences or resemblances may be, let us merely note that Pascal never seems to consider either Hobbes or Gassendi as the adversary he has in mind. Let us look at evidence of another kind: let us seek to discover, for instance, what were the actual objections of the French freethinkers of Pascal's time to the Bible. When we have done so, we shall have to admit that Pascal either chooses to neglect these objections or is imperfectly aware of them.

There are two suppositions which appear to us to have some value. First of all, Pascal's apologetic has never the strictly defensive character of actual treatises of apologetic by professional theologians, anxious above all to refute objections. Pascal is not on the defensive, he *attacks* the unbeliever, and if he has to reply to an objection, he transforms it so immediately into a positive argument that its negative value becomes contemptible. Do unbelievers use the poverty of Christ's life and its lack of outward splendour as an argument against His Divinity? Pascal immediately transforms this objection into the very proof of Christ's Divinity.

But it is probable that, to a very great degree, he was ignorant of what the philosophy of contemporary French freethinking was. He knew unbelief less through books than through experience. And what he saw at close hand, not only during his period in the great world but in his youth and after his conversion, was not so much aggressive irreligion as fashionable indifference to religion. The type of freethinker whom above all he was setting out to convert was the man like Mitton, the disillusioned pessimist who strives to forget himself in "distraction". If the note of the *Pensées* seems to us such a living and personal one, the reason is that the work sprang from Pascal's own inner life.

Moreover, not everything in the thought of this type of freethinker has to be attacked. The philosophers on whose advice he moulds his conduct can, in so far as they have really understood human nature, lead him to the only explanation of man, the Christian religion. Pascal emphasizes the importance of the Stoics, though he judges them even more severely than in the *Entretien Avec Monsieur de Saci*. Against them, he takes up the arms of Montaigne.

Montaigne has his place at the beginning of a healthy apologetic. He represents the first stage in the journey that leads to God. He has really seen the wretchedness of man, he confounds human arrogance. Thus the first chapters of the *Apology* are profoundly influenced by Montaigne. There are innumerable resemblances, in the language as well as the thought. But Montaigne, in fact, had soaked so deeply

into Pascal's mind that we find reminiscences of him throughout the work, even in the expositions of the proofs of the
truth of Christianity. Of all the influences which Pascal
underwent, that of Montaigne is perhaps the only one—
with the exception of that of the Bible—exercised more
through a book than through conversation and experience
of life.

But just how does Pascal use Montaigne, how does he
renew Montaigne's thought? We are forced to confess that
a really scholarly examination of this subject has not yet
appeared.

Pascal certainly made a system out of Montaigne's
thought, that is not to be found in Montaigne himself.
Scattered remarks of Montaigne's are organized by Pascal
round a central idea: innumerable observations on the vanity
of human knowledge illustrate a single great notion, that
of the "deceptiveness of appearances". And often apparent
resemblances between the two writers conceal profound
differences. Pascal adapts Montaigne to his own apologetic
purpose; he infuses the analyses of the great essayist with a
mode of thought which is often foreign to them. Montaigne's
reflections on habit serve to show the dual nature of man. All
man's wanderings in his search for the sovereign good are
attributed to a single principle, self-love or self-esteem, and
this recalls Jansenius rather than Montaigne. Finally, certain resemblances between Pascal and Montaigne are of
language rather than thought. Thus in Pascal's fragment
on imagination, the various passages in the *Essais* that have
inspired it do not even contain the *word* "imagination".
The effects which Pascal attributes to this deceptive power
are attributed by Montaigne to fortune. What Montaigne
placed outside man, Pascal places within him.

But for Pascal it was not enough to adapt Montaigne,
he also had to react against him. Montaigne's serious defect
had been to shut himself up in scepticism (Pascal, like the
seventeenth century generally, saw in Montaigne a complete
sceptic, and used the *Apologie de Raymond Sebon* rather than

the third book of the *Essais*). It was necessary, therefore, for Pascal, to pass beyond Montaigne's philosophy. And Pascal reproaches him vigorously for merely professing a surface faith, for leading a soft, self-indulgent life, terminated by a pagan death, and for not inspiring any questing spirit, any love of God.

Pascal's reservations about Montaigne do not conceal his profound admiration. About Descartes, on the other hand, Pascal always passes very contemptuous judgments. But we should not let ourselves be jockeyed by these judgments into forgetting the abundant resemblances of thought that link these two philosophers.

We shall not bring up again here all Pascal's criticisms of Descartes. The opposition of these two minds has been described often, and described well. "Descartes useless and uncertain", for instance, Pascal notes. What does that imply? Do not let us exaggerate the scope of the judgment. If Descartes is "useless" to Pascal, it is in the same way as geometry is "useless" because it allows itself to be drawn on by a vain "curiosity" instead of seeking out the "one thing needful". If Descartes is "uncertain", it is not that his scientific approach is not valuable but that he attributes to it an absolute value which it does not possess and bases it on a metaphysics uncertain by definition. But Descartes' "method" remains useful to Pascal and his explanation of the world is often the best one.

In fact it is not impossible to find in Pascal a rationalism which has a good deal in common with that of Descartes. When Pascal asserts the necessity of reason's submitting itself to what transcends it, to the mysteries of the faith, he does not differ from the Descartes of the *Meditations*. Moreover he admits that there is a realm with which reason can get to grips and in this realm reason must follow the rules of geometric method, very different from those of scholastic logic, and very close to those of the Cartesian "method". For Pascal, this "method" does not enable us to attain to God directly, but it is through the use of it that the value of the historical proofs of the truth of Christianity can be established.

Pascal borrowed from Descartes not only certain rules of method but also certain important ideas. Thus he often, for instance, at the end of the fragment on the two infinites, asserts the radical distinction between thought and extension. Like Descartes, Pascal considers that man's whole dignity consists in thought and that, at the merely bodily level, a strict automatism reigns; it is this principle of the animal as a machine which explains Pascal's theory of stupefaction—"abêtissement", or literally making oneself like the animals. Finally, it can be shown, as Monsieur Laporte has shown, that Pascal described the concurrence of reason and will in belief in a way that has analogies to Descartes' description.

But two observations should be made here. We ought to distinguish between what Pascal derived directly from Descartes and what he learned in the erudite circles to which he used to accompany his father. From the latter sources he could easily, without the direct influence of Descartes, have learned the rules of geometric method. On the other hand the influence of Descartes is often confused with that of Port-Royal, where Arnauld and Nicole professed a kind of diluted Cartesianism, accepting and attacking the great philosopher at once, just as Pascal does. Port-Royal, in fact—as one sometimes forgets—united to its fierce respect for tradition a love of clear method and a horror of scholasticism that must have made the men of Port-Royal look on Descartes as, in some respects, an ally.

The examination of the non-religious sources of the *Pensées* has thus led us back, in spite of ourselves, to Port-Royal. The study of the religious sources will lead us there quite naturally.

Since the *Pensées* are primarily an apology, we ought to compare Pascal with the other Christian apologists of his time. The work of Abbé Dedieu and Father Chesneau enables us to do so with some accuracy. In his scheme for combating atheism, Pascal, they tell us, had many precursors. Before him, other Christian apologists had attacked Stoicism by insisting on human weakness, sometimes even with the help of Montaigne. Before him, also, other apologists had established against the Pyrrhonists the possibility of attaining at least to some truths. Before him there had been a long development of proofs through prophecies, figurative interpretations of the Old Testament, and miracles. Before him the unbeliever had been asked to bet on the existence of God. What is more, alongside a "rational" apologetic, which claimed to demonstrate the principle dogmas of the faith by reasoned arguments, there had existed an "Augustinian" apologetic which pointed to Christianity as a religion capable of satisfying the higher needs of man, and which insisted on the necessity of submission and humility if the potential convert wished to arrive at a clear understanding of the proofs. This attitude of mind, very marked in Oratorians like Bérulle and Senault, appeared also in the Franciscan Jean Boucher's *Les Triomphes de la Religion Chrétienne*, published in 1628. Pascal was therefore not to any great extent an innovator. But we must remember what a delicate task that of the comparison of passages is. It is possible, with the help of fragments borrowed from fifty works, to put together an *Apology* that has a distant resemblance to Pascal's. But replace each of these passages in its original setting, and it wholly loses the Pascalian tone. What strikes us, rather, when one reads the apologetic treatises of the early seventeenth century is how little, either in method or spirit, they prepare us for the coming of a Pascal. If we were to retrace the history of apologetic, as the history of free-thought has been traced, without any special intention of explaining the *Pensées*, we should arrive at the same conclusions about both apologists and freethinkers; Pascal had little acquaintance with either. The researches of Father Chesneau on Father Yves de Paris show us Pascal's profound originality more clearly, for that matter, than those of the Abbé Dedieu. But we can go even further than these two scholars and say that from the other apologists of his time Pascal borrowed only—and not without reacting sharply against some of their tendencies—frameworks of thought and types of argument. As for Pascal's deeper doctrine, and the method and order of his arguments, as the arrangement of the "copy" permits us to judge of it, the traditional apologetic cannot account for it.

Nevertheless, there are two apologetic treatises of which we can affirm that Pascal made use: the *De Veritate Religionis Christianae* of Grotius and the *Pugio Fidei adversus Mauros et Judaeos* composed in the thirteenth century by the Dominican, Raymond Martini, but not published till 1651. However, what has Pascal borrowed from these two books? Only facts, a documentation. His information about Mahomet came from Grotius. The *Pugio Fidei* served him as a kind of handbook and commentary on Judaism. And how did he know these two books? Through Port-Royal. The *Pugio Fidei* was published by a friend of Arnauld's, Joseph de Voisin. Grotius's work was highly esteemed at Port-Royal; later the Abbé Goujet, a friend of Nicole's, was to make a translation of it.

Thus we cannot accept the thesis of the Abbé Dedieu and Father Chesneau, according to which Pascal, escaping from the Augustinianism of Port-Royal, attached himself to an orthodox Augustinian movement, deriving from Bérulle and culminating in Bossuet. This is an artificial distinction: the so-called "orthodox Augustinianism" and "heterodox Augustinianism" are often as alike as two peas. Do not let us reason about imaginary entities, let us reason about existing texts. Given the general background of Pascal's life, is it not more natural to suppose that Saint-Cyran rather than Bérulle influenced Pascal's thinking. We see no objection to supposing that Pascal's Augustinianism was orthodox, but the most detailed examination of the text does not enable us to maintain that it can be distinguished from that of Port-Royal.

Thus the *Pensées* as a whole are soaked in the spirit of

Port-Royal. But there is an ambiguity here which we must clear up. Would Pascal's *Apology*, when completed, have adopted a polemical tone, would it have developed the attack of *The Provincial Letters* on the Jesuits? This was the thesis of Souriau and Brunschvicg but it has been undermined by the researches of Monsieur Lafuma. No doubt when Pascal speaks of the "carnal" Christians, he has the Jesuits in mind. But the classified portion of the "copy" contains hardly any polemical writing. What is more, the whole discussion of miracles, the only argument in which polemics play an important part, turns out not to have been intended for the *Apology* but for a quite distinct work of which we have already spoken. This fact gives us a better grasp of an idea which Pascal heavily emphasizes; miracles, in the time of Jesus Christ, were necessary for the foundation of the faith; since the coming of Jesus Christ, miracles are only necessary in exceptional cases, since the fulfilment of the prophecies constitutes a "persisting miracle".

Do not let us attribute to Pascal, therefore, the confusion of kinds that would be involved in combining an apologetic address to freethinkers with a polemic directed against the Jesuits. It remains true, of course, that the Christianity to which Pascal intended to convert the freethinker is a Christianity in the spirit of Port-Royal. It is difficult to distinguish here what Pascal owes to Jansenius, to Arnauld, to Nicole, to masters of the spiritual life like Singlin and Barcos, and finally directly to Saint Augustine. Pending more detailed researches, we shall consider, here, the influence of Port-Royal as a whole on Pascal. It would be possible to discover innumerable particular links. We shall confine ourselves, however, here to dealing with three general points: the influence of Port-Royal on Pascal's conception of man, his conception of faith, and his conception of history.

We have already remarked, while describing Montaigne's influence on Pascal, that Pascal infused into Montaigne's analyses of human nature the spirit of Jansenist theology.

In fact, in the first part of the *Apology*, Pascal merely presents the Port-Royalist doctrine of human nature, with this difference, that instead of deducing man's wretchedness from the dogma of the Fall, he states man's wretchedness as a fact of general observation and leads on from it to the dogma of the Fall. The whole thesis of the first part of the *Apology* comes down to this: the man who is given freely over to his own devices is led into error, in his quest for truth as in his quest for the sovereign good, by "concupiscence" and "self-love" or "self-esteem". The only system that can explain human nature, so defined, and the only system which can bestow on man the "sovereign good" he is seeking for, is the Christian religion as taught at Port-Royal, a religion based on the interpretation of two central facts: Adam and Jesus Christ, or the Fall and the Redemption, or human concupiscence and divine Grace.

Pascal's doctrine of faith, as Mademoiselle Russier has recently expounded it, grows out of the same mental climate. Pascal is not connected with fideism, nor with religious subjectivism, nor with the school of the religion of the feelings; he is connected with Port-Royal and, through it, with a long tradition. Faith has reasonable foundations; no doubt reason cannot demonstrate the existence of God nor the other dogmas of religion, but it can demonstrate that it ought to submit to them and in addition the historical events which accompanied the revelation of the Christian faith are a guarantee of the certitude of that revelation. But even if these proofs of the truth of Christianity have a demonstrative value, their obviousness naturally escapes a reason misled by a corrupted will. If we are to perceive the validity of these proofs, our "hearts", the intimate depths of our being, must be infused with good dispositions. Only God can bestow these good dispositions and the "heart" in the long run is merely the point at which God's grace penetrates human nature. Grace is therefore a prior necessity if human reason is to be able to perceive the evidence for the truth of religion. That is the meaning of the formula:

"God felt by the heart." What use, then, is the work of a Christian apologist, like Pascal himself? We always come to the same principle: God works through human instruments. Faith comes entirely from God, and yet we must struggle and strive towards it as if it all depended on man.

But it is perhaps in Pascal's conception of history that his Jansenism appears most clearly, for in his views on history Jansenius seems to have gone further than Saint Augustine. Many theologians conceive of history as totally a movement, a progress. They think of it as a progress towards the Redemption, towards which God, like a schoolmaster with children, gently conducts fallen mankind, adapting Himself to their weakness and only revealing little by little His mysteries and the demands of His Faith. It follows that there is progress even in the very evolution of dogma and of Christian morality. Pascal retains almost nothing of this conception. For him, truth is eternal, immutable; it is whole and entire or it does not exist. The spiritual Jews pierced the veil of the figurative language, rites, and events of the Old Testament; but these "figures", properly interpreted, contain the whole of Christian dogma and morality; the "just" of all ages have known the same mysteries and practised the same law. Thus there is a sense in which history is motionless; man, like truth, is always identical with himself.

Having allowed for all these influences, can we still speak of Pascal's originality? We can, and from many points of view. First of all, in relation to what we have called "the spirit of Port-Royal", we must distinguish between the contributions of various thinkers who combined to shape that spirit. Pascal himself was one of these. If he borrowed ideas from Arnauld and Nicole, Arnauld and Nicole also borrowed ideas from him. But we must admit that there is a sad lack of serious research on this subject.

We shall repeat, therefore, two observations of Mademoiselle Russier's. Pascal was the only thinker who applied the principles of the theology of Port-Royal to an apologetic work. In this application, he is entirely original; and he was even led into presenting a wholly personal interpretation of Judaism and Paganism. Secondly, Pascal pushed the doctrine of Port-Royal to its final consequences; in his conception of the figurative interpretation of the Old Testament, in his conception of history, and also in his denial of the value of rational proofs of the existence of God, he showed himself bolder than any of his friends. We already noted this in relation to the *Ecrits sur la Grâce* and the affair of the formula. We might define Pascal's originality within the Port-Royal setting by saying that he applied the rigour of geometrical reasoning to the principles of Augustinian theology.

There is a last influence which cannot be too much emphasized—and whose importance for Pascal is another of his originalities—namely, the influence of the Bible. That influence is exercised in two ways. First, whatever might be the original source for Pascal of any great idea he always sought to rediscover it in the Bible and to meditate upon it with the aid of the sacred text. The theory of "figures", originally derived from Port-Royal, was thought out afresh by Pascal with the aid of certain texts from the great Old Testament prophets and from the Gospels. In the picture of the wretchedness of man the pessimism of Montaigne and Jansenius reinforces that of Ecclesiastes. To conclude his chapter, "Opinions du Peuple Saines", Pascal recalls the Gospel notion of the supreme wisdom consisting of a return to a childlike state. Secondly, however, the Bible for Pascal was not merely a source of intellectual light; it inflamed his imagination and his sensibility. The patriarchs, the prophets, and above all Jesus Christ were for him living people to whom he was linked in a close bond. The note of the "Mystère de Jesus" is found in many other fragments of the *Apology*. In mentioning this Biblical mysticism, we are in touch with the very depths of Pascal's soul, and his assiduous meditation of Scripture is betrayed even in the very style of the *Pensées*, in which we can often recognize the vocabulary and the movement of the holy sentences.

But the deepest originality of the *Pensées* lies in the powerful personality of their author. It is that personality which organizes ideas that have come from so many various sources, which enters into these ideas more fully, which infuses them with a new spirit, which discovers in them an unexpected scope, and which enriches them with its whole religious experience. It is that personality which we rediscover, also, in the prose style which it has so strongly marked. That style is coloured by a powerful imagination, which transforms every idea into a concrete vision, every demonstration into an analysis of facts, which knows how to emphasize a representative type of man, the judge at the sermon, the king who is bored, and then to rough out a picture of the whole human comedy: a masquerade of judges and doctors in their strange robes and caps, the feverish bustle of a humanity that tries to forget itself in distractions. Pascal's style is that both of a scientist and a mystic; a style whose perfection, especially in its rhythmic movement and its control of sound, derives from a faultless technique, but a style nevertheless perpetually animated by passion, violent or restrained, and one that gives expression to the slightest motion of an exceptionally sensitive soul.

CONCLUSION

THIS patient examination has, I hope, enabled us to follow Pascal through the actions of his life in detail, and to appreciate the intrinsic originality of each of his works; so that we are now in a position to take a general view of his genius. At the same time, we shall try to show, in relation to a number of important problems, just what were his influence on, and his reputation among, the generations that succeeded him. These two tasks, in any case, are complementary to each other; for if we want to define the exact importance of any writer's work we must do so by considering the various interpretations that have been given of it and reactions it has excited.

I. *The Man*

"Pascal, not the writer, but the man": with this phrase the Swiss moral philosopher, Vinet, drawing his inspiration from one of the most famous of the *Pensées*, headed one of the chapters of his *Etudes sur Pascal*. It is, indeed, one of the most notable facts about Pascal's astonishing personality that, however great his genius as a mere writer may appear to us to be, it is Pascal the man, in the end, whom we really wish to grasp; even more than Pascal's thought, it is the soul of Pascal that criticism seeks to revive for us. Let us, in our turn, seek to lay bare his secret.

Though there have been numerous reactions against the romantic critics, modern criticism is on the whole still obsessed with their picture of Pascal as himself a romantic, first brilliantly sketched by Chateaubriand, more methodically worked out by Victor Cousin, and finished off in several different styles by the various Pascal enthusiasts of the last century. This romantic picture is that of a man tending in all directions towards excess; using up his strength in the pursuit of science, flinging himself madly into the fashionable world, and then suddenly won over by a kind of fanaticism and wasting himself away in austerities. Full of anguish when confronted with the silence of the world and the mystery of God's grace, this romantic Pascal is thought of as having been assailed by doubt and having rescued himself from misery by rushing headlong into belief. Finally, this romantic Pascal is thought of as above all a sick man, a "sublime madman", in the phrase of Voltaire which Chateaubriand repeated; as a man owing his genius to his excessively neurotic temperament, to the hallucinatory vividness of his imagination; as a man writing in pain and fever.

Such a picture of Pascal bears too obviously the marks of the age which conceived it to remain a really authoritative one. A biographical study, like our own, which aims at precision is obliged to tone down these glaring colourings and to depict the inner life of Pascal and its development with a more delicate balance of light and shade. What critics have taken as Pascal's personal anguish is, after all, only the anguish of humanity deprived of God, as it is described at the outset of the *Apology*. The famous cry, "The everlasting silence of these infinite spaces frightens me," ought to be placed, as Tourneur has shown, in the mouth of the unbeliever whose plight Pascal is considering; or even if it was a cry from Pascal's own heart, it could only be considered as expressing a transitional moment in a process of thought soon to conclude in triumphant certainty. In a word, it is futile to seek to explain Pascal by his illness. Nobody, in fact, has been able to say exactly what the nature of this illness was. In a recent work, Dr. Onfray diagnoses it as ophthalmic migraine; an attractive hypothesis, and valid up to a point, but one which does not appear to us to take account of the whole range of documented facts about the illness. While we are still waiting for really decisive medical researches on Pascal, let us confine ourselves to asking a single question: what is it, in Pascal's life and his work, that betrays the sick man? It must be admitted that, in their answers to this question, critics have been rather lax in their notions of what constitutes evidence and also rather simple-minded. How many facts have been attributed to Pascal's illness for which there is a much simpler explanation if one consults the relevant documents or even places oneself in the climate of Pascal's age! Here is an example: Pascal's handwriting, which is, we are told, "shaken by fever". Let us compare it, however, with other typical handwritings of the time. It is a thin, regular handwriting, very similar to other seventeenth-century cursive scripts, much more legible than that of many Parliamentary records and many legal documents. Is it generally known that Pascal's will, written by the hand of his attorney, Guineau, is much harder to decipher than the manuscript of the *Pensées*? Finally, we ought once more to make a close study of contemporary descriptions of Pascal's illness, notably those of Boulliau. It is obvious from these that physical suffering, far from producing a sort of nervous exaltation in Pascal, crushed and overwhelmed him and made him incapable of any sort of work—and less capable, if possible, of intellectual work than of any other kind. Such descriptions appear to us to have a symbolic value: Pascal's life and work were, in fact, the fruit of a constant victorious struggle *against* his illness. Pascal's genius is not to be explained by his illness; on the contrary it was able to expand and achieve itself *in spite* of his illness.

It is starting, therefore, from other premises that we shall sketch out the broad lines of our portrait of this extraordinarily striking figure.

Incontestably, Pascal was in the first place a *violent* man. This violence, however, was not that of a neurotic, but the violence proper to that tough and vigorous generation of the first half of the seventeenth century in France; his was the violence which one also discovers in his father and in Jacqueline—in this, truly the female counterpart of her brother—in the Arnaulds, and in the men of the Fronde. Basically, this violence is an ardent zest for life. We are wrong to think of Pascal as always shut up within the four walls of a study, a literary drawing-room, a cell. He was a traveller; he travelled from Clermont to Paris and from Paris to Rouen more often than has been generally noticed; we find him at Poitiers and at Fontenay-le-Comte, taking the waters at Bourbon, certainly also at Dieppe and possibly at Lyons, visiting his friend Desargues. He had the temperament of a man of action, a love for grandiose undertakings; he carried out spectacular experiments, tried to exploit his calculating machine commercially, had a share in the project for draining the Poitou marshes, formed a project of his own for the education of a prince, established in Paris a carriage service at a fare of five sols. This ardent zest for life, moreover, was often transformed in Pascal into a dominating pride. Conscious of his own supreme genius, Pascal as a scientist could brook no contradiction and showed himself merciless to such adversaries as Father Noël or Father Lalouère. Pascal the convert was never able, moreover, wholly to root out and destroy this natural arrogance; in a moment of anger he could terrify Singlin, whose inadequacies on the intellectual plane could not escape him; he humiliated Arnauld and Nicole when he made it clear that he thought their conduct pusillanimous. This need to dominate over other souls, though much purified by Pascal's conversion, explains, no doubt, his violence and impetuosity as a religious apologist. But this violence and impetuosity can also be considered as a kind of passion. There is, in Pascal, a passion for truth in all its shapes; this is seen as clearly, in spite of the reservations we have occasionally thought fit to make, in Pascal's investigations into the nature of a vacuum as in his controversies about the formula. Even more, there is in Pascal a passion for the infinite; thanks to that, transcending the rather elementary common sense with which average minds content themselves, he was able to pave the way for the discovery of the infinitesimal calculus, to denounce the vanity of every kind of merely human social organization, and to define one of the highest forms of the religious ideal.

This fundamental violence was linked, however, in Pascal's nature to a profound *sensibility*. This sensibility, however, found hardly any satisfaction in the outer natural world. Intellectually, Pascal was able to appreciate the picturesque aspects of nature, but he got no profound enjoyment out of them. The social sentiments were far more deeply rooted in him. We know the tenderness of his feelings for his family, a tenderness sometimes a little exclusive and self-centred, which led to his at first opposing Jacqueline's entry into Port-Royal; but a tenderness all the more moving because the seventeenth century offers us hardly any other famous examples of such united families. Pascal's tender feelings towards friends were hardly less strong. Gilberte Périer bears witness to this, and it is proved also by the attachment which Pascal always showed towards the Duc de Roannez and his sister; we should be in a better position to appreciate this tenderness if the greater part of Pascal's correspondence were not lost.

But a sensibility so profound could only, in the end, be satisfied by an infinite object: it could reach its real flowering only in the attitude of the mystic. Nature, which in itself did not touch Pascal's feelings, nevertheless nourished this mysticism of his to the degree in which it is itself only a "forest of symbols", a *figurative* representation of the Infinite that has created it. "Invisible things" are represented in "the visible". God hides himself under the veil of sensible appearances. But the chief source of Pascal's profounder emotions lay in the sense of communication with God, with the living God of the Bible. The *Mémorial* is an impulse of love reaching out towards the God of Abraham, of Isaac and of Jacob; in *The Mystery of Jesus* the note of exaltation becomes so deep that the crucified Christ is caught up in a dialogue with the penitent human soul.

It is from this unique and individual sensibility that all

the sublimity of the Pascalian sense of disquiet arises. It is the expression, by a man of genius, of a more general Christian disquiet. There is a sense of disquiet about one's own salvation: who can be certain of persevering in the ways of grace, and who does not feel in himself the fountain-head of these evil desires that cause divine grace to be lost? Ought Pascal not to be all the more fearful, in that he had already fallen? However, on this point, he remained strongly confident. What troubled him much more was disquiet about the salvation of others; when he put himself, in fancy, in the place of the unbeliever, Pascal felt a kind of shudder; the moment when he appreciated the position of the un-believer from his own believer's point of view was also the moment in which a sense of the tragedy of human fate gripped him with a kind of anguish. Here and there this disquiet already lends feeling to *The Provincial Letters*; and it is what gives the *Pensées* their gripping note.

But Pascal would not be a true contemporary of Corneille, of the author of *Cinna* and *Polyeucte*, if this inner violence and this profound sensibility of his were not linked to a great *self-mastery*. This violent man is not a man who acts on his instincts; this "man of feeling" reflects on his emotions. Pascal's natural impetuosity very rarely carries him beyond the boundaries which it has fixed for itself; at the moment of the most intense ecstasy, the lucidity of reason does not lose its rights. Pascal dominates both his own life and his own work through the strength of his will and the clarity of his intelligence.

It would not be surprising if such a man, in his youth, had been strongly influenced by Stoicism: when Jacqueline in her *Stances contre l'Amour* exalts the power of reason over the passions, it is very probable that she is expressing an ideal she shared with her brother. In the *salons*, those who preached the ideal of the *honnête homme* tended to intellectualize the emotions and demanded from their disciples first submission to others, and then self-control and self-transcendence. After his second conversion, Pascal sought to check and tame a sensibility which he knew to be sometimes excessive and an inner violence which kept him at a distance from Christian humility. If he did succeed in the end in becoming "as simple as a child", it was at the price of patient effort and not without numerous fallings by the way. It was the strength of his will that enabled him to attain the state in which he had, as it were, stripped himself of worldliness.

This self-mastery is to be found also in Pascal's literary work, which is wholly and in every part governed by his intelligence. In this connection, the unfinished state of the *Pensées* ought not to deceive us. There can be no longer any question of considering these as a "shapeless heap of materials". The *Pensées* were methodically prepared, and even methodically grouped, by a genius who had a complete mastery of his own gifts and was extremely conscious of the effects he sought to obtain. Pascal was never tempted to equate sincerity with spontaneity or art with self-abandonment to instinct. If he hastens towards truth with a sort of violent passion, he nevertheless conducts his investigations into what may be truth with an extremely acute critical spirit and shows himself as strict as can be in his weighing of evidence. If his thinking aspires towards an infinite God, it remains none the less the thinking of a man who is a scientist as well as a mystic, and it also tends to express itself in an artistically perfect form. The completed *Pensées* would have had all the finish of *The Provincial Letters*; the violence of the feeling would have been wedded to a subtle elaboration of form.

From Pascal's whole personality there emanates a kind of imperious attraction. He attracted by imposing himself. We know what an ascendancy he gained over the Duc de Roannez, how this great nobleman made himself Pascal's humble disciple and retained all his life a touching fidelity to his master. We know also, through many witnesses, how Pascal's spoken words remained, as it were, engraved in the memories of those who heard him. Having moved his contemporaries so strongly, he could not fail to exercise a strong fascination over posterity.

II. *The Thinker*

But Pascal does not attract us only by the vigour of his personality; he possesses in addition the prestige which properly belongs to every powerful and original thinker. Not that he was, strictly speaking, a philosopher; he did not organize his notions into a complete and coherent system. But his work carries a "message", if one understands by that certain great ideas which Pascal grasped profoundly and to which he gave a lasting life; exciting enthusiasm on the one hand, and arousing violent opposition on the other.

One primary aspect of this message can be defined as *the primacy of experience and the experimental method.* This is already, in his purely scientific work, one of the chief lessons he has to teach us. "Experiments are the only basis of physical science." In opposition to Descartes, for whom physical science rests on mathematical deductions from purely rational principles, and for whom experiments merely confirm these deductions, Pascal claims that the explanation of phenomena must rest on experiments only, and not on any system of thought that may claim priority to experience; we must not assert anything more than our experiments allow us to. In all this, Pascal made a much more important contribution than Descartes to the separation of physics from metaphysics and towards laying the foundations of modern science.

The habit of mind of Pascal, the man of science, can also be discovered in Pascal, the theologian. Just as he disallows purely deductive reasoning in physics, so he disallows it in theology. The theologian confines himself to acquiring knowledge of *the facts* contained in Revelation and Tradition. Experience is the basis of human science, revelation of divine science; in both cases, reason, as such, has a limited part to play. Revelation and experience thus, taken to-

gether, define two classes of facts which are totally independent of each other and between which, therefore, no
contradiction is possible. Nothing which is accessible to
experience has been revealed: that is the basis of the attitude
of Pascal and his friends on "the question of fact". But
the theologian may have to take simultaneous cognizance
of these two classes of facts, experiential and revealed.
Thus no theologian's theory of the nature of the moral
act may contradict psychological realities; every system
of casuistry must be based at once on a scrupulous fidelity
to Tradition and on an exact knowledge of human nature.
Pascal reproaches the Jesuits not only with forgetting the
lessons of the Christian Fathers, but also with being ignorant
of man's real nature.

In a word, Pascal's religious apologetic is based on the
principle: God is accessible to us through facts and not
through reasonings. This does not mean that Pascal denies
any value at all to human reason; he merely takes note of
the fact that, in the world as we find it, it is not reasonings
that convince men; if the reign of true justice should commence on earth, men would still oppose that justice; and
though the argument from the orderliness of the universe
may really prove the existence of a God, it does so in vain,
since men do not believe any more firmly in God because
of that proof. The facts of the case, on the other hand, are
of a nature to constrain any mind that is not made blind by
concupiscence. Thus the whole dialectic of the *Apology*
rests on two facts: the fact of man and the fact of history.
What is it that experience reveals to us about man? It is
essentially his dual nature, his wretchedness and his greatness. Only one system can explain this fact of man's dual
nature, and that system is Christianity. What does the
examination of history reveal to us? The fulfilment of
Biblical prophecies, the perpetuity of a religion opposed to
the passions of man, and therefore the presence of a miracle,
of the divine, in the world. And this note of the divine is
attached to the Christian religion alone, under its two

forms, which an analysis of the documents shows to be identical with each other: the Jewish form, and the strictly Christian form. In all this argument of Pascal's there has been no place anywhere for abstract deduction.

But if we pass from the methodological realm of discourse to that of philosophy, the primacy of experience can be equated with the primacy of *existence*. As has often been noticed, Pascal is in effect a precursor of contemporary existentialism. Like the existentialists, he takes his stance in concrete living, he strives to consider the situation of man with fresh eyes, to get back to the primitive feeling of existence: and in fact he manages to make us feel astonished that we *do* exist. We discover in the *Pensées* one of the most cherished topics of existentialism: the absurdity of the human condition, expressed by Pascal in terms like "contrariness" or "disproportion"; the anguish that results from this absurdity; even M. Sartre's "nausea" to which Pascal's "weariness" (*ennui*), taken in the strong, seventeenth-century sense, corresponds; we discover also the necessity of choice, of commitment, of "the wager". Pascal's Christianity can also be called an existential Christianity. It is through reflecting on his own existence that man discovers the necessity of God, who is alone capable of filling the emptiness which man feels in himself: a living, incarnate God, who lives in each of us, members of His Mystical Body. Nevertheless, Pascal's existentialism is a very original existentialism. It widely transcends the limits of modern types of existentialism, even if only through its concern for the universal.

The existentialist attitude is nearly always combined with a profound pessimism, as the themes touched on above have already made clear. In fact, a second aspect of Pascal's message may be expressed in the words: *the wretchedness of man without God*. Among all his writings, it may be that the pages devoted to the description of this wretchedness have awakened the profoundest echo.

But in the *Pensées* this idea is brought forward in a very original and precise shape. The essence of man's wretchedness lies in his *powerlessness*. And man's wretchedness, also is caused by his greatness. Man resembles the animals, and these are not wretched; but he finds himself in a far loftier station than they and the vague memory which he retains of his first state makes his present condition unbearable to him. The wretchedness of man comes from the contradiction between the reality of what he is and the ideal to which he aspires. He aspires to truth and finds only error; he aspires towards real justice and finds only false justice; he aspires towards the infinite and finds only the finite. Man is therefore a divided being; his life is a perpetual drama.

Pascal is, however, at the opposite pole to Kierkegaard in that he never gives the impression that man is necessarily crushed under the weight of his destiny, necessarily condemned to a perpetual painful anxiety. His description of man's wretchedness is an invitation to man to transcend himself, to discover that infinite towards which he aspires. Thus even the most pessimistic pages at the outset of the *Apology* contain an appeal to the heroic element in human nature, an appeal to man to turn towards God. Man's wretchedness is merely the wretchedness of man "without God". Everything evil comes from man, everything good from God; to be delivered from his wretchedness, man must renounce himself.

Pascal's dramatic vision of humanity awakens a deep echo in all unsatisfied souls, particularly in "times of troubles", when man becomes tragically aware of his own destiny. But it is also this part of his argument that arouses the most lively opposition. There are two groups of thinkers who react against the harshness, the naked heroism, of his portrait of human nature; on the one hand, those who uphold a kind of optimistic rationalism; and on the other, the partisans of "the pursuit of happiness", and, in general, those who assign to man no other end, or aim, than himself.

The best representative of the first group, the upholders

of an optimistic rationalism, is obviously Voltaire. His famous "observations" on Pascal, contained in the twenty-fifth of his *Lettres Philosophiques*, are familiar to most readers, at least in France. To Pascal's assertion that man is wretched, Voltaire opposes the assertion that human happiness is a reality; and he appears to himself to be stating a plain fact. Our impulses, according to Voltaire, are in themselves good; nothing, for instance, is healthier than that human self-esteem, or self-love, which Pascal hated. Rational self-love is the foundation of social life, of, indeed, every form of human activity; it alone really makes us exist. There is nothing, again, for Voltaire, disquieting about human destiny; our destiny is marked out for us by our place in the great chain of being, a little above the animals, a little below pure spirits like the angels. There is nothing that we need worry and torment ourselves about in the riddle of the universe; why not simply trust ourselves to a bene-volent Providence? Voltaire's optimistic rationalism issues, therefore, in a kind of exaggerated Molinism. These critic-isms have been repeated, since Voltaire's time, in a hundred different styles; some of them have been brilliantly restated in our own day by the early Aldous Huxley.

In our second group, that of the humanist opponents of Pascal, we include those thinkers who are less concerned to attack Pascal's picture of the wretchedness of man than to refute the moral he draws from it. They substitute for Pascal's ideal of human self-transcendence a new ideal of human completeness or fulfilment. Life for them is like the elaboration of a work of art, which must draw as near as it can to perfection, but to a perfection that will always remain finite. This is the common note of Nietzsche who, putting forward the ideal of the superman, comes sharply up against Pascal, whose sheer power nevertheless overawes him, and of Gide, who refuses to "work out his salvation with fear and trembling", and who, without failing to recognize the element of illusion in it, nevertheless re-habilitates the notion of "diversion", of amusement or distraction, in its forms of sport or art. These, in spite of everything, do enable man to fulfil himself.

These are the two principal lines of opposition to Pascal. There is no place here for a discussion of the validity of these criticisms. Let us repeat, merely, an observation that has often been made before; in the end, the thinker who really raises man up to the highest level, who sets before him the highest aim, is the very thinker who insists most strongly on man's "lowly" and "wretched" condition; the thinker who shows the greatest humanity, the greatest understanding of man, in that he refuses to betray, by denying, man's secret suffering, is the very thinker who demands that man should die to himself.

While the adversaries of Pascal have always concentrated on the problem of man's wretchedness, it is Pascal's strictly religious message which has gained him his warmest adherents. If the reading of the *Pensées* occasionally leads to religious conversions, it is less because it disquiets the soul than because it offers to the religious need and impulse in man the highest conceivable ideal. For the third aspect of Pascal's message is: "There is no religion without love". Without love, which is to say, without charity or love of God. In that are summed up "all the law and the Prophets".

The principle of the love of God plays an essential part in Pascal's apologetic. True religion can consist only of the love of God. "If there is a single principle underlying everything, a single end set for everything, then everything exists through that principle and everything exists for the sake of it. It is therefore necessary that true religion should teach us to adore nothing but this principle, to love only it." Every religion which does not put the love of God in the first place is false, since it is incapable of satisfying that need for the infinite which our intellect and our emotions both experience: love, in fact, is precisely this human gift or capacity for the infinite. That is why, for instance, the religion of Mahomet appears to Pascal "absurd". But, somewhere between the true religions and the false ones, there exists, problematically, the religion of the Jews. Can we halt, in our religious development, at the letter of the Law and of the ceremonies of the Old Testament? One cannot, in fact, say about these that they had charity as their sole aim; and therefore the religion of the Jews would be, according to Pascal's criterion, a false one. But an exact interpretation of the Biblical texts enables Pascal to reach this conclusion: "Everything (in the Bible) that does not make for charity is figurative." All the precepts of the Mosaic Law are only various expressions of the central precept of charity. "The one end at which Holy Scripture aims is charity." In its basis, therefore, the Jewish religion is true; it is identical with the Christian religion.

But let us leave the plane of apologetic for that of the moral life. How can we define in terms of psychology the presence of the love of God in a soul? As we have already said, the love of God for Pascal is primarily and essentially a good direction of the will: a faithfulness in man to the call which he has heard leading him towards something higher than himself, his response to his "vocation".

Thus it is love which conducts the infidel towards faith. It is love which leads us to undertake that quest for the truly Good which is nothing other than the quest for God Himself. Whoever feels his own wretchedness and has a deeply-rooted desire to cure it; whoever feels that he cannot find any real consolation in created things; such a man in the end will find his "Liberator". It is not the evidence for the truth of Christianity that by itself convinces the unbeliever; the love of God must clarify his reasoning faculty before he will be able to perceive the truth of the evidence.

In the same way, with the believer, it is only love that gives religious practice life. That is the real lesson of *The Provincial Letters*. It was by no means Pascal's intention merely to substitute an austere religious formalism for the lax religious formalism of the Jesuits; he repudiates formalism in all its shapes. Nothing is really at a more opposite

B.^{se} PASCAL.

Dessiné et Gravé par Aug. St Aubin d'après la Statue en Marbre faite par Pajou

pole than Jansenism to that middle-class Puritanism of seventeenth-century Protestant countries with which historians too often tend to confuse it. For Jansenism, the sacraments, if they are really going to be the instruments of grace, must be received with a purified heart; for absolution to be valid, the penitent must manifest a sincere goodwill in relation to his future conduct. In order to act morally, we must be ready to respond to the stirrings of a conscience which we have taken care to orientate towards the quest for truth, and to make more scrupulous by the practice of putting ourselves under spiritual direction. This is the lesson which Pascal repeats at the end of his *Apology*, in the chapter called "Christian Morals", where he allots their respective shares to external practice and the inner life in the conduct of the Christian. The leading image in this chapter is that of the Mystical Body. The limbs, the members, live only through the body as a whole; man lives only through God. If I wish to attain to the true life of the spirit, "I must love only God and hate only myself."

Though Pascal puts this ideal forward to all men, it is an ideal which is likely to be realized only by an *élite*. This fact does not diminish the sympathy which many Protestants feel for Pascal, but it does worry some Roman Catholics. It worries them because it tends to lessen the importance of external rites and ceremonies, because it bases religion on a personal link between man and God, and because it demands of the believer that he should seek to be perfect. Thus Pascal has aroused a certain mistrust, which has been formulated now more, and now less, clearly, among those who prefer, to a reflective Christianity, or a Christianity of the inner man, the faith of the simple, a popular piety, even if that has to be mingled with a certain amount of superstition. It has excited distrust also among those who think of the Church as a kind of sacred army, regulated, like an army, by the law of unquestioning obedience; and finally by those who fear that, by demanding too much, Pascal will discourage the weaker brethren. With these

O

reservations, we have to admit that Roman Catholic opinion in general has always considered Pascal as one of the masters of the spiritual life and has always considered his apologetic as a model.

III. *The Artist*

However many opponents the thought of Pascal may have encountered, his art as a writer has been universally admired. However, this powerful and subtle art of his does not lend itself easily to analysis; it is extremely spontaneous and yet it has been carefully thought out; it is the art of a man who possessed in the highest degree the two essential gifts of a writer, richness of invention and sureness of taste. These two qualities are united in Pascal, balancing each other in a way that is extremely rare in literary history. He is always the master of his inspiration even when it surges forth most strongly; the innumerable corrections in the manuscript of the *Pensées* never destroy the freshness of the original vision. Thus, if the literary art of Pascal is based on a few grand and general aesthetic principles, it none the less expresses also the man himself in the very essence of his soul.

Certain theoretical writings help us to grasp some aspects of the ideal which Pascal, as a typical man of good taste of his century, had accepted for himself. We have already shown, in analysing *L'Art de Persuader*, what is the philosophical foundation of what has been called Pascal's "rhetoric". Some of the *Pensées* define the practical consequences of these rhetorical theories. Two ideas are outlined with particular sharpness and clarity: that of "order", as an element of good style, and that of "naturalness".

In arranging his papers with his *Apology* in mind, Pascal had formed a first chapter called "Order", in which he grouped together all his reflections about the disposition of the material in his intended work. But, in repeating the word "order" so often, Pascal had not in any sense in mind the trite idea that a work of literature ought to be clearly and solidly composed. On the contrary, he thought the rigorous divisions of topics which he discovered in scholastic treatises artificial and therefore to be condemned. Order for him was not an abstraction, not something independent of the idea to be expressed. A thought, for Pascal, could not receive a faithful expression, nor attain the purpose which the writer had in mind in expressing it, unless a certain "order" had been imposed on it. "The same words differently arranged convey different meanings, and the same meanings differently arranged have different effects on the reader." In the same way, a chapter, or a work taken as a whole, ought to develop itself in an orderly fashion, in harmony with the subject treated, or the leading idea to be emphasized. Thus, wishing to speak of Pyrrhonism, Pascal warns his reader: "I shall put down my thoughts here without any order, and yet perhaps not in mere purposeless confusion; this is the proper order, which, by its very disorder, indicates my theme." Apparent disorder is also a kind of order; in this sense disorder can be not only a source of beauty, as Boileau had already seen, but also of truth. It is therefore in the search for a proper order that a thinker's labours achieve their purpose; it is in its order that the real originality of a work of literature lies. "Let nobody say that I have said nothing new. The arrangement of the material is new."

Thus "order" in writing, though primarily intended to convey the author's idea faithfully, in the end also expresses his personality. And to find the right order for what one has to say is to achieve "naturalness". Here we have the formulation of Pascal's grand aesthetic principle. All useless ornaments ought to be lopped away; the writer must eschew "false beauties", "mock windows put in for the sake of symmetry". He must also eschew everything that smacks of specialization. "We must be able to say of a writer neither that he is a mathematician, nor a preacher, nor an able orator, but that he is an honest man. Only that universal quality pleases me." Finally "the author" must give way to "the man". No doubt he must seek to please, but it is only naturalness that really pleases. "We need both what is pleasant and what is solid, but what is pleasant must be itself based on truth." Pointed sentences and brilliant antitheses excite only an artificial and transitory pleasure. On the contrary, the writer who paints the passions in their natural colours makes his readers recognize, in their own inner selves, the truth of his observations; he pleases in the real sense of the phrase, he makes himself loved. All these ideas, partly inspired perhaps by the Chevalier de Méré, show that Pascal belonged completely to the seventeenth-century French classical tradition.

In his actual writing, moreover, Pascal was able to put his theories of composition magnificently into practice. If there is order and naturalness in everything he writes, the reason is that in his writing he is always profoundly himself. In Pascal's literary art, we find Pascal the man completely expressed; the temperament of a scientist blended with that of a poet.

The scientific habit of Pascal's mind can be traced in his eagerness to define his terms strictly, an eagerness which we see demonstrated at the beginning of the fourth "Provincial Letter", or in the mathematical precision of some of his formulas. We shall attempt to draw attention, especially, to the influence of this scientific habit of mind on Pascal's methods of composition. The method of the physicist explains the development of a fragment, like that in the *Pensées* on the subject of "diversion", of amusement or distraction. Pascal begins by noting facts, which, taken together, permit him to assert that men suffer from a kind of restlessness which is not linked to any coherent sense of need or purpose. Then he postulates a hypothesis to explain this restlessness; man is seeking to forget his wretched condition. The hypothesis is then demonstrated in an extreme and crucial case; that of a king, who, though the most favoured of mortals, must nevertheless seek distraction like other men to avoid unhappiness. Finally, the demonstration of this hypothesis is followed by a return to the facts which Pascal started with. But a new light has been shed on these; every kind of human activity can be explained by the great principle of man's need for distraction. A similar movement of thought can often be discovered in Montaigne, but it lacks in him this scientific character. The same method appears in other fragments of the *Pensées*, like that on imagination. Other passages make us think less of the experimental method of natural science than of that of pure mathematics. In the fragment on the two kinds of infinity, we see the universe working outwards or inwards in concentric circles; it is the geometrical method which is our model. Elsewhere, we have indicated the sources in geometry of Pascal's idea of the three orders of greatness. The presentation of the idea, however, has its model in an arithmethical symbolism, the sum in proportion: as flesh is to spirit, so is spirit to charity. The whole development of the thought consists in the postulation of the equality of these relations in eight different fashions. (The problem is made more complex, of course, by the fact that these relations, unlike those in a sum in proportion, are relationships between infinite values.) We can see that Pascal's thought has a natural tendency to shape itself in a scientific mould.

It might be feared that methods of exposition borrowed from the sciences would entail a certain dryness. But as the fragment on the three orders wonderfully proves, the method has an opposite result. Pascal's prose acquires through his scientific approach a purity and nakedness of line which brings out the whole substance of his thought and feeling. The strictness of the approach assists, rather than hinders, the lyrical impetus.

In fact Pascal was primarily a poet, He was a poet above all through his gift for creating images. But these images, in his case, are never used merely to adorn an abstract idea, or even to make it clearer by a concrete example; the image in Pascal, is of one flesh with the idea, it is summoned by the idea. It is the warmth of the argument that gives birth to the vision; it is the emotion excited by the idea that begets the image. In his genius for the powerful and original metaphor, Pascal is closely related to the great French romantics.

What is the nature of these images? Some of them reveal a gift of penetrating observation, an observation turned on outward nature, on the pictorial aspects of the world, as much as on the moral attitudes of men. In his descriptions of the "human comedy", Pascal's minute realism sometimes even verges on triviality—though not to the extent which certain blundering editors of the romantic period might make us believe, who read "trognes d'armées" (high-coloured faces of armies, flushed as if with drink) where Pascal had merely written "troupes d'armées" and "foisons de religions" (heaps of religions) where he had merely written "faiseurs de religions". But there *are* descriptions like those of the magistrates with "their red robes, their ermines, in which they swaddle themselves like cats in their fur"; or there is the spectacle of the dance, one of the best means man has of forgetting his condition: "You have to think carefully where you put your feet." More often, however, external reality is transcended. Pascal's imagination is superior even to his gift of observation, and starting with some concrete detail we reach up towards an infinity which is, as it were, made palpable to us: the "atomic tininess" which we reach in dissecting as thoroughly as we can the body of an alimentary parasite suddenly expands into an "infinity of universes".

How are these images fitted into the general pattern of the development of Pascal's thought? Usually, the metaphor is rapidly sketched in. Pascal asks himself whether our reason is abused by our imagination. "Ridiculous reason that the wind shifts, and shifts in every direction!" The spectacle of the search for distraction extorts from him the cry: "How hollow the heart of man is, and how full of filth!" Sometimes the metaphor is expressed through a violent foreshortening and thus becomes all the more striking. Compared to the infinity of celestial space this familiar universe of ours is only "a prison cell". Finally, in certain images which he has allowed himself to develop with more elaboration, Pascal touches the height of his powers: "We drift on a vast scene, always uncertain and floating, thrust from one goal towards another. If there is some boundary to which we think we can hold on and there assert ourselves, it shakes us off and leaves us and, if we follow it, it escapes our grasp, glides away from us and flees with an eternal flight."

Pascal is a poet, also, through his acute sense of rhythm. If we read the sentence just quoted, in French, we find ourselves in the presence of what is really a strophe, beginning with two octosyllables, "Nous voguons sur un milieu vaste, toujours incertains et flottants", and the various climaxes of this fantastic voyage, as Tourneur has remarked, are evoked by "the balance of the sentence, its jolts, its prolonged development, its cadences and the sounds of the individual words". There are very many passages of the *Pensées* and also of *The Provincial Letters* which, if arranged on the page in "free verse" form, would at once reveal their cunning management of sound and rhythm. The French alexandrine itself is often "in ambush" in this poetic prose. Here is an example, a line of piercing harmony, which concludes a discussion of reality and dreams: *Car la vie est un songe un peu moins inconstant.* (This also comes naturally over into an English heroic line: *Life is a slightly less inconstant dream.*) Pascal, therefore, is a poet not only through his visionary power but because he makes use of the poet's actual techniques.

But Pascal is a poet, above all, through the emotional power which animates his sentences. The *Pensées* are one huge poem in the lyrical mode. We can distinguish in them two different kinds of lyricism, differing according to the nature of the underlying emotion. In the first part of the

Apology, we have the lyricism of man's wretchedness. By a kind of act of poetic substitution, Pascal identifies himself with that humanity deprived of God, whose distress he lives through. Elsewhere, there is a *mystical* lyricism, nourished by an ardent love for the person of Christ, humble and poor throughout His life, in the end pouring out His Blood on the Cross for the salvation of sinners. Pascal reaches his emotional heights when he most completely strips himself.

Thus Pascal is very profoundly a literary artist in the classical tradition: classical in the theoretical principles of his art, classical in his concern for perfection of form, classical in that he considers reflection inseparable from the creative task. But through the sheer power of his genius he so infinitely transcends all the groups and schools of his time that the romantics, later, were able to claim him as one of themselves.

One lesson, we believe, emerges from this study: that there is a profound unity between Pascal's life and his work. All critical efforts to divide Pascal from himself have ended in failure. We cannot radically oppose the scientist to the man of the world, or the scientist or the man of the world to the Christian; Pascal, was always, in various fashions, a scientist, a man of the world, *and* a Christian. It is futile to try to set the doctrine of *The Provincial Letters* against that of the *Pensées,* or to try to set the dying Pascal against the living Pascal. The foregoing examination of Pascal's life and writings has shown, on the contrary, that the same doctrines, the same topics, the same habits of mind are found throughout his works and link them together. Pascal's art cannot be explained without considering his science, nor his efforts as a Christian apologist without considering his polemics and his theology. In the unity of his personality and his work, Pascal, like Corneille, expresses in a very original fashion the trends and the aspirations of the age, in France, of Louis XIII and the minority of Louis XIV. He expresses the spirit of that ardent and sturdy generation,

CONCLUSION

proud and independent, setting out like explorers towards the discovery of the physical and moral worlds; a generation with a passion for concrete reality and yet an idealistic generation, men who disciplined their natural impetuosity by accepting the authority of reason, who were eager for distinction and in love with fine manners, but eager also for, and in love with, heroism and sanctity.

SUMMARY BIBLIOGRAPHY

ONE of the difficulties that faces the student of Pascal is the huge literature of the subject. Happily there is a good guide:

> A. MAIRE, *Bibliographie générale des oeuvres de Blaise Pascal*, Paris, 1925–7. Five volumes.

This work can be supplemented up to 1935 by:

> J. GIRAUD, *Manuel de Bibliographie littéraire pour les XVIe, XVIIe, et XVIIIe siècles français*, pp. 148–161, Paris.

We shall here give a list of the most useful works up to 1935 and a few notable studies of more recent date. (In principle, we are leaving out articles in scholarly journals and literary reviews.)

I. *The Period*

(A) For a general view:

> G. MONGREDIEN, *La vie littéraire au XVIIe siècle*, Paris, 1947.
>
> A. ADAM, *Histoire de la littérature française au XVIIe siècle, L'époque de Henri IV et de Louis XIII*, Paris, 1948.
>
> A second volume of this work will be devoted to *Pascal et son Temps*.

(B) Fashionable life:

> M. MAGENDIE, *La politesse mondaine et les théories de l'honnêteté en France au XVIIe siècle de 1600 à 1660*, Paris, 1925.

(C) The learned circles and free thought:

> R. PINTARD, *Le libertinage érudit en France dans la première moitié du XVIIe siècle*, Paris, 1943.

(D) The scientific movement:

> R. LENOBLE, *Mersenne ou la naissance du mécanisme*, Paris, 1943.

SUMMARY BIBLIOGRAPHY

(E) The religious movement:

H. BREMOND, *Histoire littéraire du sentiment religieux en France*, Paris, 1916–36, twelve volumes.

H. BUSSON, *La pensée religieuse française de Charron à Pascal*, Paris, 1933.

J. CALVET, *La littérature religieuse de François de Sales a Fénelon*. Paris, 1938.

CHARLES CHESNEAU, *Le Père Yves de Paris et son temps*, Paris, 1946, two volumes. Volume one studies the apologetic movement before Pascal.

L. COGNET, *Les Origines de la spiritualité française au XVIIe siècle*, Paris, 1948.

(F) Port-Royal and Jansenism:

RACINE, *Abrégé de l'histoire de Port-Royal*, ed. Gazier, Paris, 1908.

SAINTE-BEUVE, *Port-Royal*, third edition, Paris, 1888, seven volumes.

This still indispensable masterpiece should be supplemented by:

J. LAPORTE, *La Doctrine de Port-Royal.*

1. *Saint-Cyran*, Paris, 1923.

2. *Les Vérités de la Grace*, Paris, 1923.

J. ORCIBAL, *Les origines du jansénisme.*

1. *Correspondance de Jansénius*, Louvain-Paris, 1947.

2 and 3. *Jean Duvergier de Hauranne, Abbé de Saint-Cyran et son temps* (1581–1636), Louvain-Paris, 1947 and 1948. Two volumes.

Two further volumes are to bring the story up to 1644.

MONSIEUR ORCIBAL also promises us an *Introduction à Port-Royal.*

L. COGNET: *La réforme de Port-Royal*, Paris, 1950. This is the first of a series of studies on *La Mère Angélique et son temps.*

Claude Lancelot, solitaire de Port-Royal, Paris, 1950.

II. *Sources*

Manuscripts:

The French Bibliothèque Nationale possesses:

The manuscripts of the *Pensées*: *Recueil original* (no. 9,202) and two *Copies* (nos. 9,203 and 12,449). The manuscripts of the *Discours sur les passions de l'amour* (nos. 19,303 and the recently acquired 4,015).

Three *Recueils Guerrier* (nos. 12,988; 13,913; 15,281).

The *Mémoires* of the Jansenist BEAUBRUN, essential for the history of *The Provincial Letters*.

The Bibliothèque Mazarine possesses an important Faugère bequest (nos. 4,259 to 4,558). Nos. 4,546; 4,550; 4,551; 4,552; 4,556, in particular, should be consulted.

In private collections, there are certain essential documents:

Two important *Recueils Guerrier* communicated to FAUGERE and BRUNSCHVICG by the Bellaigue family.

The valuable *Manuscrit de l'Abbé Périer* which has luckily fallen into the hands of MONSIEUR LAFUMA.

The Minutier Central des Notaires de Paris contains a good number of legal documents signed by Pascal. Some are already well known, but we have discovered many unpublished ones, which will appear very shortly in a series of studies.

Printed sources:

BARBEAU DE LA BRUYERE, *Recueil de plusieurs pièces pour servir à l'histoire de Port-Royal*, Utrecht, 1740.

This is the famous *Recueil d'Utrecht* which contains, among other items, an important biography of Pascal.

III. *Editions*

Complete Works:

Ed. BOSSUT, Hague, 1779, five volumes.
Ed. BRUNSCHVICG-BOUTROUX-GAZIER, Paris, 1904–14.
Ed. STROWSKI, Paris, 1923–31.

SUMMARY BIBLIOGRAPHY

Discours sur les passions de l'amour
> Ed. SAULNIER, Paris, 1947.
> Ed. LAFUMA, Paris, 1950.

Entretien avec Monsieur Saci
> Ed. J. GUITTON, Paris, 1930.

Provinciales

These first appeared separately in pamphlets, and were published in collected form for the first time in 1657.

A serious study of the *Provinciales* will involve consulting the Latin translation accompanied by notes by NICOLE (WENDROCK), which appeared in 1658. The fourth or fifth edition should be used and MADEMOISELLE DE JONCOUX' translation of the Latin consulted. Consult also the modern editions of:

> MAYNARD, Paris, 1851.
> TOURNEUR, Paris, 1944.

Abrégé de la Vie de Jésus-Christ
> Ed. MICHAUT, Paris, 1942.

Pensées

We have grouped the editions according to the method of classification. Those marked with an asterisk have particularly interesting commentaries.

(a) *Order chosen by the editor*: PORT-ROYAL (1670 and 1678), CONDORCET (1776), *CONDORCET-VOLTAIRE (1778), BOSSUT (1779), *HAVET (1852), *ASTIE (1857), DRIOUX (1881), *BRUNSCHVICG (1897 and 1904), GAZIER (1907), MARGIVAL (1911), STROWSKI (1931), *DEDIEU (1937).

(b) *Attempts to reconstitute Pascal's scheme*: DUCREUX (1785), FRANTIN (1835), FAUGÈRE (1844), LOUANDRE (1854), *ROCHER (1873), MOLLINIER (1877), JEANNIN (1883), VIALARD (1895), *GUTHLIN (1896), DIDIOT (1897), CHEVALIER (1925, 1936, and 1949), MASSIS (1929), SOURIAU (1933), STEWART (1950).

(c) *Objective editions:* order of the *Recueil Original*: MICHAUT (1896). Order of the *Copie* (partially modified): TOURNEUR (1938 and 1942): LAFUMA (1947).

IV. *The Principal Pascal Studies*

A general view of the development of Pascalian studies will be found in:

B. AMOUDRU, *La vie posthume des Pensées*, Paris, 1936.

Till the end of the eighteenth century

From the publication of the *Pensées* onwards, critics tended to divide into Pascalians and anti-Pascalians. There were few really useful studies.

Among the adversaries of Pascal, we should note:

ABBE DE VILLARS, *Traité de la délicatesse*, Paris, 1671.

VOLTAIRE, *Lettres philosophiques*, *XXV*, Paris, 1734.

CONDORCET, *Eloge de Pascal*, introducing his edition of 1776.

The best defender of Pascal was:

F. BOULLIER, *Défense des Pensées de Pascal*, Amsterdam, 1741.

The romantic epoch

A few pages by Chateaubriand bring forward the theme of Pascal as a romantic. The essential problem is now that of Pascal's *scepticism*.

V. COUSIN, *Rapport à l'Académie francaise*, Paris, 1842.

ABBE FLOTTES, *Etudes sur Pascal*, Montpelier, 1844.

ABBE MAYNARD, *Pascal*, Paris, 1850.

A. VINET, *Etudes sur Blaise Pascal*, Paris, no date.

E. DROZ, *Etude sur le scepticisme de Pascal*. Paris, 1886.

The great period

At the end of the nineteenth century, Pascal studies took a magnificent stride forward. The leading figures were university teachers. The essential problem was becoming that of Pascal's *Jansenism*.

(1) *Under University auspices:*

V. GIRAUD, *Pascal, l'homme, l'oeuvre, l'influence*, Fribourg, 1898, *La Vie heroique de Blaise Pascal*, Paris, 1923.

G. LANSON, "Pascal" (article in the *Grande Encyclopédie*).

E. BOUTROUX, *Pascal*, Paris, 1900.

G. MICHAUT, *Les époques de la pensée de Pascal*. Second edition, Paris, 1902.

F. STROWSKI, *Pascal et son temps*, Paris, 1907–8. *Les Pensées de Pascal*, Paris, 1930.

A. GAZIER, *Les Derniers Jours de Blaise Pascal*. Paris, 1911.

E. CHEVALIER, *Pascal*, Paris, 1922. "Etudes sur Pascal" (*Revue de métaphysique et de morale*, April to June, 1923).

L. BRUNSCHVICG, *Le Génie de Pascal*, Paris, 1924. *Pascal*, 1932.

J. LHERMET, *Pascal et la Bible*, Paris, 1931.

(2) *Not under University auspices:*

(*a*) Learned works:

E. JOVY, *Pascal inédit*, Vitry-le-François, 1908–12, five volumes.

ETUDES PASCALLIENES, Paris, 1927–36, nine volumes.

Consult also the remarkable articles of CHARLES-HENRI BOUDHORS and the researches of regional scholars.

(*b*) Works of Catholic inspiration:

H. PETITOT, *Pascal, sa vie religieuse et son Apologie du Christianisme*, Paris, 1911.

J. DEDIEU, "Survivances et influences de l'apologétique traditionelle dans les Pensées", in the *Revue d'hist. litt.*, 1930–31.

F. MAURIAC, *Blaise Pascal et sa soeur Jacqueline*, Paris, 1931.

ABBE CONSTANTIN, "Pascal" (article in the *Dictionnaire de Théologie Catholique*).

(*c*) Works on Pascal's "worldly" period:

E. CHAMAILLARD, *Pascal mondain et amoureux*, Paris, 1923.

J. D'ORLIAC, *Le coeur humain, inhumain, surhumain de Blaise Pascal*, Paris, 1931.

PASCAL: HIS LIFE AND WORK

The search for a new Pascal

Around 1935, the Universities ceased to take the lead in Pascalian studies. There are at present almost no links between the pure scholars and the literary critics in their approach to Pascal. The leading current problem is that of Pascal's *originality*.

(*a*) Works of Scholarship:

z. TOURNEUR, as well as his editions of the *Pensées*, has published two curious and very uneven studies:

"Beauté poétique", *histoire critique d'une pensée de Pascal et de ses annexes*, Melun, 1933.

Une vie avec Blaise Pascal. Paris, 1942.

P. L. COUCHOUD has attempted to reconstitute, with the aid of the more important fragments of the *Pensées*, a *Discours sur la condition de l'homme*, Paris, 1948.

The essence of LOUIS LAFUMA's researches is condensed in his *Recherches pascaliennes*, Paris, 1949.

MONSIEUR LAFUMA has kindly kept us in touch with his most recent discoveries and let us see his unpublished collation of Mme Périer's *Vie de Pascal*.

(*b*) Works of criticism:

E. BAUDIN, *La philosophie de Pascal*, Neuchatel, 1946–7, four volumes.

P. HUMBERT, *L'oeuvre scientifique de Blaise Pascal*, Paris, 1947.

G. CHINARD, *En lisant Pascal*, Lille-Geneve, 1948.

G. TRUC, *Pascal, son temps et le nôtre*, Paris, 1949.

J. RUSSIER, *La foi selon Pascal*, Paris, 1949, two volumes.

H. LEFEBVRE, *Pascal*, Paris, 1949. One volume of a series has so far appeared.

J. LAPORTE, *Le coeur et la raison selon Pascal*, Paris, 1950. (Posthumous republication of an article printed in the *Revue Philosophique* of 1927.)

Let us mention finally the most recent work on Pascal's illness:

R. ONFRAY, *L'abîme de Pascal*, Alençon, 1949.

APPENDIX

L'an de grâce 1654

Lundi 23 novembre jour de St Clément pape et martyr et autres au Martyrologie.

Veille de St Chrysogone martyr et autres.

Depuis environ dix heures et demie du soir jusques environ minuit et demi.

Feu

Dieu d'Abraham, Dieu d'Isaac, Dieu de Jacob.

non des philosophes et des savants.

Certitude, certitude; sentiment, joie, paix.

Dieu de Jésus-Christ.

Deum meum et deum vestrum

Ton Dieu sera mon Dieu.

Oubli du monde et de tout hormis Dieu.

Il ne se trouve que par les voies enseignées dans l'évangile.

Grandeur de l'âme humaine.

Père juste le monde ne t'a point connu mais je t'ai connu.

Joie joie joie pleurs de joie.

Je m'en suis séparé.

Dereliquerunt me fontem aquae vivae.

Mon Dieu me quitterez-vous?

Que je n'en sois pas séparé éternellement

Cette est la vie éternelle qu'ils te connaissent seul vrai

Dieu et Celui que tu as envoyé, Jésus-Christ

Jésus-Christ

Jésus-Christ